THE LIFE
AFTER
1

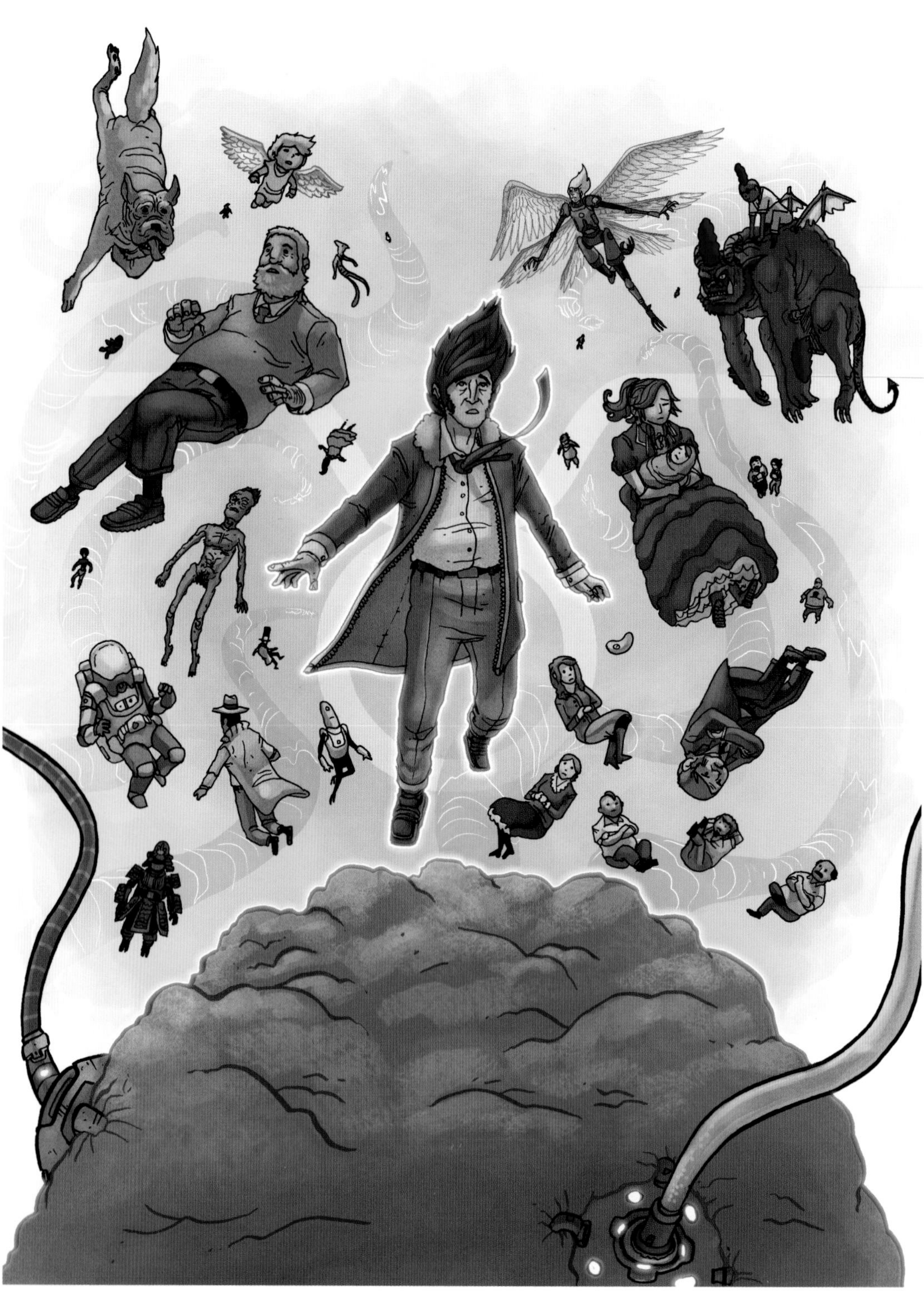

The Life After

THE LIFE AFTER

1

Written by
JOSHUA HALE FIALKOV

Illustrated and colored by
GABO

Lettered by
CRANK!

Designed by
KEITH WOOD

Edited by
JAMES LUCAS JONES &
ARI YARWOOD

AN ONI PRESS PUBLICATION

PUBLISHED BY ONI PRESS, INC.

JOE NOZEMACK publisher

JAMES LUCAS JONES editor in chief

TIM WIESCH v.p. of business development

CHEYENNE ALLOTT director of sales

JOHN SCHORK director of publicity

TROY LOOK production manager

JASON STOREY senior designer

JARED JONES production assistant

CHARLIE CHU editor

ROBIN HERRERA editor

ARI YARWOOD associate editor

BRAD ROOKS inventory coordinator

JUNG LEE office assistant

onipress.com • facebook.com/onipress
twitter.com/onipress • onipress.tumblr.com

thefialkov.com • @joshfialkov
yogabogabo.com • @galvosaur

This volume collects issues #1-5 of the
Oni Press series *The Life After*.

Chapter breaks by

NICK PITARRA & MEGAN WILSON and GABO.

Oni Press, Inc.
1305 SE Martin Luther King Jr. Blvd.
Suite A
Portland, OR 97214
USA

First edition: January 2015

General release • ISBN 978-1-62010-214-5
Direct market • ISBN 978-1-62010-195-7
eISBN 978-1-62010-198-8

Library of Congress Control Number: 2014944756

1 2 3 4 5 6 7 8 9 10

PRINTED IN CHINA.

To the great potato in the sky, and
the sweet potato in my home.
- JOSHUA

To Leah, for helping me break
out of the cycle.
- GABO

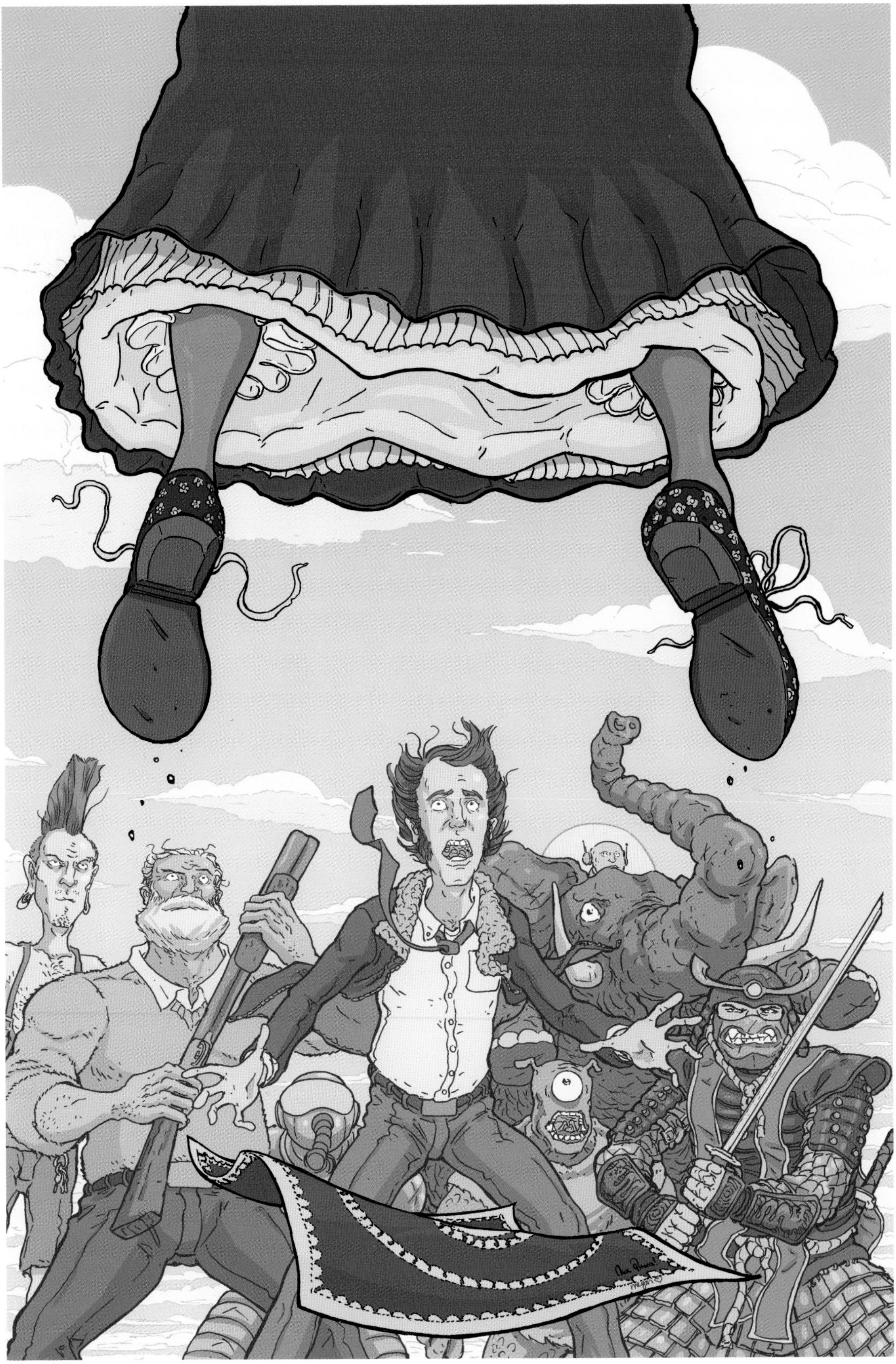

Chapter One

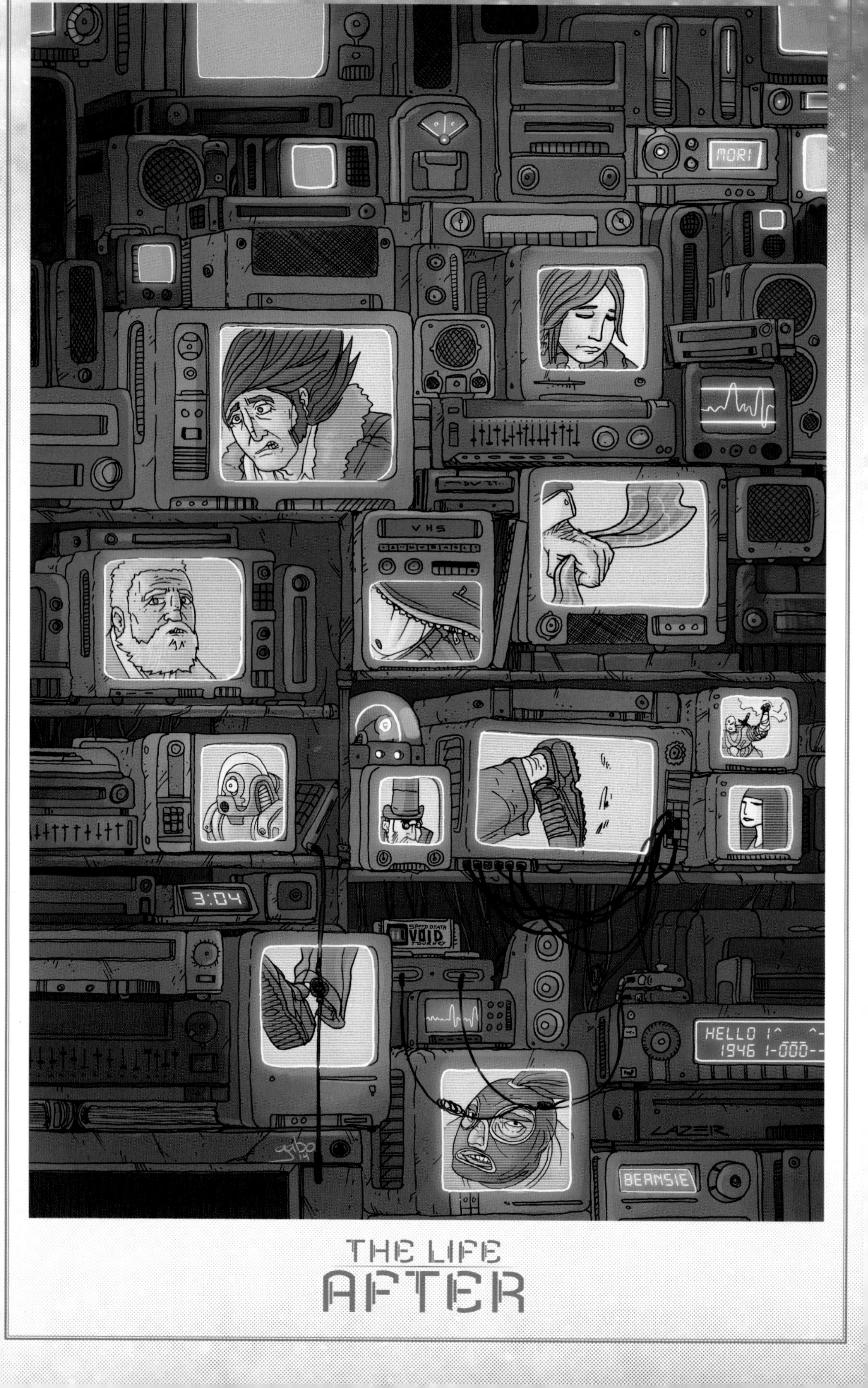
MORI
VHS
3:04
SPEED DEATH
VOID
TOURNEY
LAZER
BEANSIE

THE LIFE AFTER

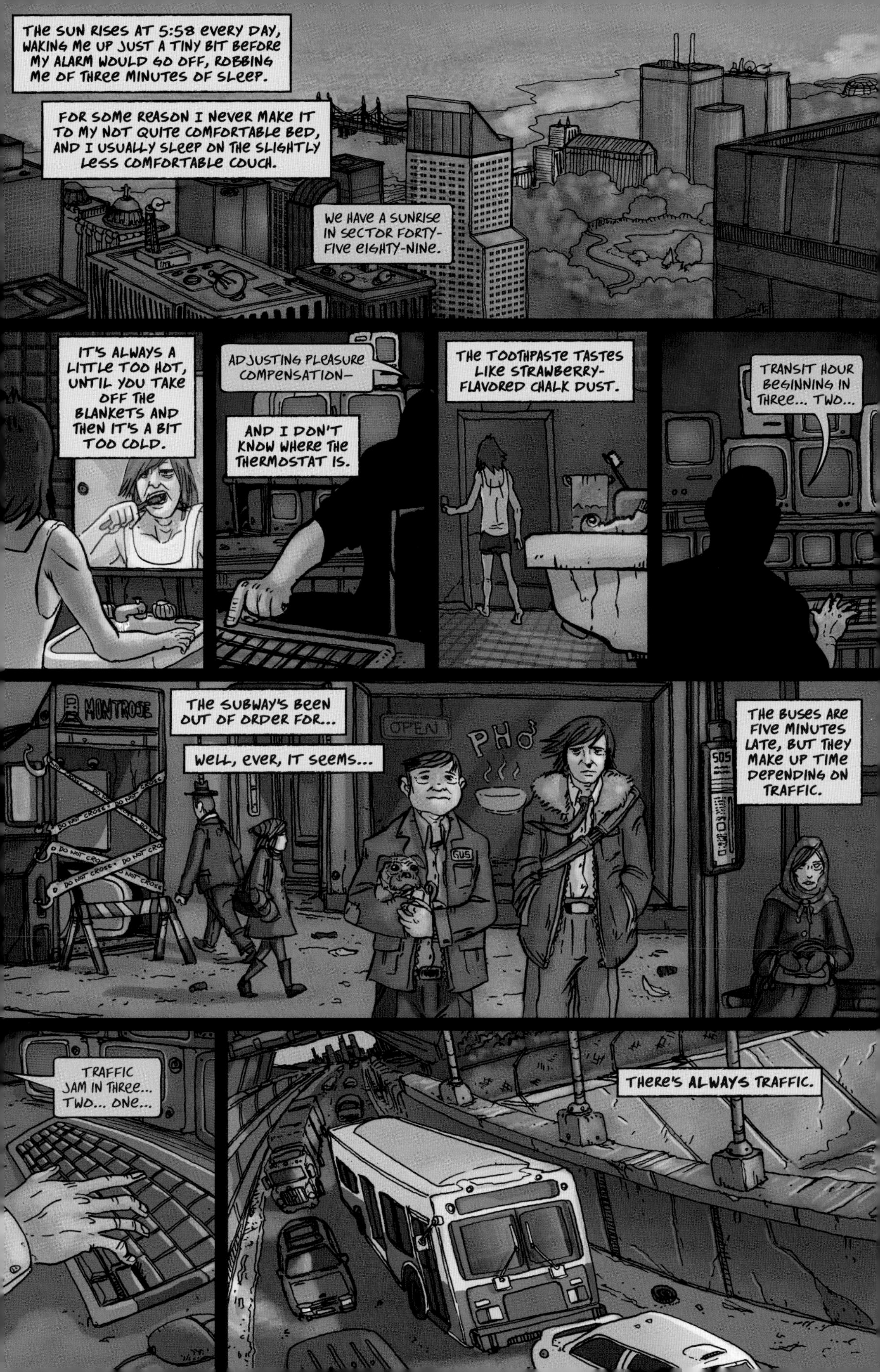
THE SUN RISES AT 5:58 EVERY DAY, WAKING ME UP JUST A TINY BIT BEFORE MY ALARM WOULD GO OFF, ROBBING ME OF THREE MINUTES OF SLEEP.
FOR SOME REASON I NEVER MAKE IT TO MY NOT QUITE COMFORTABLE BED, AND I USUALLY SLEEP ON THE SLIGHTLY LESS COMFORTABLE COUCH.
WE HAVE A SUNRISE IN SECTOR FORTY-FIVE EIGHTY-NINE.
IT'S ALWAYS A LITTLE TOO HOT, UNTIL YOU TAKE OFF THE BLANKETS AND THEN IT'S A BIT TOO COLD.
ADJUSTING PLEASURE COMPENSATION—
AND I DON'T KNOW WHERE THE THERMOSTAT IS.
THE TOOTHPASTE TASTES LIKE STRAWBERRY-FLAVORED CHALK DUST.
TRANSIT HOUR BEGINNING IN THREE... TWO...
MONTROSE
DO NOT CROSS
THE SUBWAY'S BEEN OUT OF ORDER FOR...
WELL, EVER, IT SEEMS...
OPEN
PHỞ
GUS
SOS
THE BUSES ARE FIVE MINUTES LATE, BUT THEY MAKE UP TIME DEPENDING ON TRAFFIC.
TRAFFIC JAM IN THREE... TWO... ONE...
THERE'S ALWAYS TRAFFIC.

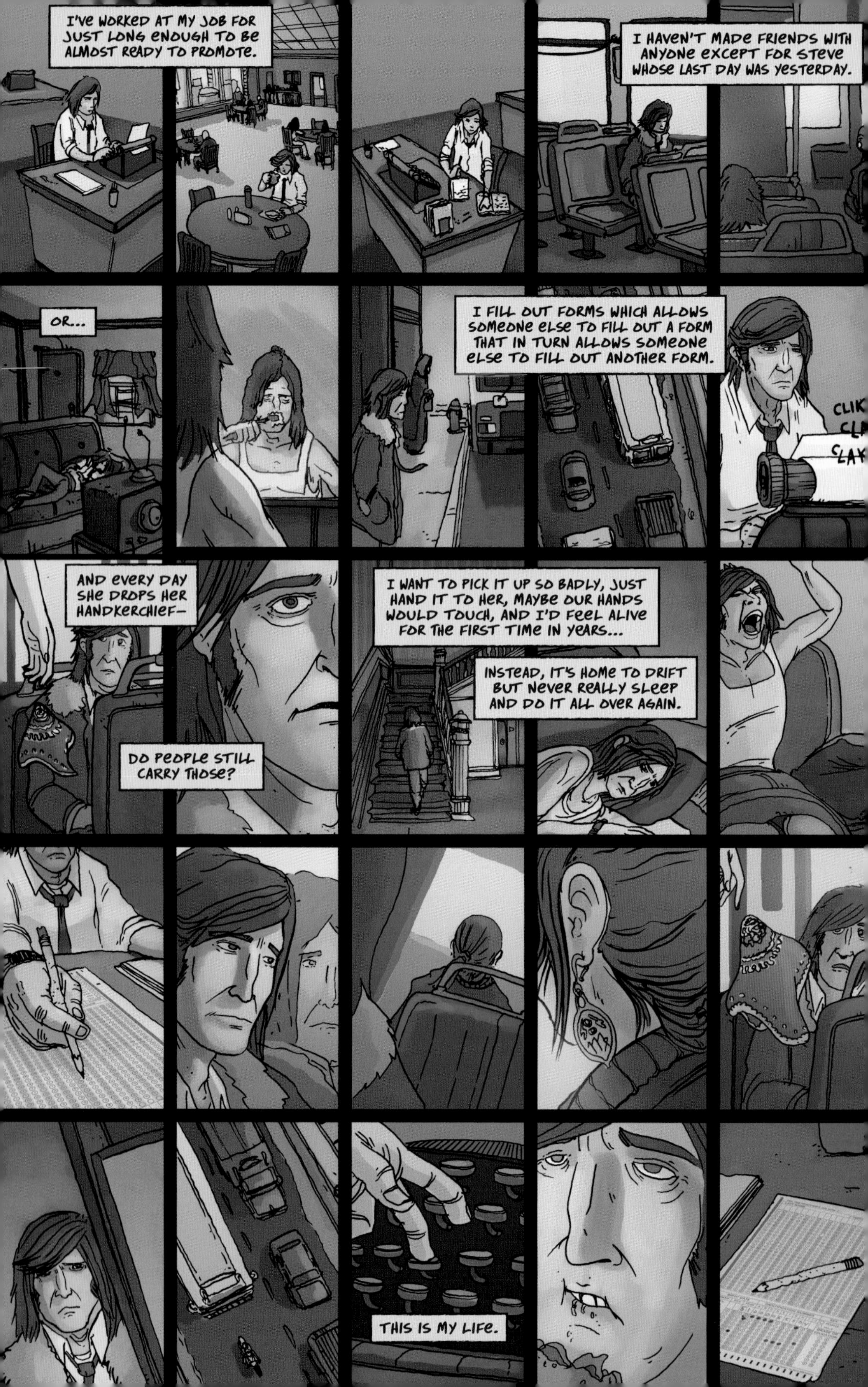

I'VE WORKED AT MY JOB FOR JUST LONG ENOUGH TO BE ALMOST READY TO PROMOTE.
I HAVEN'T MADE FRIENDS WITH ANYONE EXCEPT FOR STEVE WHOSE LAST DAY WAS YESTERDAY.
OR...
I FILL OUT FORMS WHICH ALLOWS SOMEONE ELSE TO FILL OUT A FORM THAT IN TURN ALLOWS SOMEONE ELSE TO FILL OUT ANOTHER FORM.
CLIK
AND EVERY DAY SHE DROPS HER HANDKERCHIEF—
DO PEOPLE STILL CARRY THOSE?
I WANT TO PICK IT UP SO BADLY, JUST HAND IT TO HER, MAYBE OUR HANDS WOULD TOUCH, AND I'D FEEL ALIVE FOR THE FIRST TIME IN YEARS...
INSTEAD, IT'S HOME TO DRIFT BUT NEVER REALLY SLEEP AND DO IT ALL OVER AGAIN.
THIS IS MY LIFE.

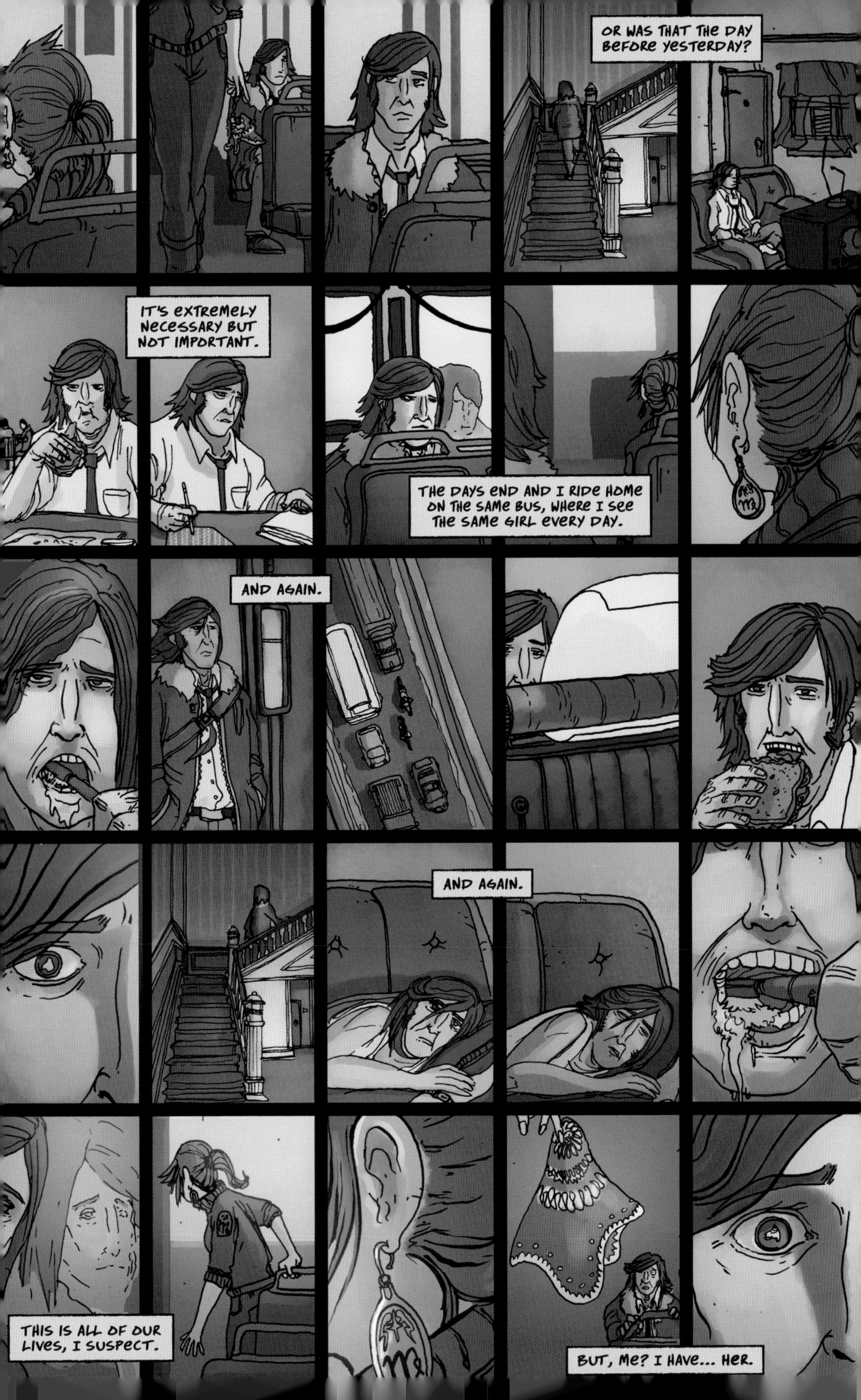
OR WAS THAT THE DAY BEFORE YESTERDAY?
IT'S EXTREMELY NECESSARY BUT NOT IMPORTANT.
THE DAYS END AND I RIDE HOME ON THE SAME BUS, WHERE I SEE THE SAME GIRL EVERY DAY.
AND AGAIN.
AND AGAIN.
THIS IS ALL OF OUR LIVES, I SUSPECT.
BUT, ME? I HAVE... HER.

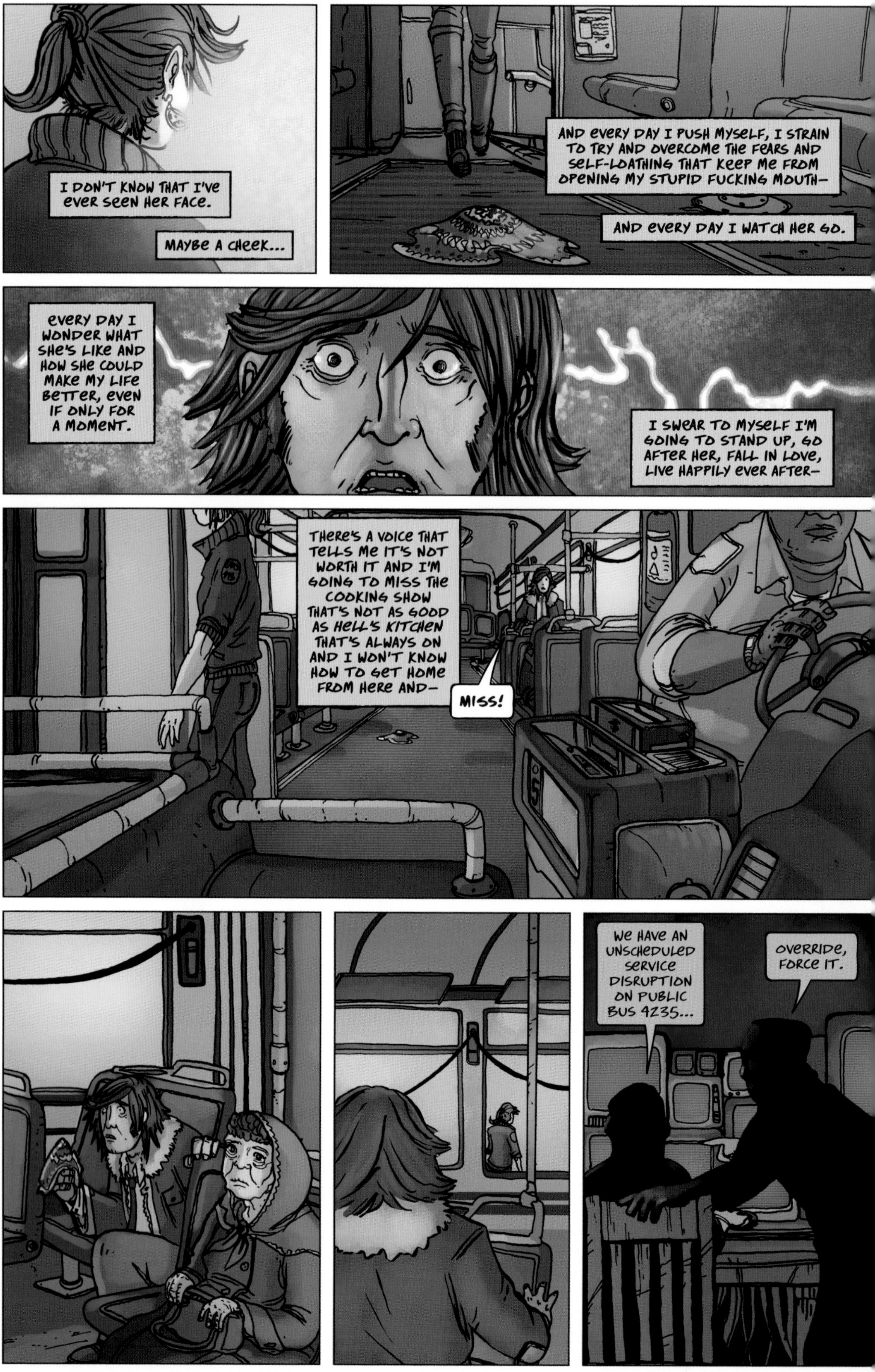

I DON'T KNOW THAT I'VE EVER SEEN HER FACE.
MAYBE A CHEEK...
AND EVERY DAY I PUSH MYSELF, I STRAIN TO TRY AND OVERCOME THE FEARS AND SELF-LOATHING THAT KEEP ME FROM OPENING MY STUPID FUCKING MOUTH—
AND EVERY DAY I WATCH HER GO.
EVERY DAY I WONDER WHAT SHE'S LIKE AND HOW SHE COULD MAKE MY LIFE BETTER, EVEN IF ONLY FOR A MOMENT.
I SWEAR TO MYSELF I'M GOING TO STAND UP, GO AFTER HER, FALL IN LOVE, LIVE HAPPILY EVER AFTER—
THERE'S A VOICE THAT TELLS ME IT'S NOT WORTH IT AND I'M GOING TO MISS THE COOKING SHOW THAT'S NOT AS GOOD AS HELL'S KITCHEN THAT'S ALWAYS ON AND I WON'T KNOW HOW TO GET HOME FROM HERE AND—
MISS!
WE HAVE AN UNSCHEDULED SERVICE DISRUPTION ON PUBLIC BUS 4235...
OVERRIDE, FORCE IT.

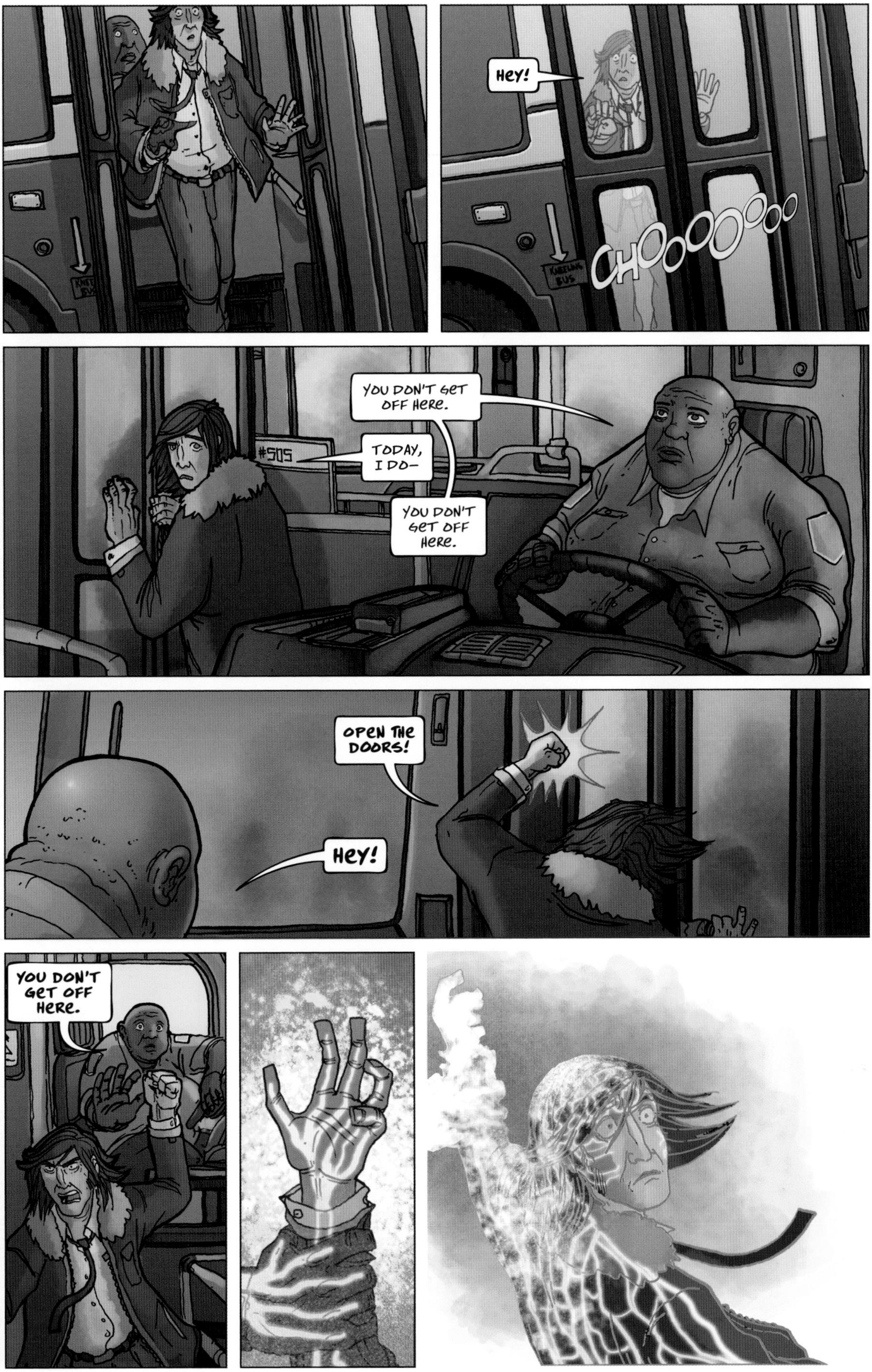
Hey!
CHOOOOOOOO
YOU DON'T GET OFF HERE.
TODAY, I DO—
YOU DON'T GET OFF HERE.
OPEN THE DOORS!
Hey!
YOU DON'T GET OFF HERE.

LAST STOP. EVERYBODY OFF.

ANYBODY ELSE?

HURM.

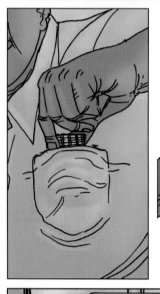

FUCK 'EM.

WHAT THE HELL WAS THAT?!

YOU DON'T GET OFF HERE.

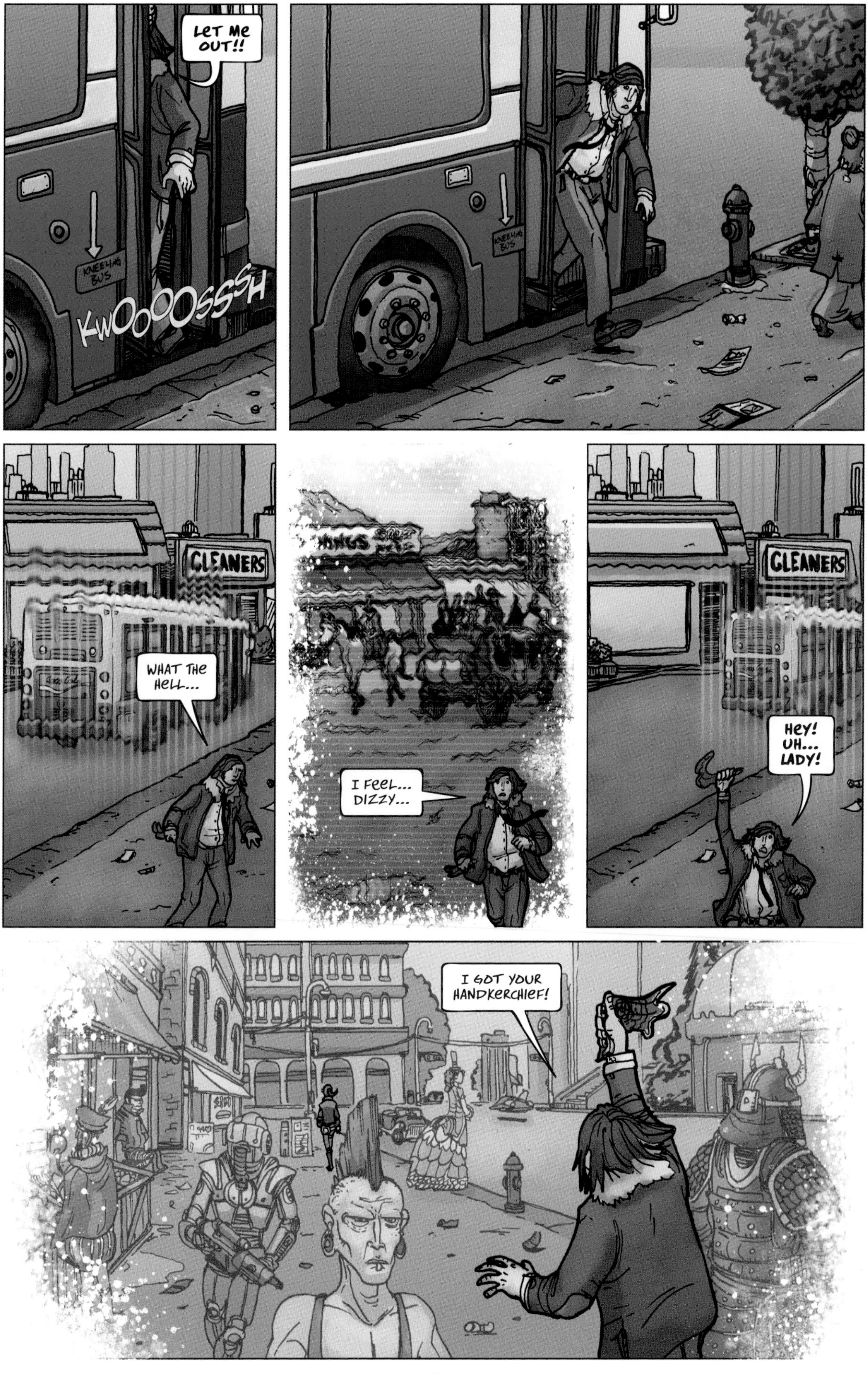
LET ME OUT!!
KWOOOOSSSH
CLEANERS
WHAT THE HELL...
I FEEL... DIZZY...
CLEANERS
HEY! UH... LADY!
I GOT YOUR HANDKERCHIEF!

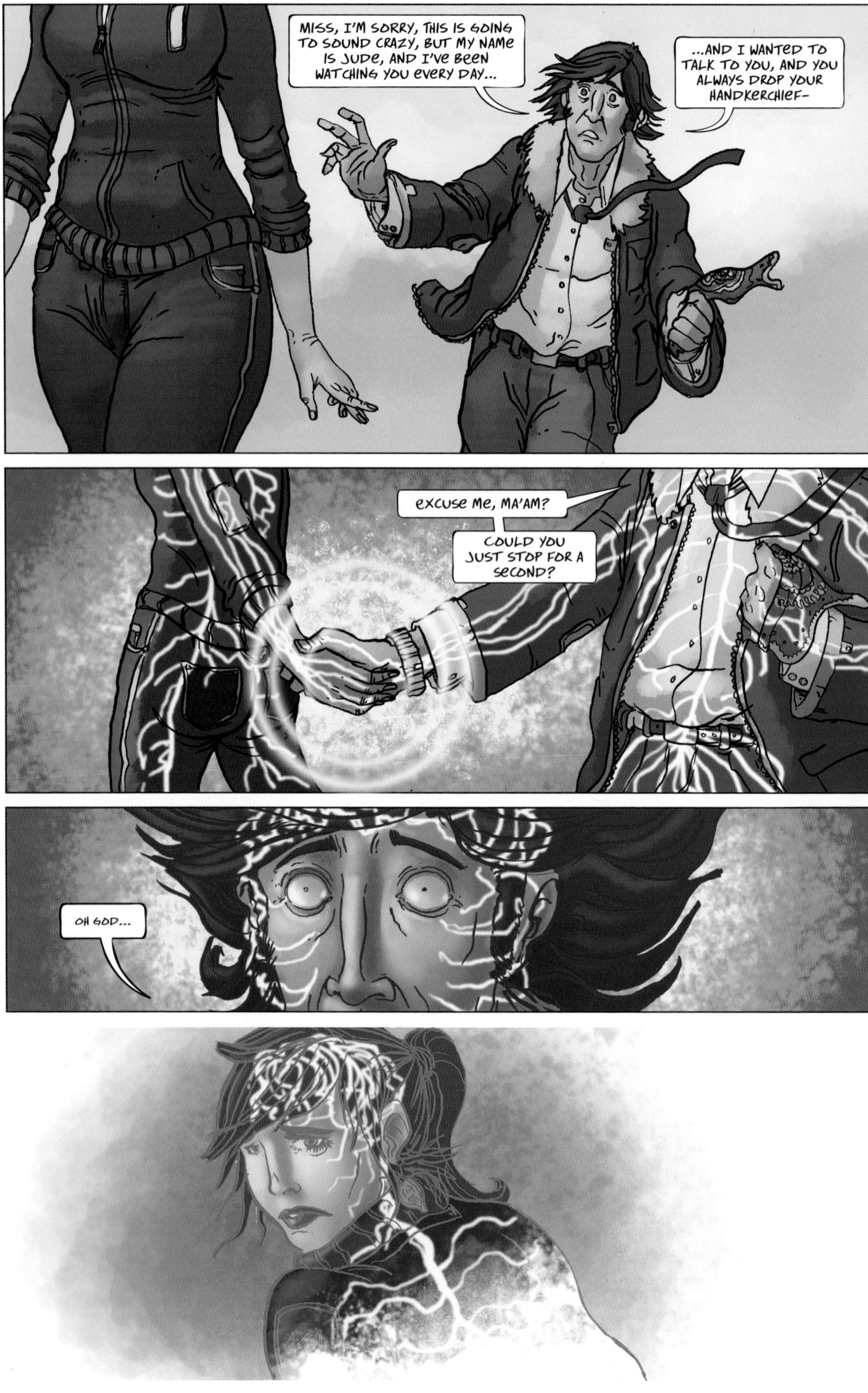
MISS, I'M SORRY, THIS IS GOING TO SOUND CRAZY, BUT MY NAME IS JUDE, AND I'VE BEEN WATCHING YOU EVERY DAY...
...AND I WANTED TO TALK TO YOU, AND YOU ALWAYS DROP YOUR HANDKERCHIEF-
EXCUSE ME, MA'AM?
COULD YOU JUST STOP FOR A SECOND?
OH GOD...

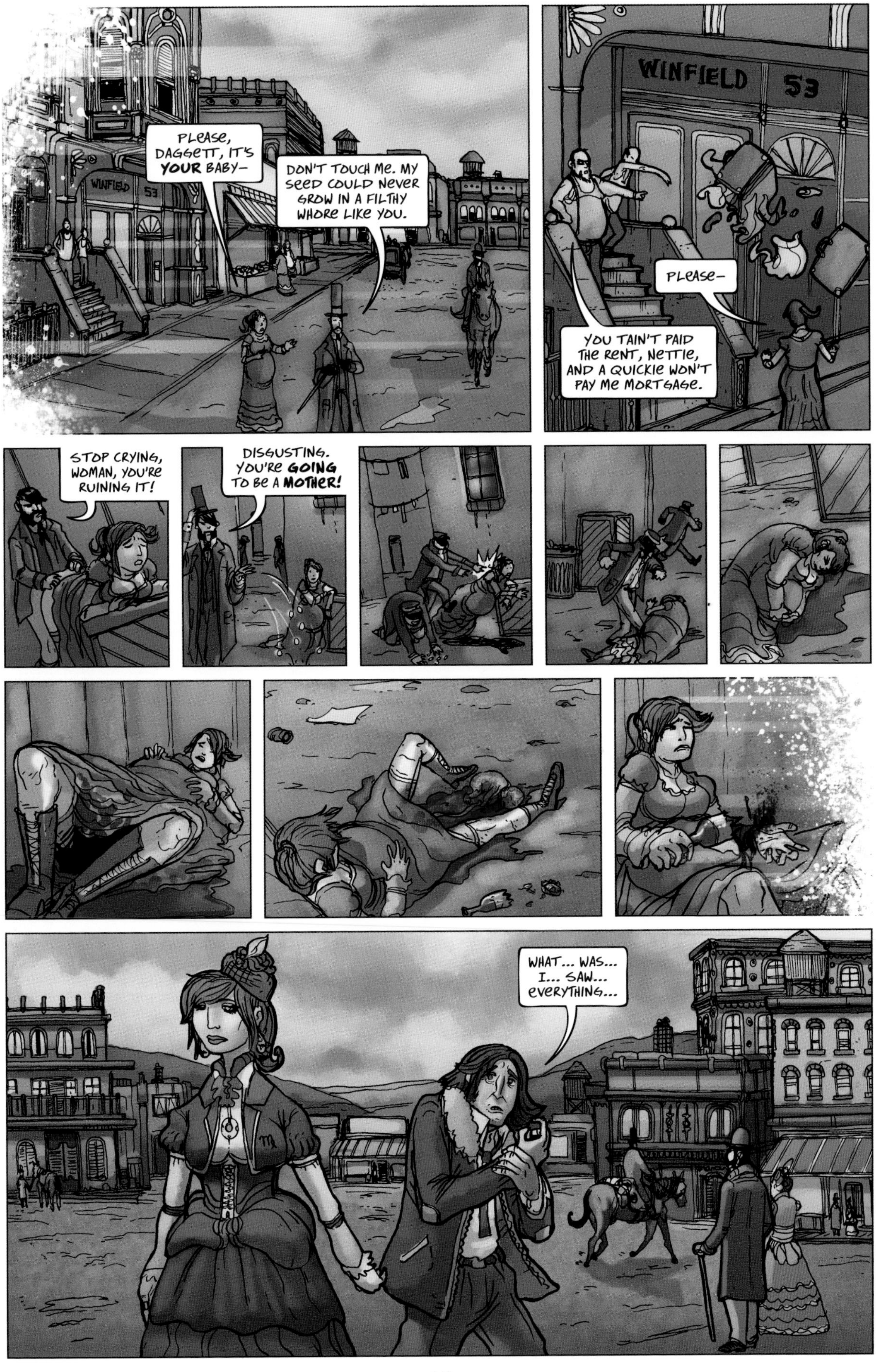
WINFIELD 53
PLEASE, DAGGETT, IT'S YOUR BABY–
DON'T TOUCH ME. MY SEED COULD NEVER GROW IN A FILTHY WHORE LIKE YOU.
WINFIELD 53
PLEASE–
YOU TAIN'T PAID THE RENT, NETTIE, AND A QUICKIE WON'T PAY ME MORTGAGE.
STOP CRYING, WOMAN, YOU'RE RUINING IT!
DISGUSTING. YOU'RE GOING TO BE A MOTHER!
WHAT... WAS... I... SAW... EVERYTHING...

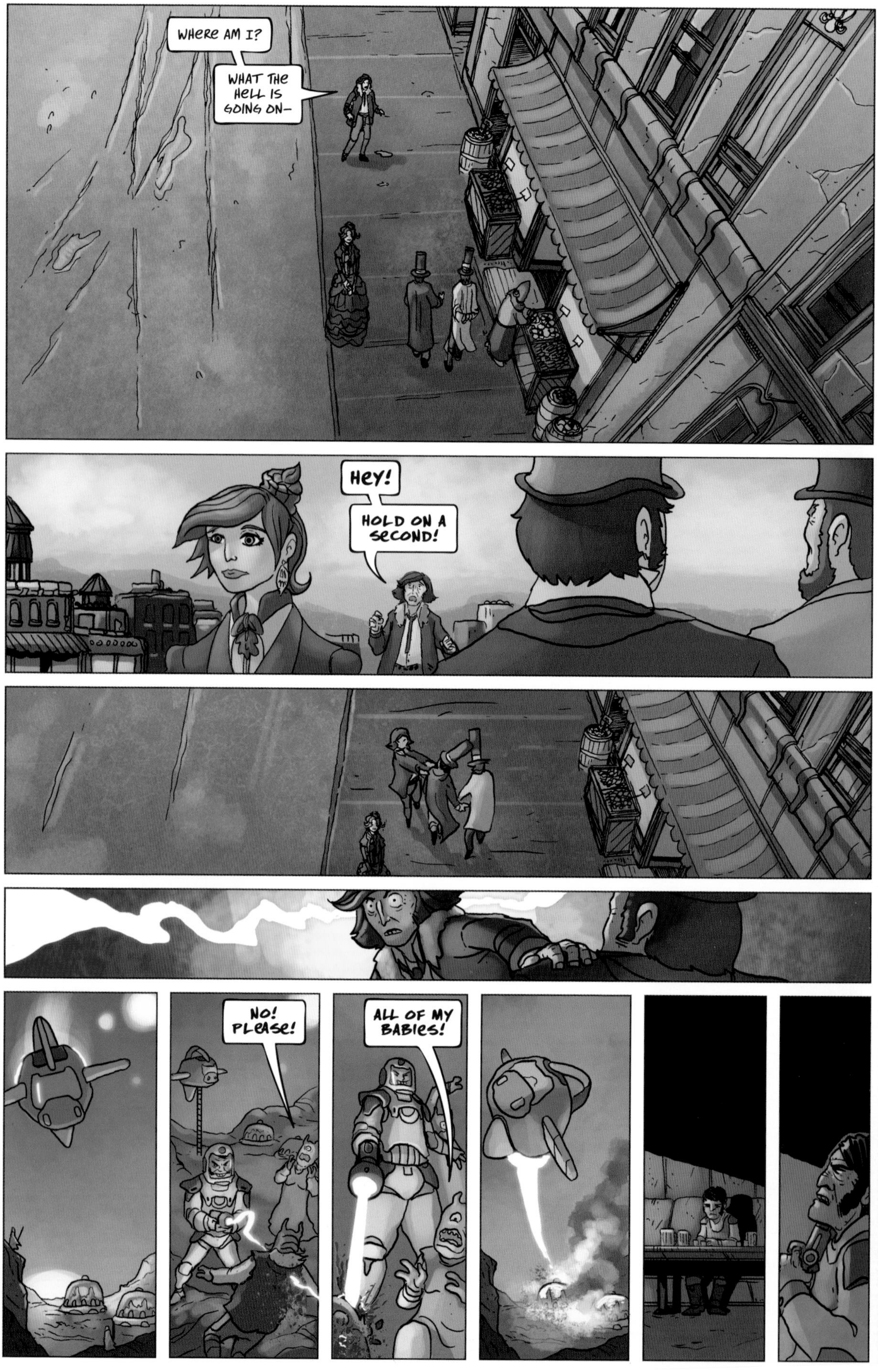
WHERE AM I?
WHAT THE HELL IS GOING ON—
HEY!
HOLD ON A SECOND!
NO! PLEASE!
ALL OF MY BABIES!

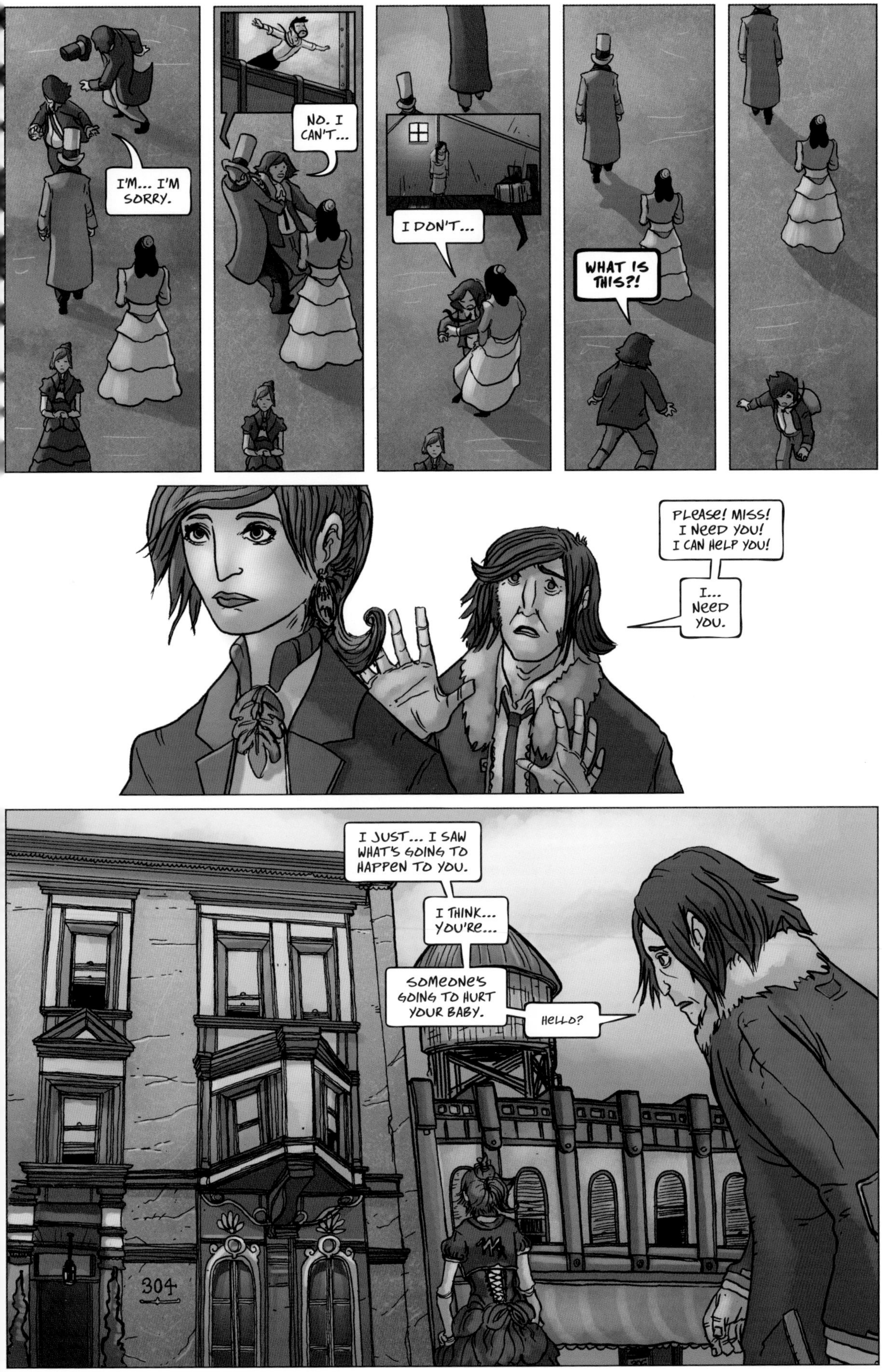
I'M... I'M SORRY.
NO. I CAN'T...
I DON'T...
WHAT IS THIS?!
PLEASE! MISS! I NEED YOU! I CAN HELP YOU!
I... NEED YOU.
I JUST... I SAW WHAT'S GOING TO HAPPEN TO YOU.
I THINK... YOU'RE...
SOMEONE'S GOING TO HURT YOUR BABY.
HELLO?
304

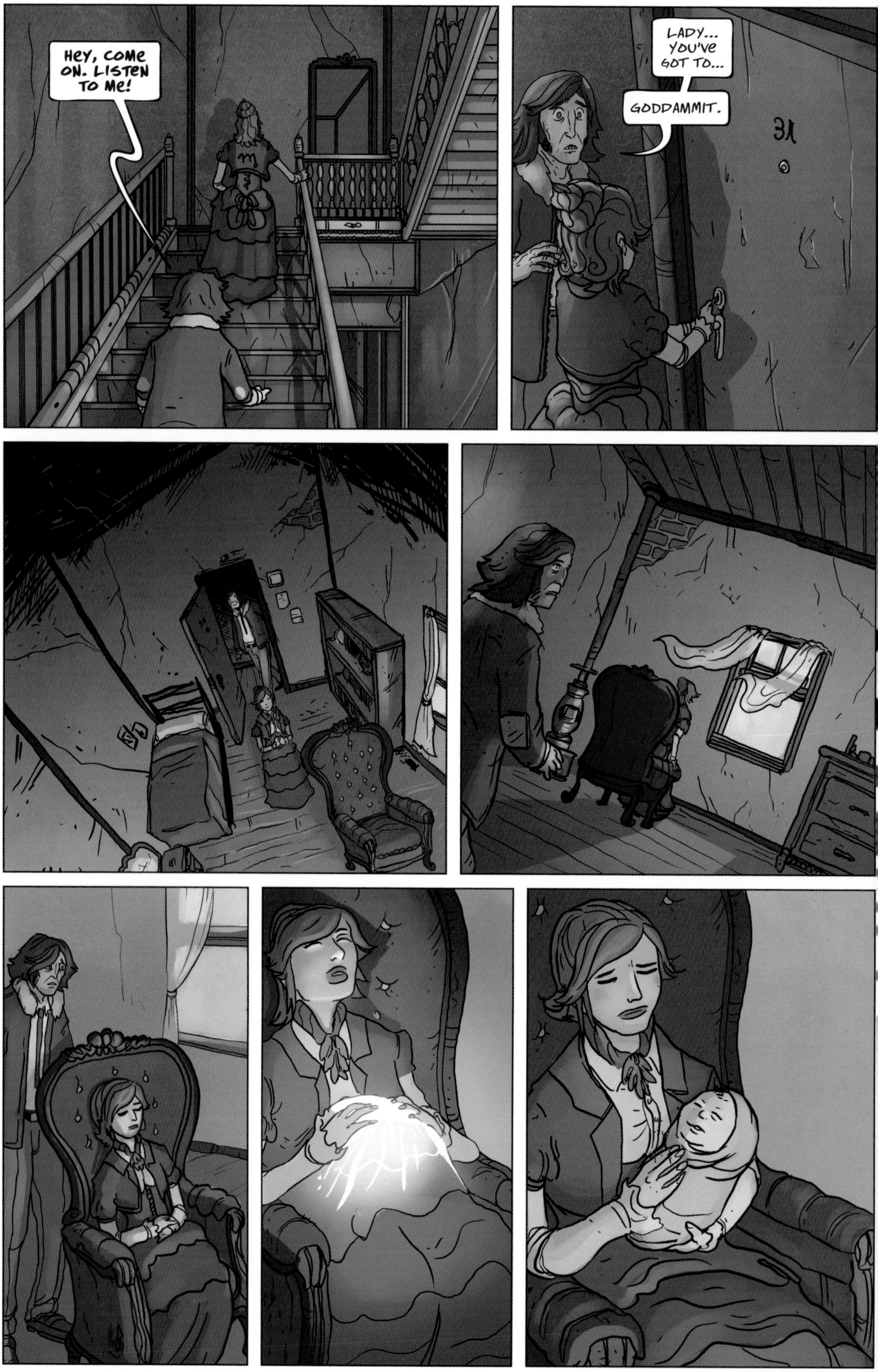
HEY, COME ON. LISTEN TO ME!
LADY... YOU'VE GOT TO...
GODDAMMIT.
31

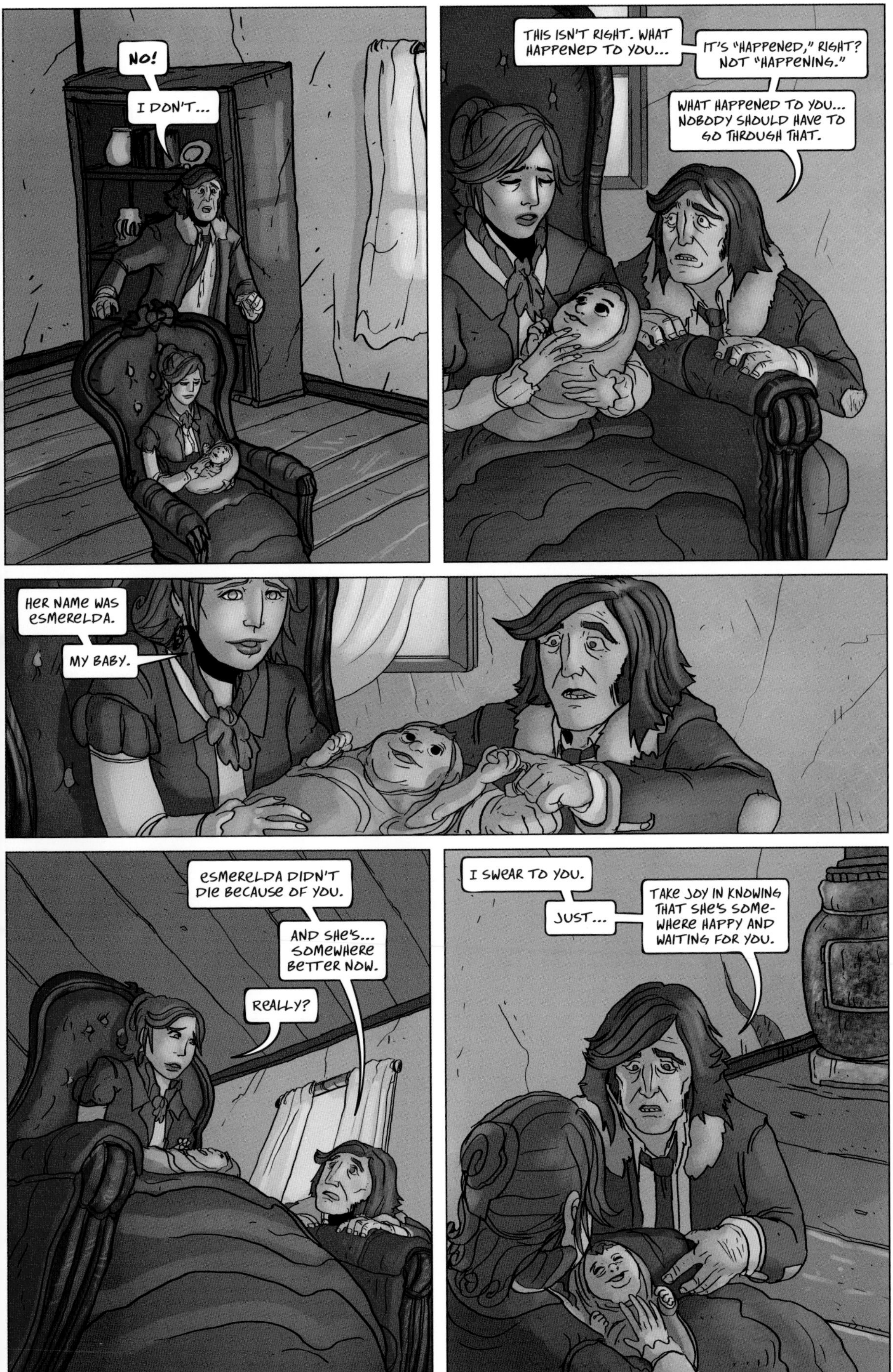
NO!
I DON'T...
THIS ISN'T RIGHT. WHAT HAPPENED TO YOU...
IT'S "HAPPENED," RIGHT? NOT "HAPPENING."
WHAT HAPPENED TO YOU... NOBODY SHOULD HAVE TO GO THROUGH THAT.
HER NAME WAS ESMERELDA.
MY BABY.
ESMERELDA DIDN'T DIE BECAUSE OF YOU.
AND SHE'S... SOMEWHERE BETTER NOW.
REALLY?
I SWEAR TO YOU.
JUST...
TAKE JOY IN KNOWING THAT SHE'S SOME-WHERE HAPPY AND WAITING FOR YOU.

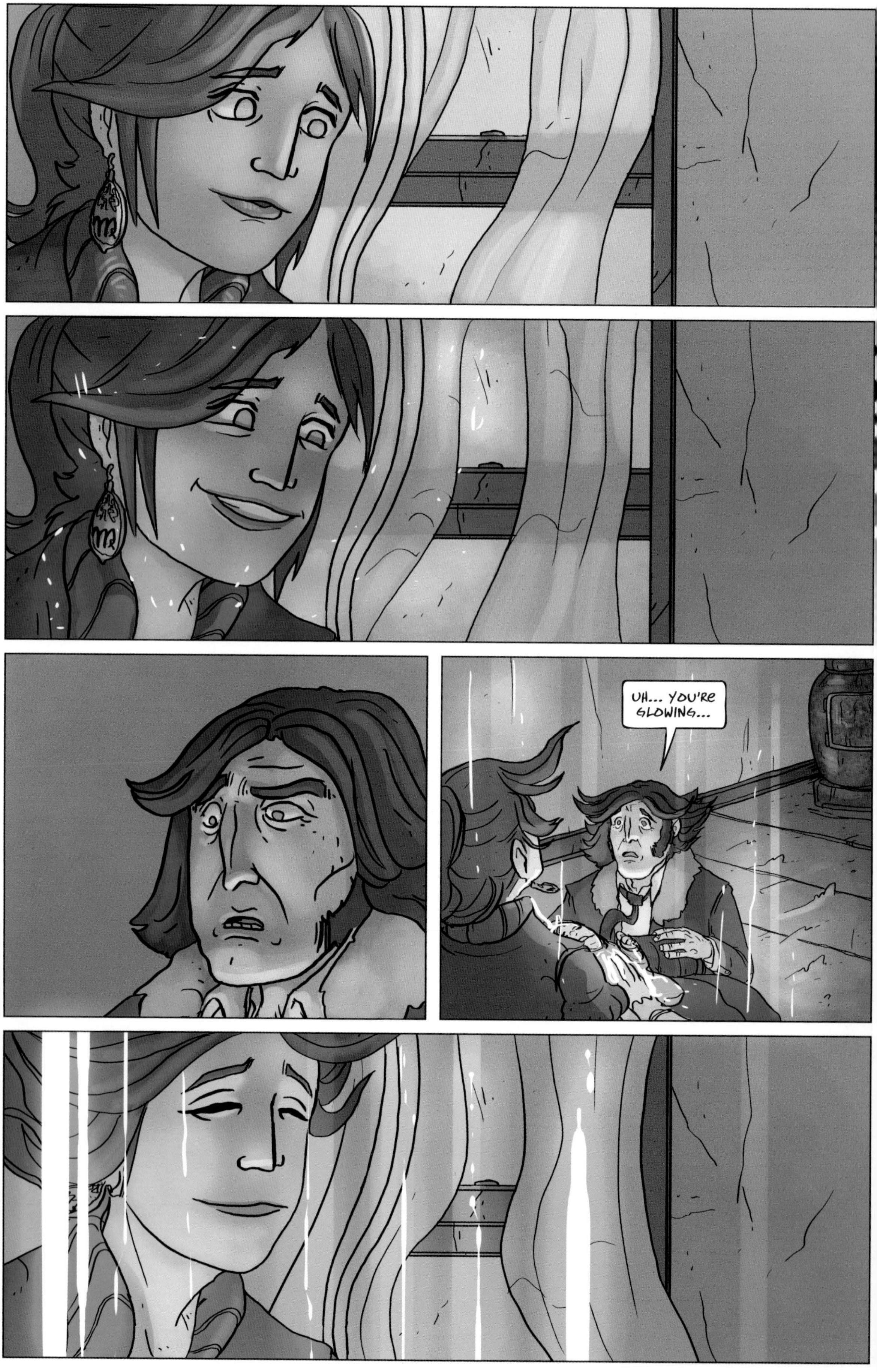
UH... YOU'RE GLOWING...

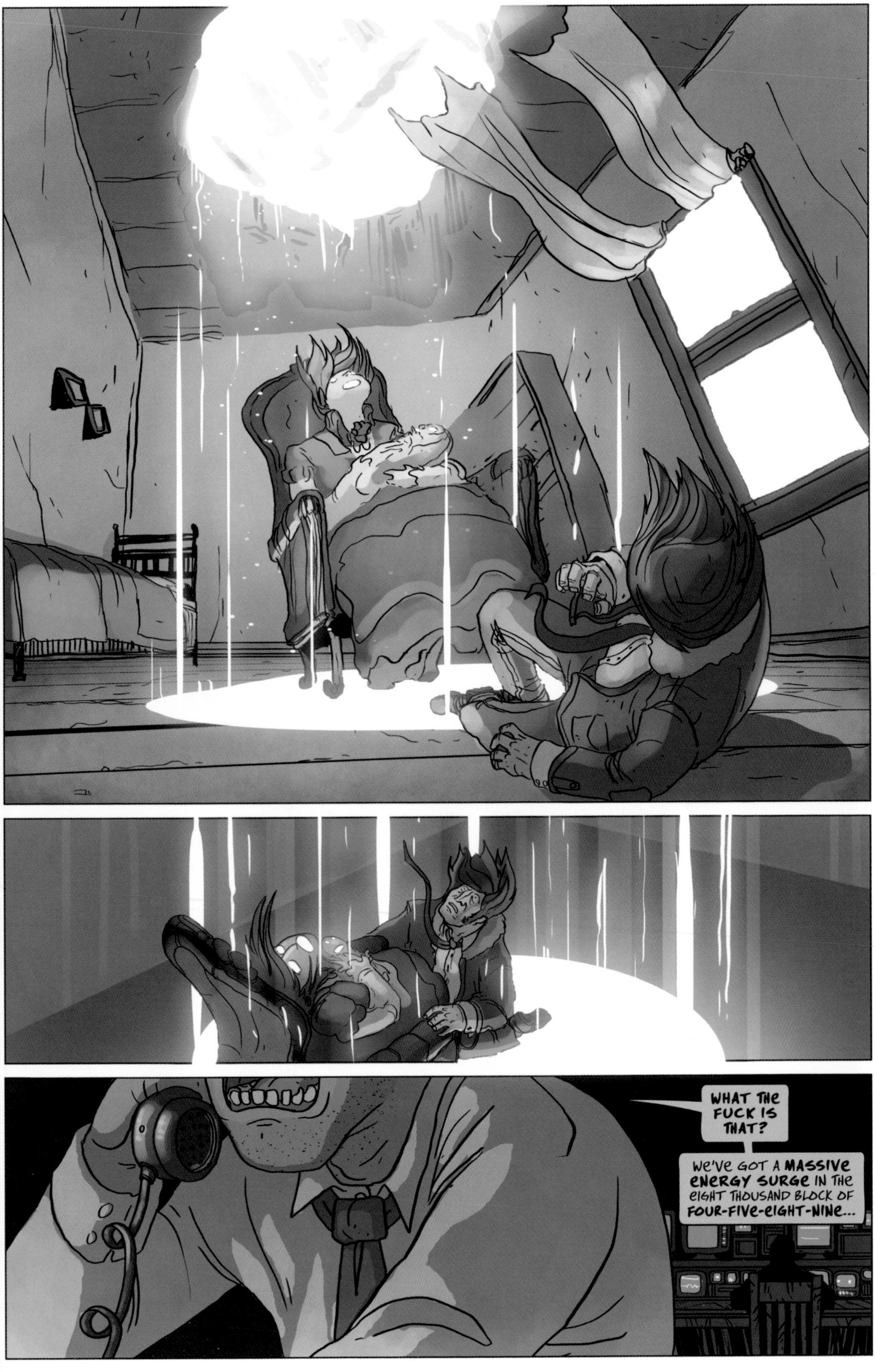
WHAT THE FUCK IS THAT?
WE'VE GOT A MASSIVE ENERGY SURGE IN THE EIGHT THOUSAND BLOCK OF FOUR-FIVE-EIGHT-NINE...

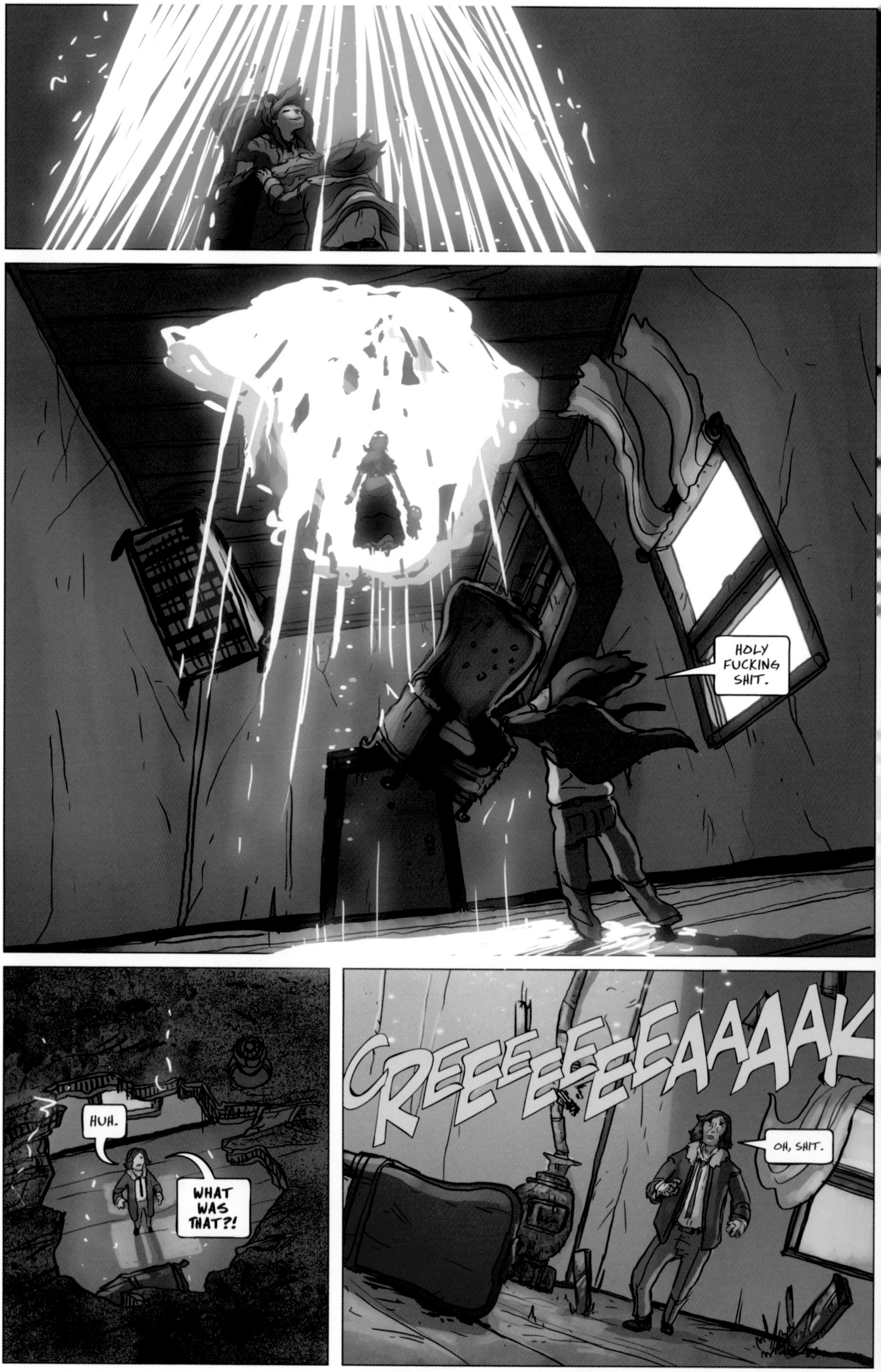

HOLY FUCKING SHIT.
HUH.
WHAT WAS THAT?!
CREEEEEEEEAAAAK
OH, SHIT.

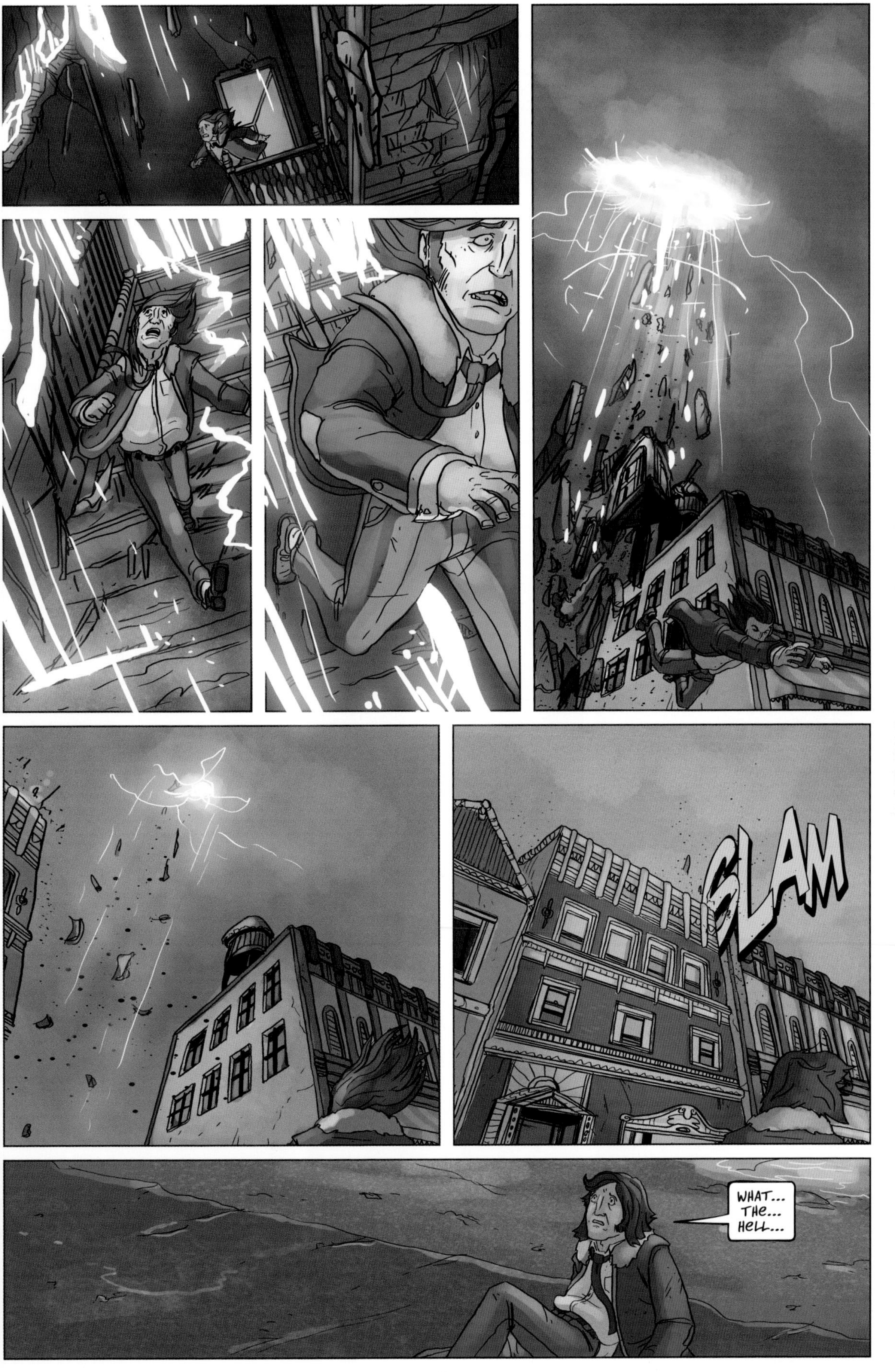
SLAM
WHAT... THE... HELL...

AM I...
DEAD?

WHERE
AM I?

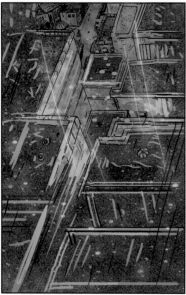

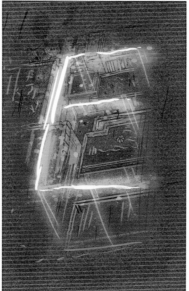

SECTOR 4589
ALPHA CENTARI

ERROR...
CLASS UPPER LEFT
CRASH SECTOR ALP

HUH.

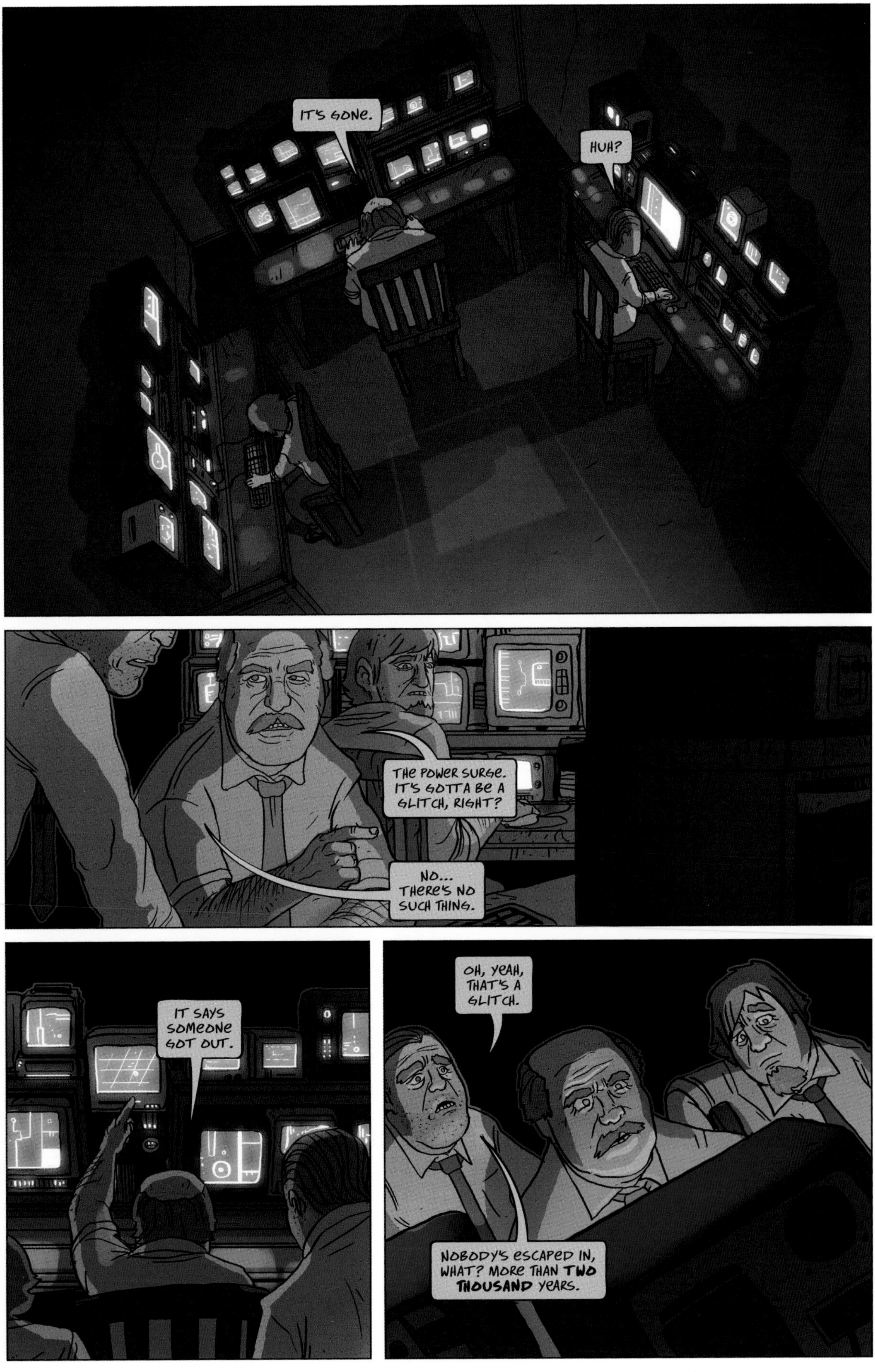
IT'S GONE.
HUH?
THE POWER SURGE. IT'S GOTTA BE A GLITCH, RIGHT?
NO... THERE'S NO SUCH THING.
IT SAYS SOMEONE GOT OUT.
OH, YEAH, THAT'S A GLITCH.
NOBODY'S ESCAPED IN, WHAT? MORE THAN TWO THOUSAND YEARS.

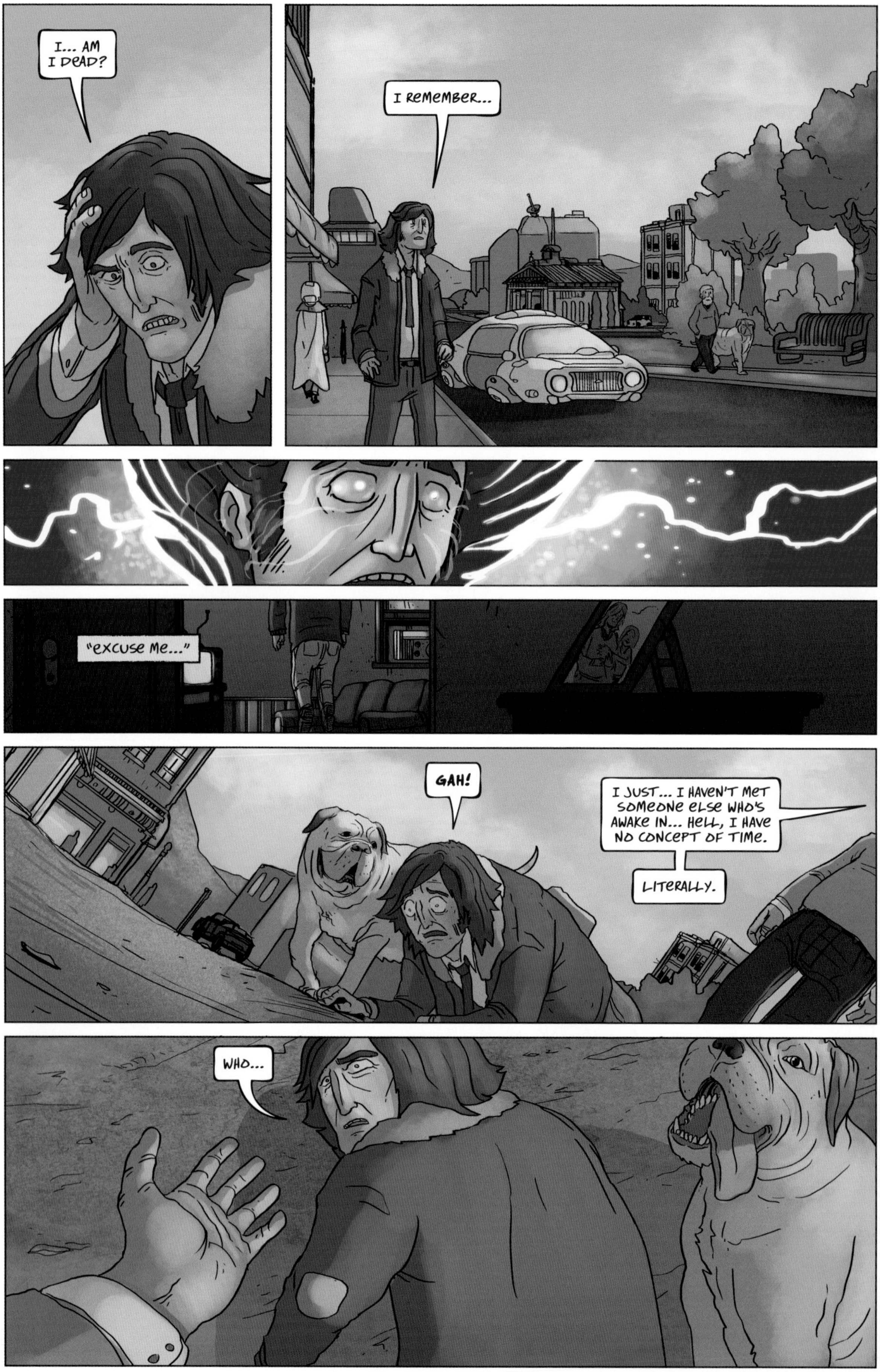
I... AM I DEAD?
I REMEMBER...
"EXCUSE ME..."
GAH!
I JUST... I HAVEN'T MET SOMEONE ELSE WHO'S AWAKE IN... HELL, I HAVE NO CONCEPT OF TIME.
LITERALLY.
WHO...

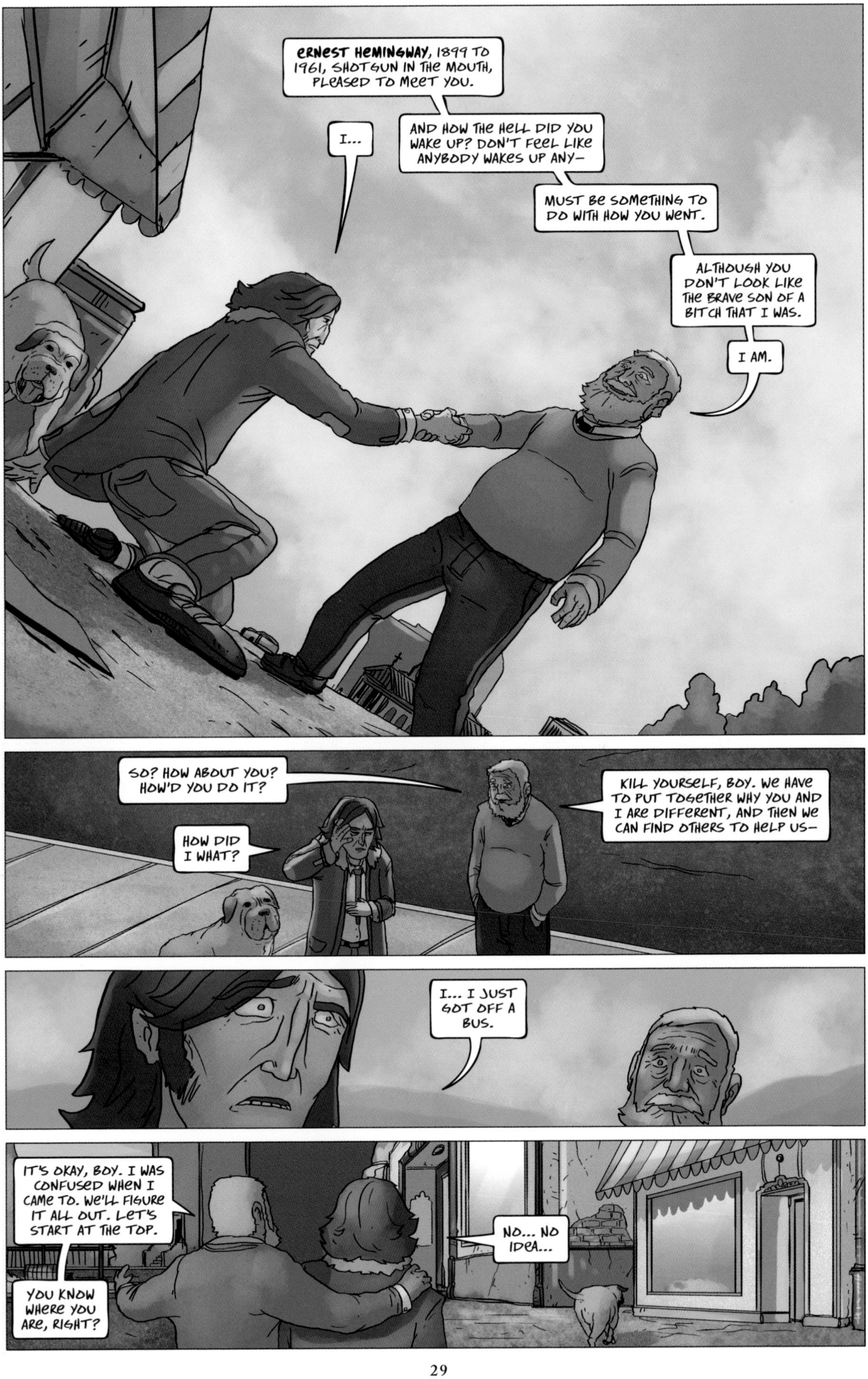
ERNEST HEMINGWAY, 1899 TO 1961, SHOTGUN IN THE MOUTH, PLEASED TO MEET YOU.
I...
AND HOW THE HELL DID YOU WAKE UP? DON'T FEEL LIKE ANYBODY WAKES UP ANY—
MUST BE SOMETHING TO DO WITH HOW YOU WENT.
ALTHOUGH YOU DON'T LOOK LIKE THE BRAVE SON OF A BITCH THAT I WAS.
I AM.
SO? HOW ABOUT YOU? HOW'D YOU DO IT?
HOW DID I WHAT?
KILL YOURSELF, BOY. WE HAVE TO PUT TOGETHER WHY YOU AND I ARE DIFFERENT, AND THEN WE CAN FIND OTHERS TO HELP US—
I... I JUST GOT OFF A BUS.
IT'S OKAY, BOY. I WAS CONFUSED WHEN I CAME TO. WE'LL FIGURE IT ALL OUT. LET'S START AT THE TOP.
YOU KNOW WHERE YOU ARE, RIGHT?
NO... NO IDEA...

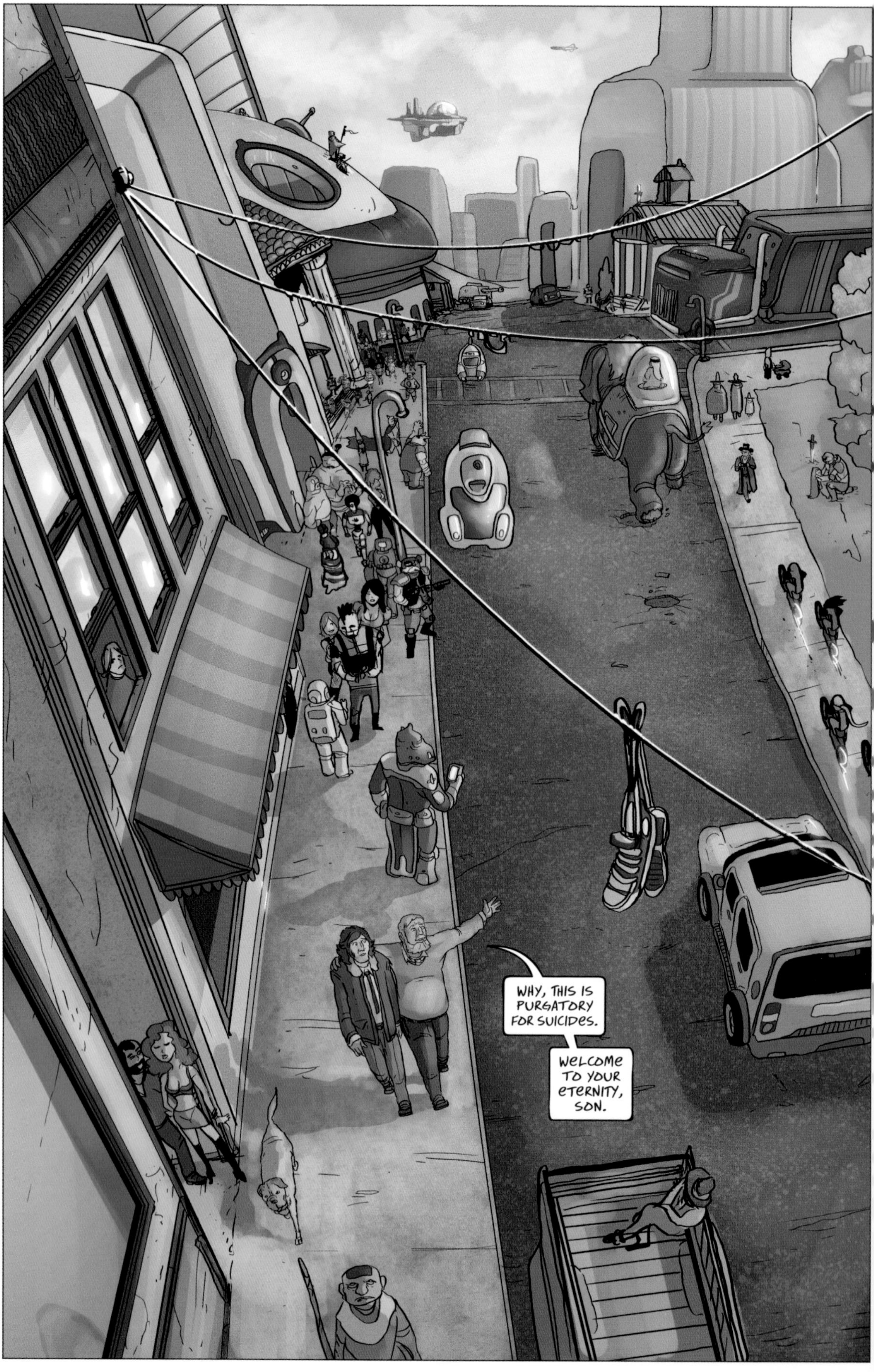
WHY, THIS IS PURGATORY FOR SUICIDES.
WELCOME TO YOUR ETERNITY, SON.

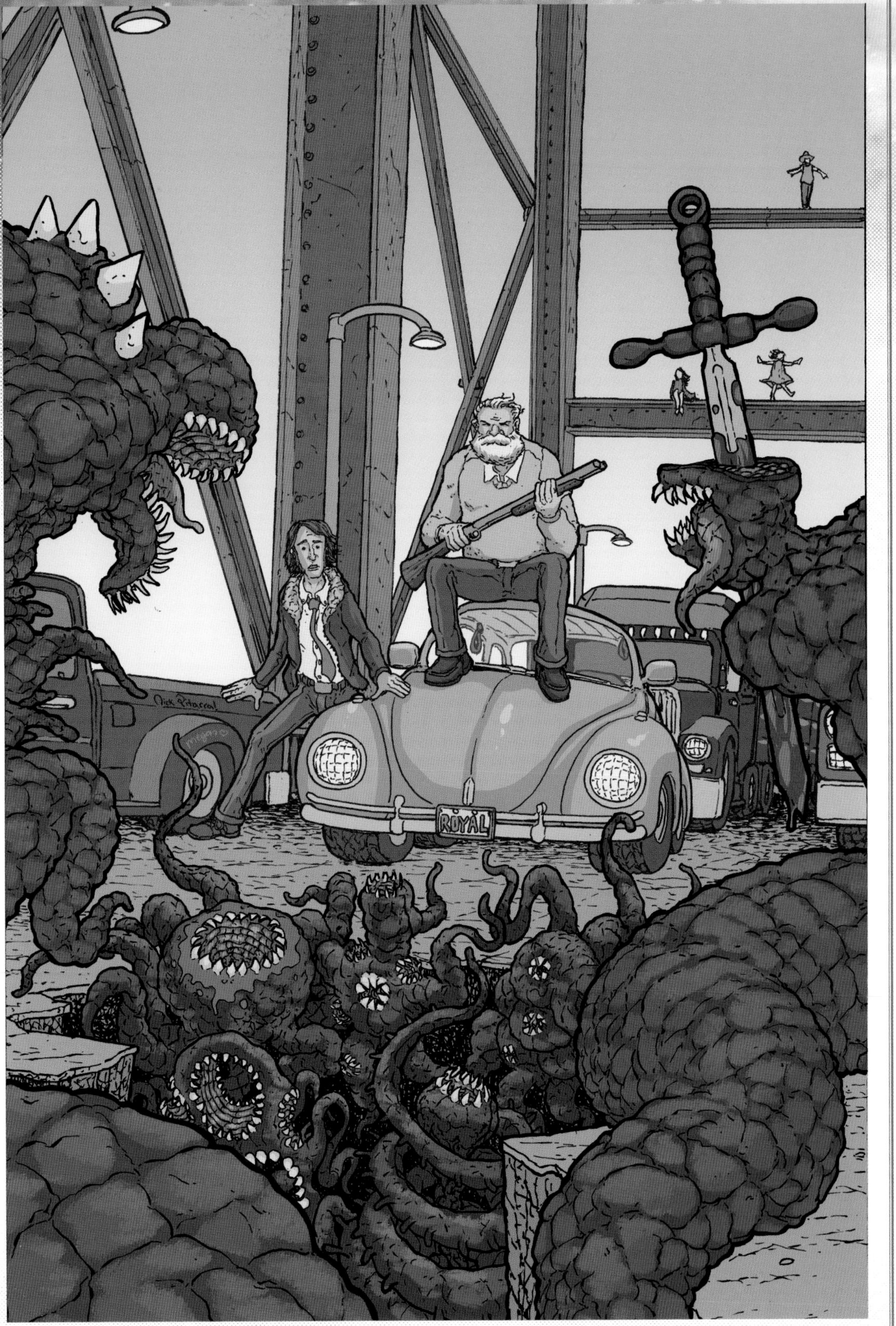
ROYAL

Chapter Two

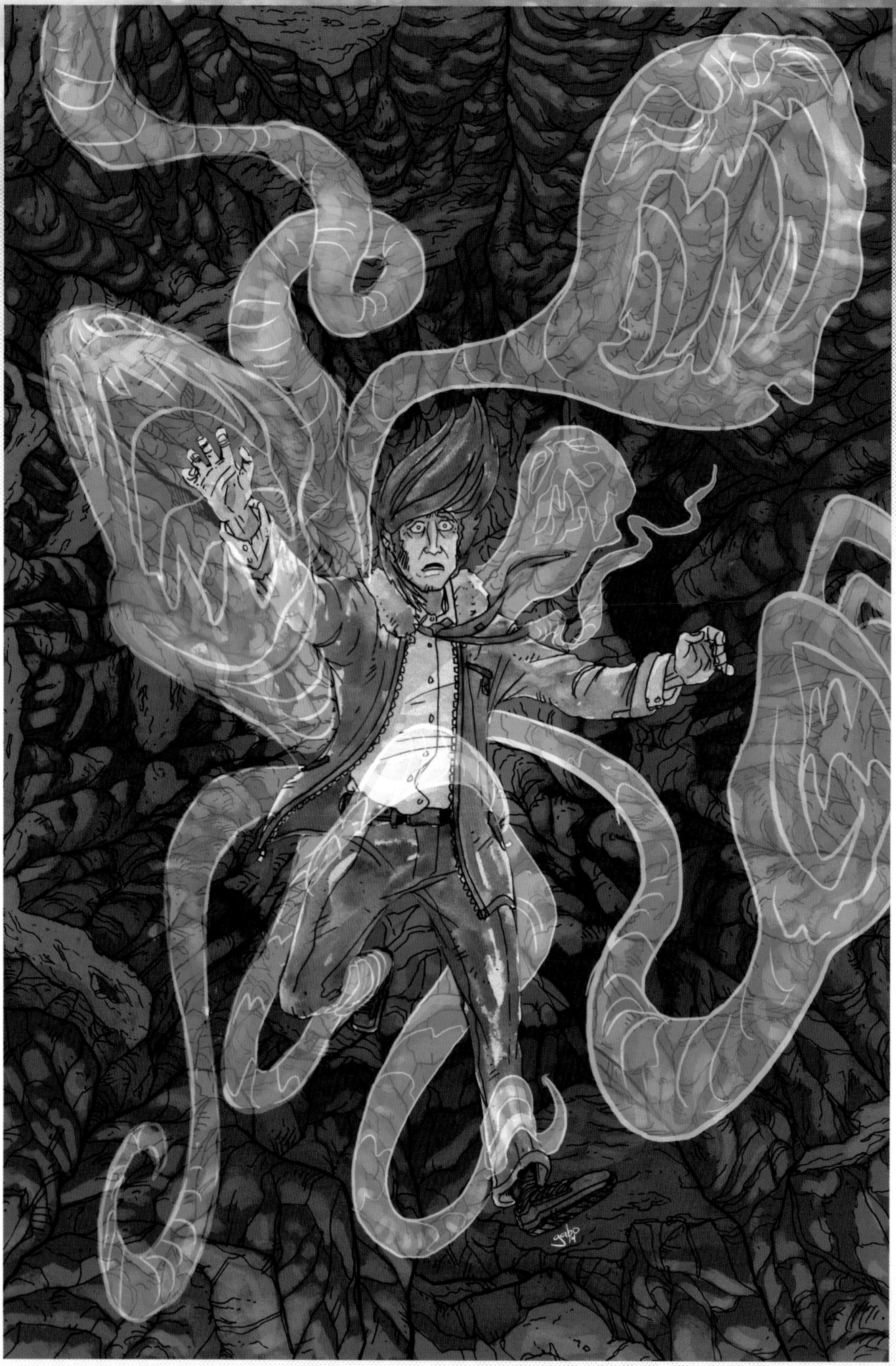

THE LIFE
AFTER

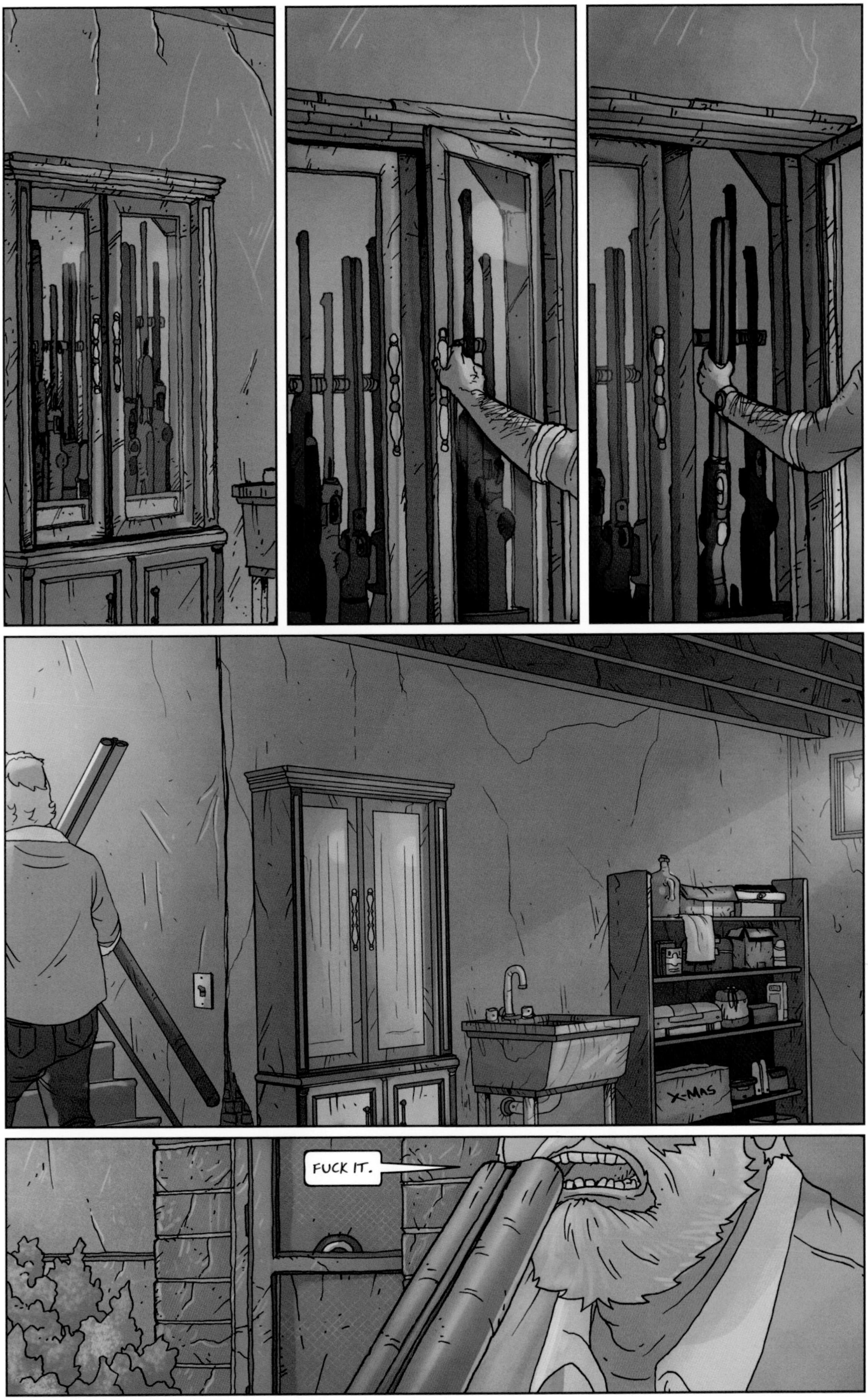
X-MAS
FUCK IT.

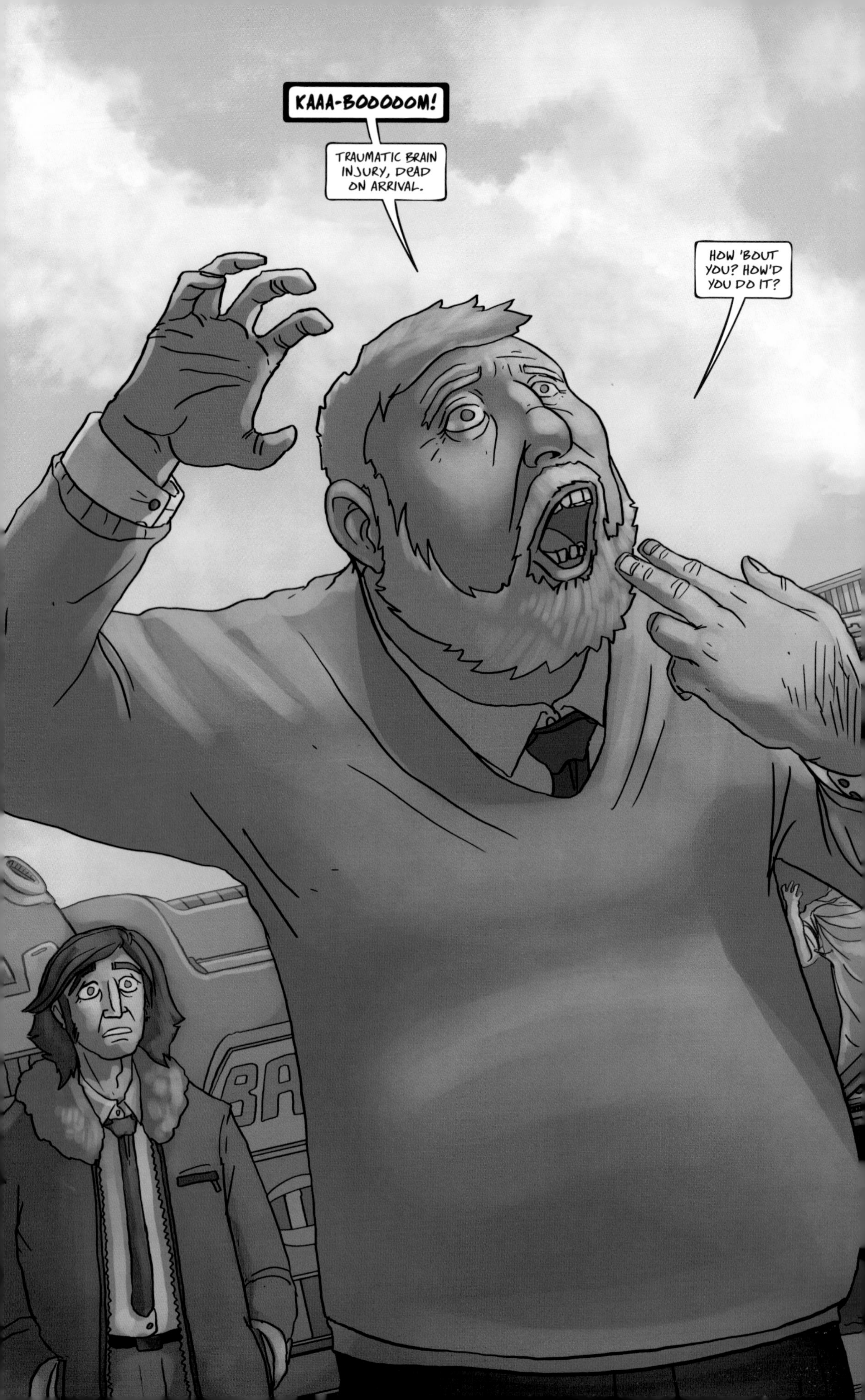
KAAA-BOOOOOM!
TRAUMATIC BRAIN INJURY, DEAD ON ARRIVAL.
HOW 'BOUT YOU? HOW'D YOU DO IT?

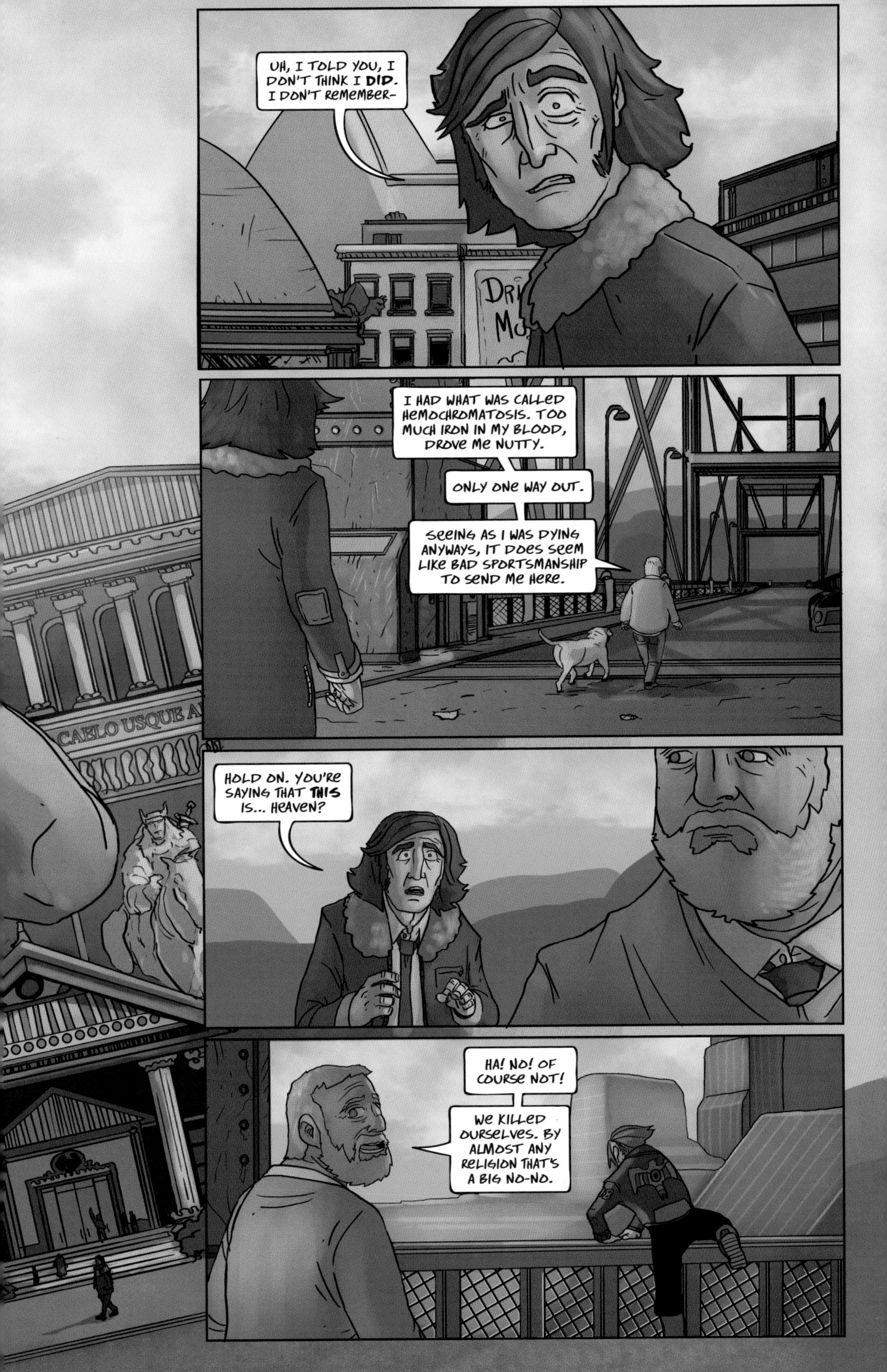

UH, I TOLD YOU, I DON'T THINK I **DID**. I DON'T REMEMBER-
DRI
MO
I HAD WHAT WAS CALLED HEMOCHROMATOSIS. TOO MUCH IRON IN MY BLOOD, DROVE ME NUTTY.
ONLY ONE WAY OUT.
SEEING AS I WAS DYING ANYWAYS, IT DOES SEEM LIKE BAD SPORTSMANSHIP TO SEND ME HERE.
CAELO USQUE A
HOLD ON. YOU'RE SAYING THAT **THIS** IS... HEAVEN?
HA! NO! OF COURSE NOT!
WE KILLED OURSELVES. BY ALMOST ANY RELIGION THAT'S A BIG NO-NO.

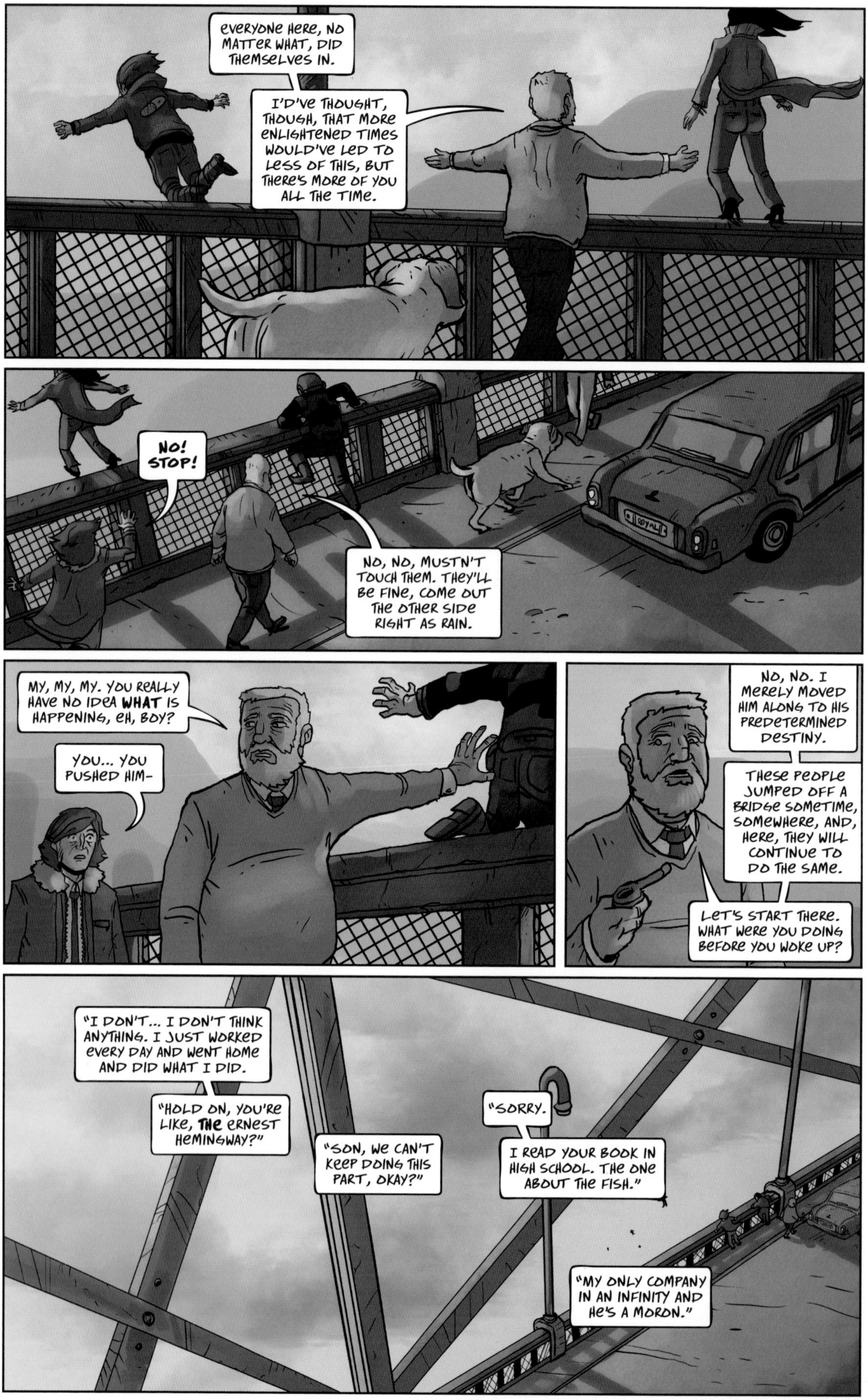
EVERYONE HERE, NO MATTER WHAT, DID THEMSELVES IN.
I'D'VE THOUGHT, THOUGH, THAT MORE ENLIGHTENED TIMES WOULD'VE LED TO LESS OF THIS, BUT THERE'S MORE OF YOU ALL THE TIME.
NO! STOP!
NO, NO, MUSTN'T TOUCH THEM. THEY'LL BE FINE, COME OUT THE OTHER SIDE RIGHT AS RAIN.
MY, MY, MY. YOU REALLY HAVE NO IDEA **WHAT** IS HAPPENING, EH, BOY?
YOU... YOU PUSHED HIM-
NO, NO. I MERELY MOVED HIM ALONG TO HIS PREDETERMINED DESTINY.
THESE PEOPLE JUMPED OFF A BRIDGE SOMETIME, SOMEWHERE, AND, HERE, THEY WILL CONTINUE TO DO THE SAME.
LET'S START THERE. WHAT WERE YOU DOING BEFORE YOU WOKE UP?
"I DON'T... I DON'T THINK ANYTHING. I JUST WORKED EVERY DAY AND WENT HOME AND DID WHAT I DID.
"HOLD ON, YOU'RE LIKE, **THE** ERNEST HEMINGWAY?"
"SON, WE CAN'T KEEP DOING THIS PART, OKAY?"
"SORRY.
I READ YOUR BOOK IN HIGH SCHOOL. THE ONE ABOUT THE FISH."
"MY ONLY COMPANY IN AN INFINITY AND HE'S A MORON."

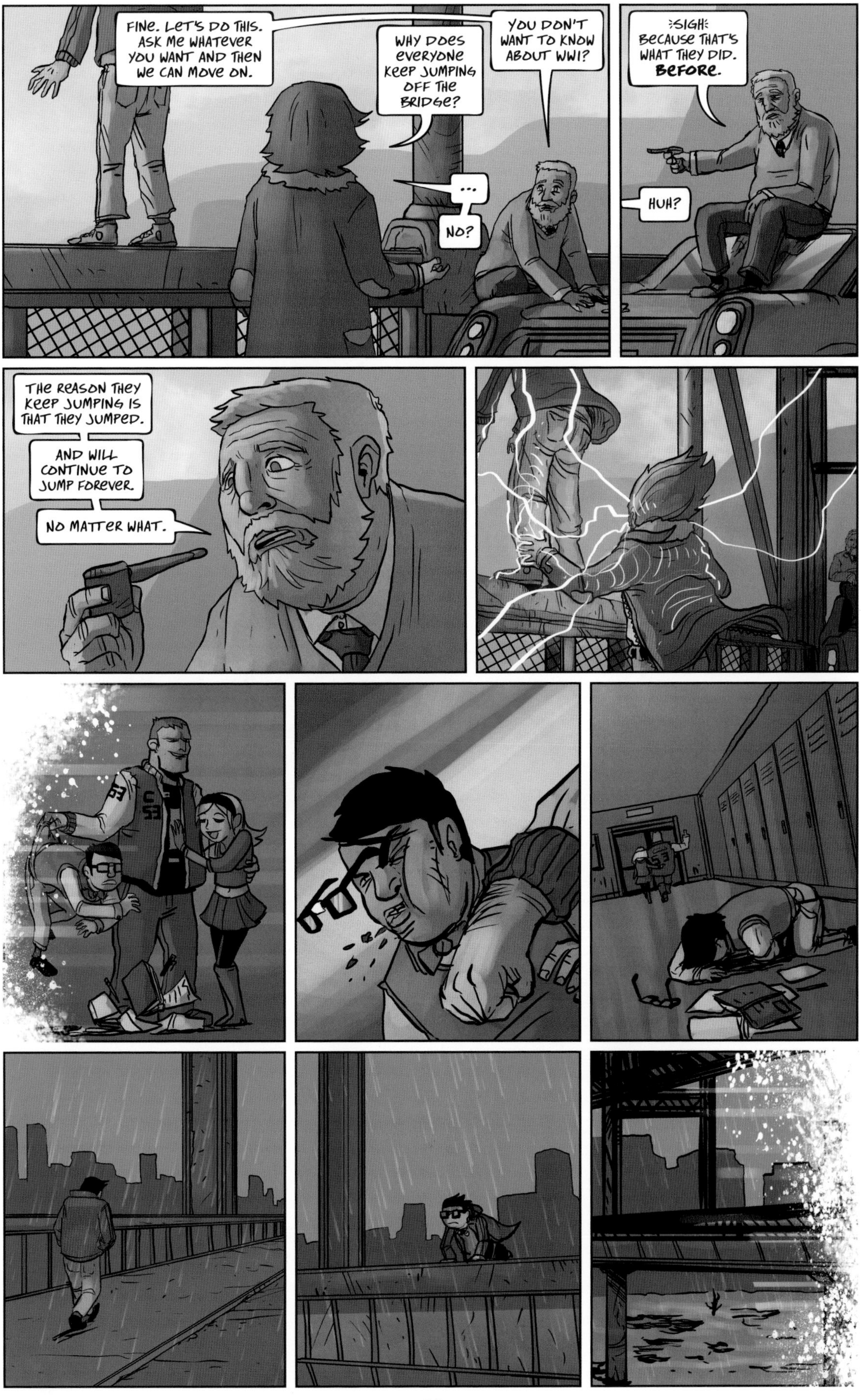
FINE. LET'S DO THIS. ASK ME WHATEVER YOU WANT AND THEN WE CAN MOVE ON.
WHY DOES EVERYONE KEEP JUMPING OFF THE BRIDGE?
YOU DON'T WANT TO KNOW ABOUT WWI?
...
NO?
SIGH
BECAUSE THAT'S WHAT THEY DID. BEFORE.
HUH?
THE REASON THEY KEEP JUMPING IS THAT THEY JUMPED.
AND WILL CONTINUE TO JUMP FOREVER.
NO MATTER WHAT.

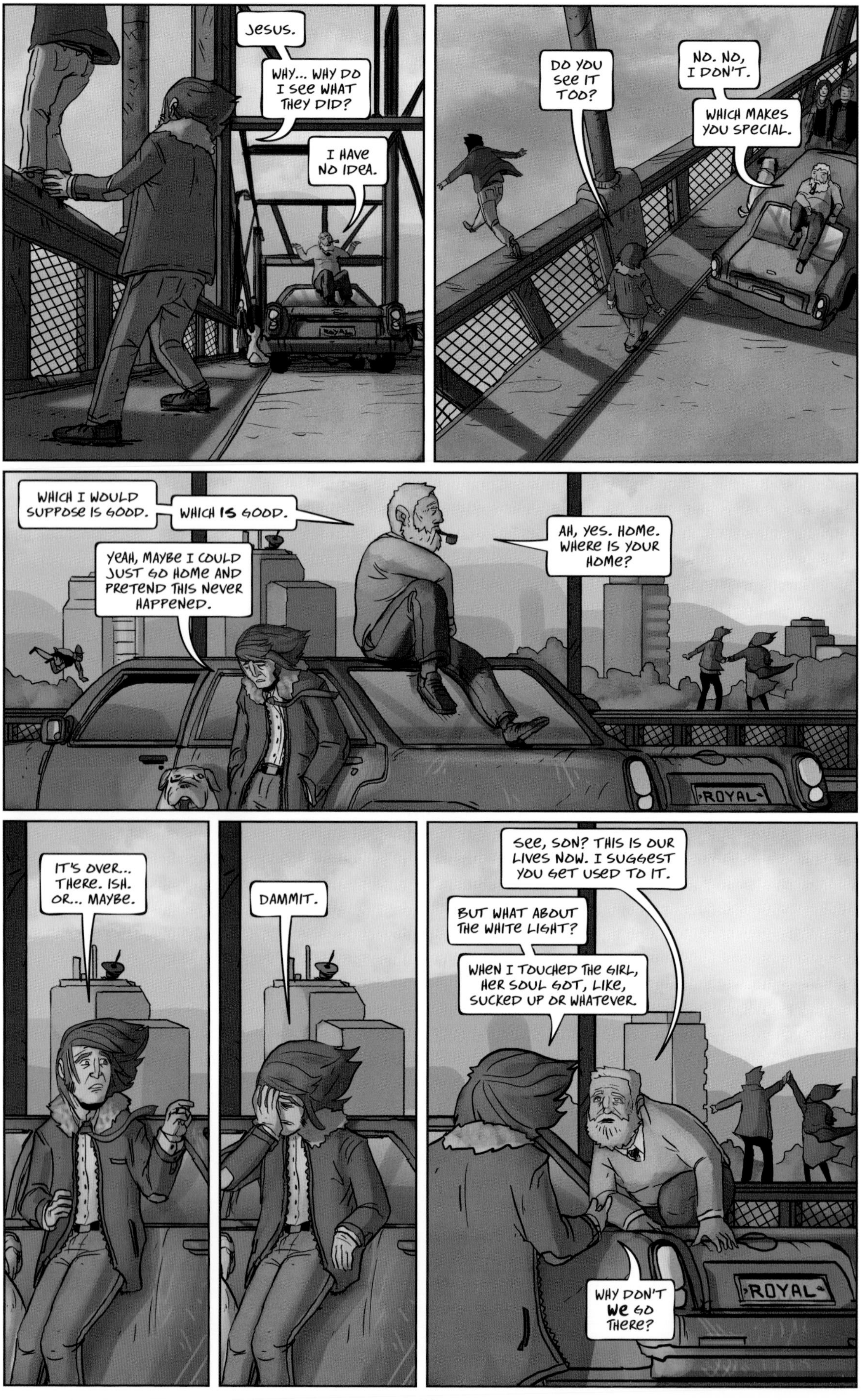
Jesus.
Why... why do I see what they did?
I have no idea.
Do you see it too?
No. No, I don't.
Which makes you special.
Which I would suppose is good.
Which **is** good.
Yeah, maybe I could just go home and pretend this never happened.
Ah, yes. Home. Where is your home?
ROYAL
It's over... there. Ish. Or... maybe.
Dammit.
See, son? This is our lives now. I suggest you get used to it.
But what about the white light?
When I touched the girl, her soul got, like, sucked up or whatever.
Why don't **we** go there?
ROYAL

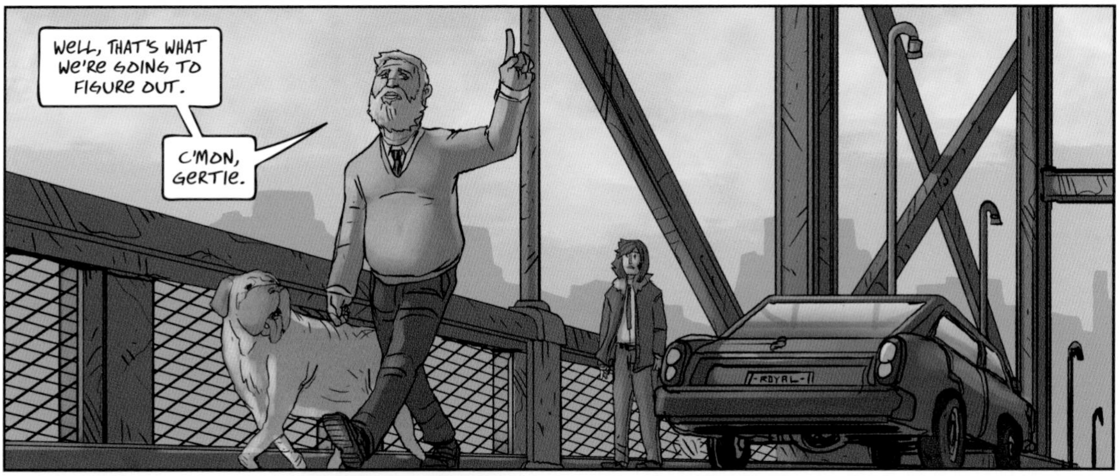
WELL, THAT'S WHAT WE'RE GOING TO FIGURE OUT.
C'MON, GERTIE.

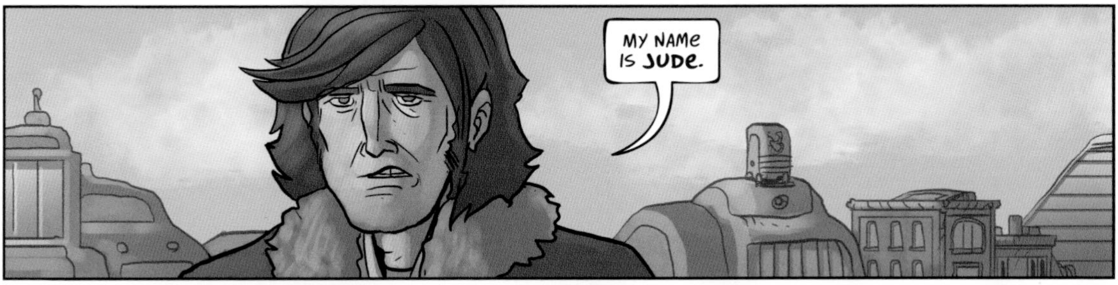
MY NAME IS **JUDE**.

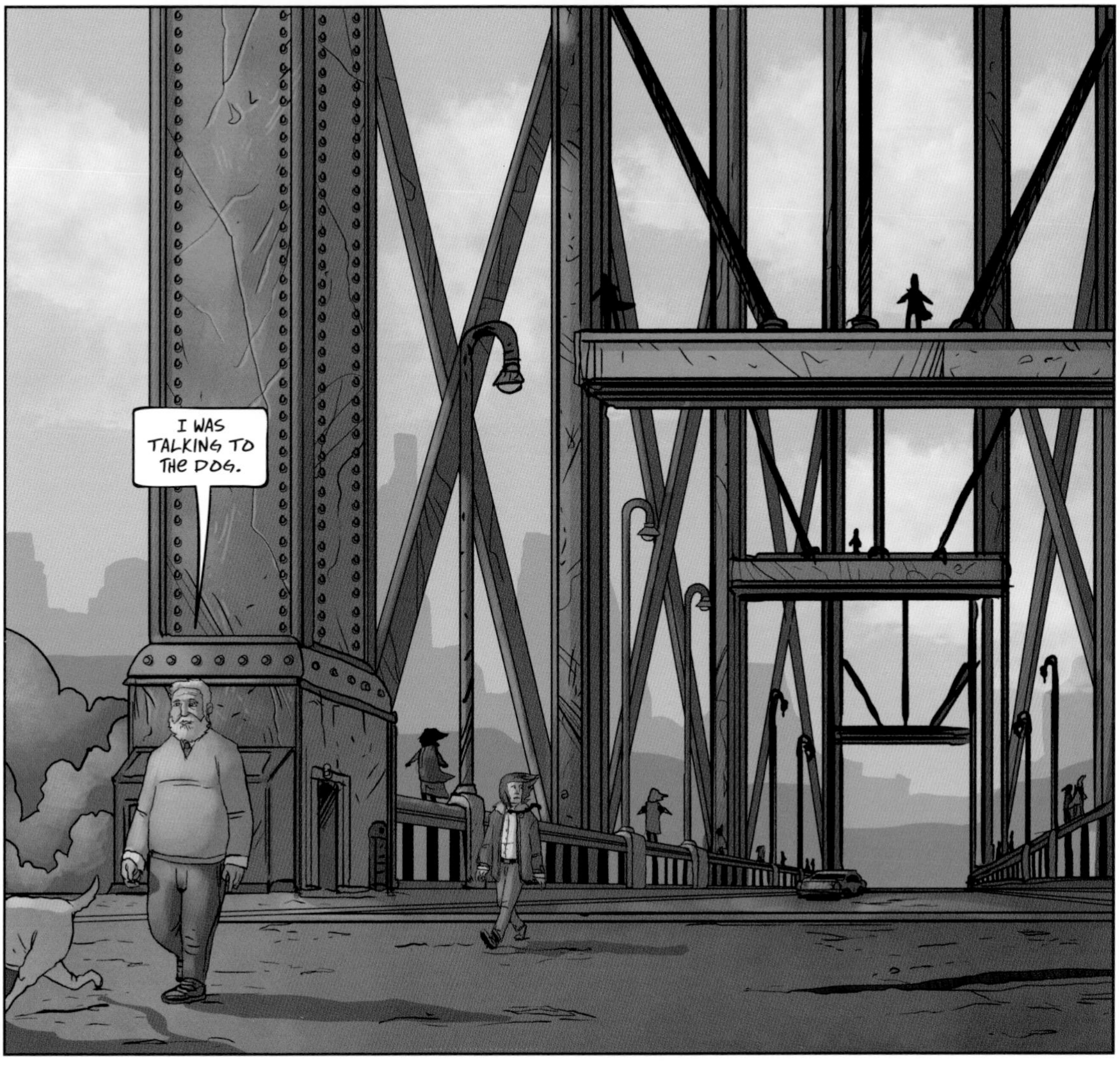
I WAS TALKING TO THE DOG.

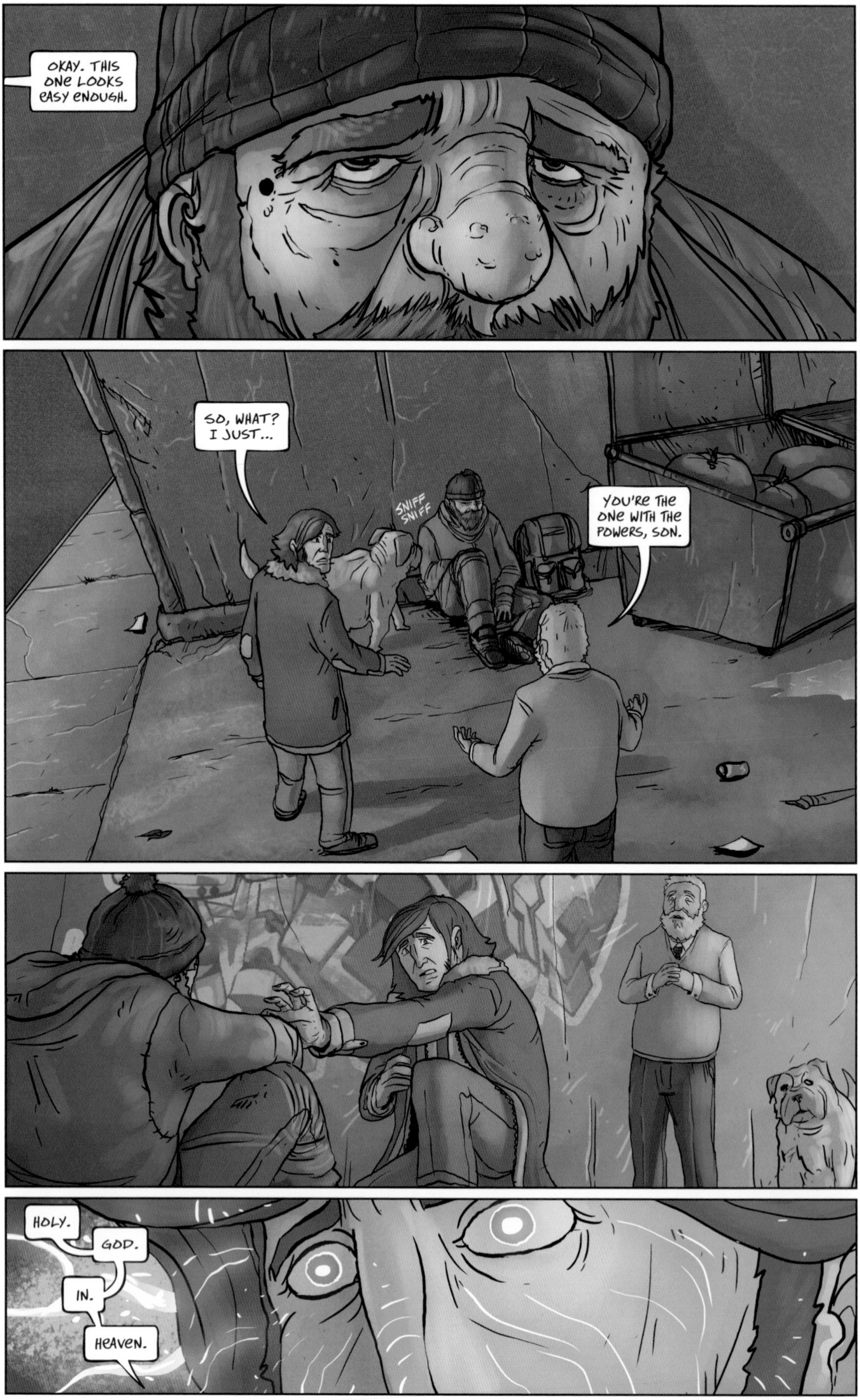
OKAY. THIS ONE LOOKS EASY ENOUGH.
SO, WHAT? I JUST...
SNIFF SNIFF
YOU'RE THE ONE WITH THE POWERS, SON.
HOLY.
GOD.
IN.
HEAVEN.

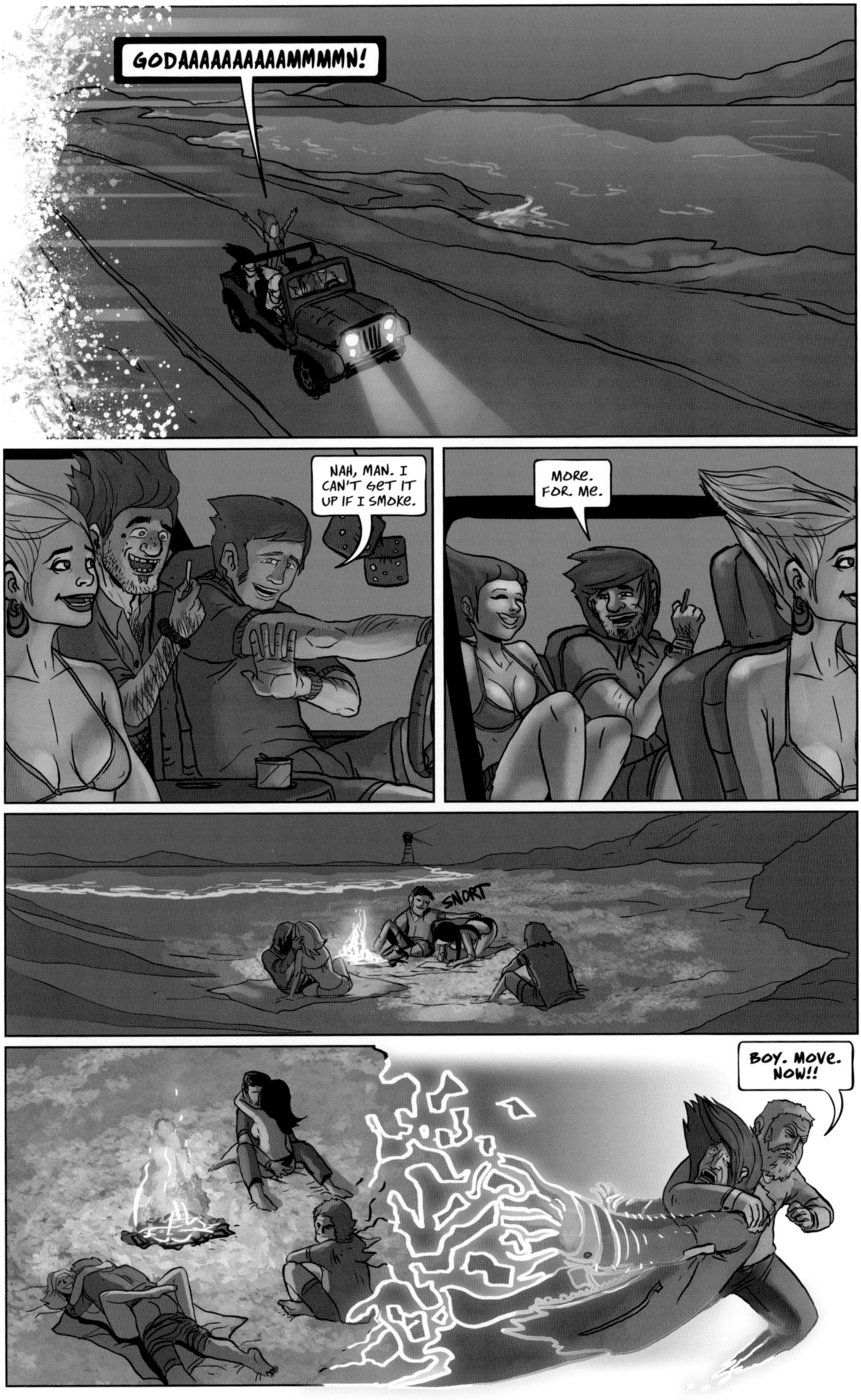
GODAAAAAAAAAAMMMMN!
NAH, MAN. I CAN'T GET IT UP IF I SMOKE.
MORE. FOR. ME.
SNORT
BOY. MOVE. NOW!!

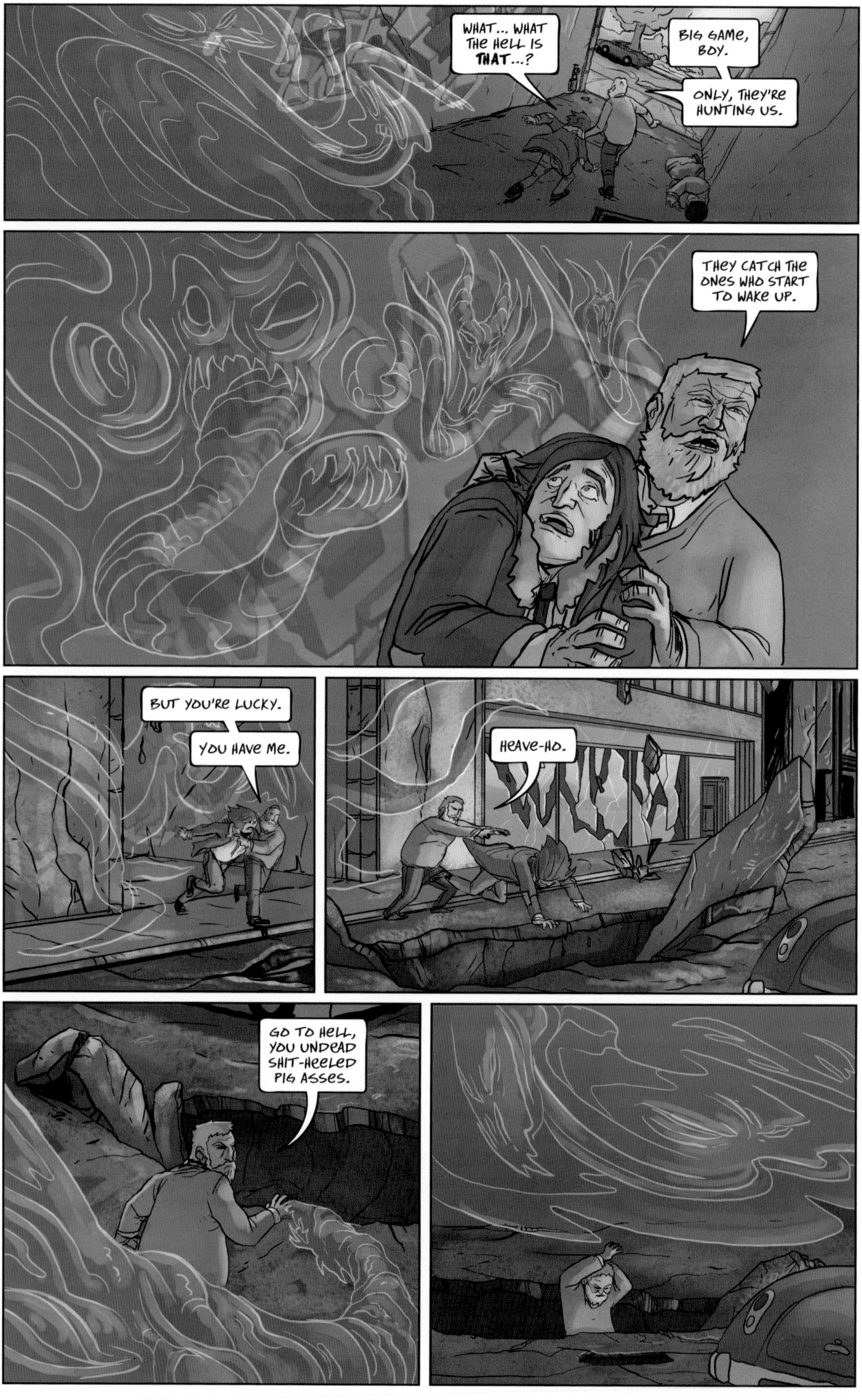
WHAT... WHAT THE HELL IS THAT...?
BIG GAME, BOY.
ONLY, THEY'RE HUNTING US.
THEY CATCH THE ONES WHO START TO WAKE UP.
BUT YOU'RE LUCKY.
YOU HAVE ME.
HEAVE-HO.
GO TO HELL, YOU UNDEAD SHIT-HEELED PIG ASSES.

WE'VE GOT THE MONITOR TO HIS LOCATION.

WE SHOULD BE BACK ONLINE AND ABLE TO SEE WHAT WE'RE DEALING WITH IN A COUPLE MINUTES.

SO NOW WE'VE GOT **TWO** WAKERS WALKING AROUND.

WELL, THE CLEANING PROGRAM WILL GET THEM OUT.

I THINK WE NEED TO REPORT THIS TO UPSTAIRS.

HELL NO.

REPORT WHAT?

OH. SIR. NOTHING. WE DON'T WANT TO BOTHER THE FOREMAN—

NONSENSE, PLAWSKY—

UH, I'M PLAWSKY, SIR.

OF COURSE, MY MISTAKE.

SO, WHAT? WE GLITCHING AGAIN?

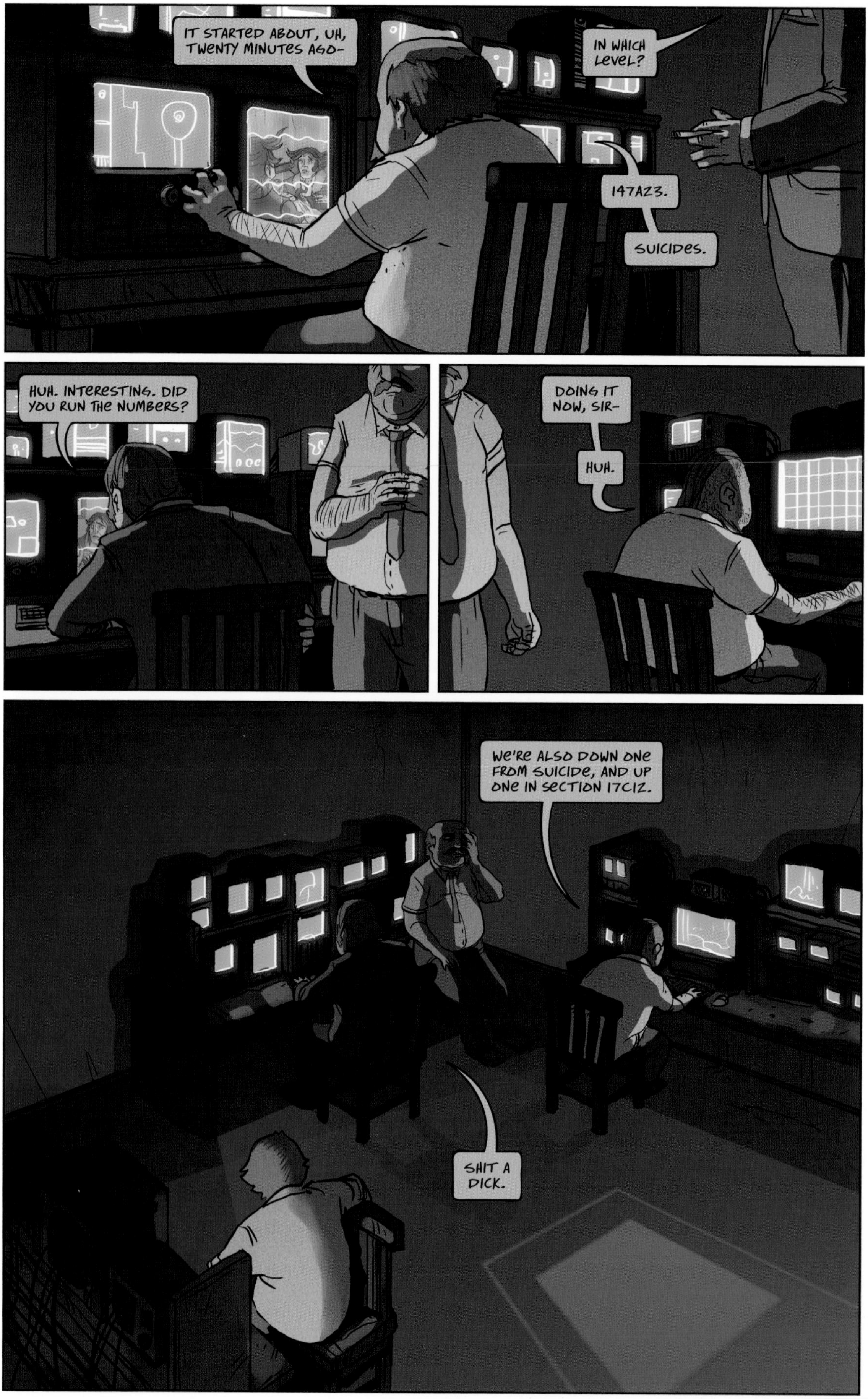
IT STARTED ABOUT, UH, TWENTY MINUTES AGO-
IN WHICH LEVEL?
147A23.
SUICIDES.
HUH. INTERESTING. DID YOU RUN THE NUMBERS?
DOING IT NOW, SIR-
HUH.
WE'RE ALSO DOWN ONE FROM SUICIDE, AND UP ONE IN SECTION 17C12.
SHIT A DICK.

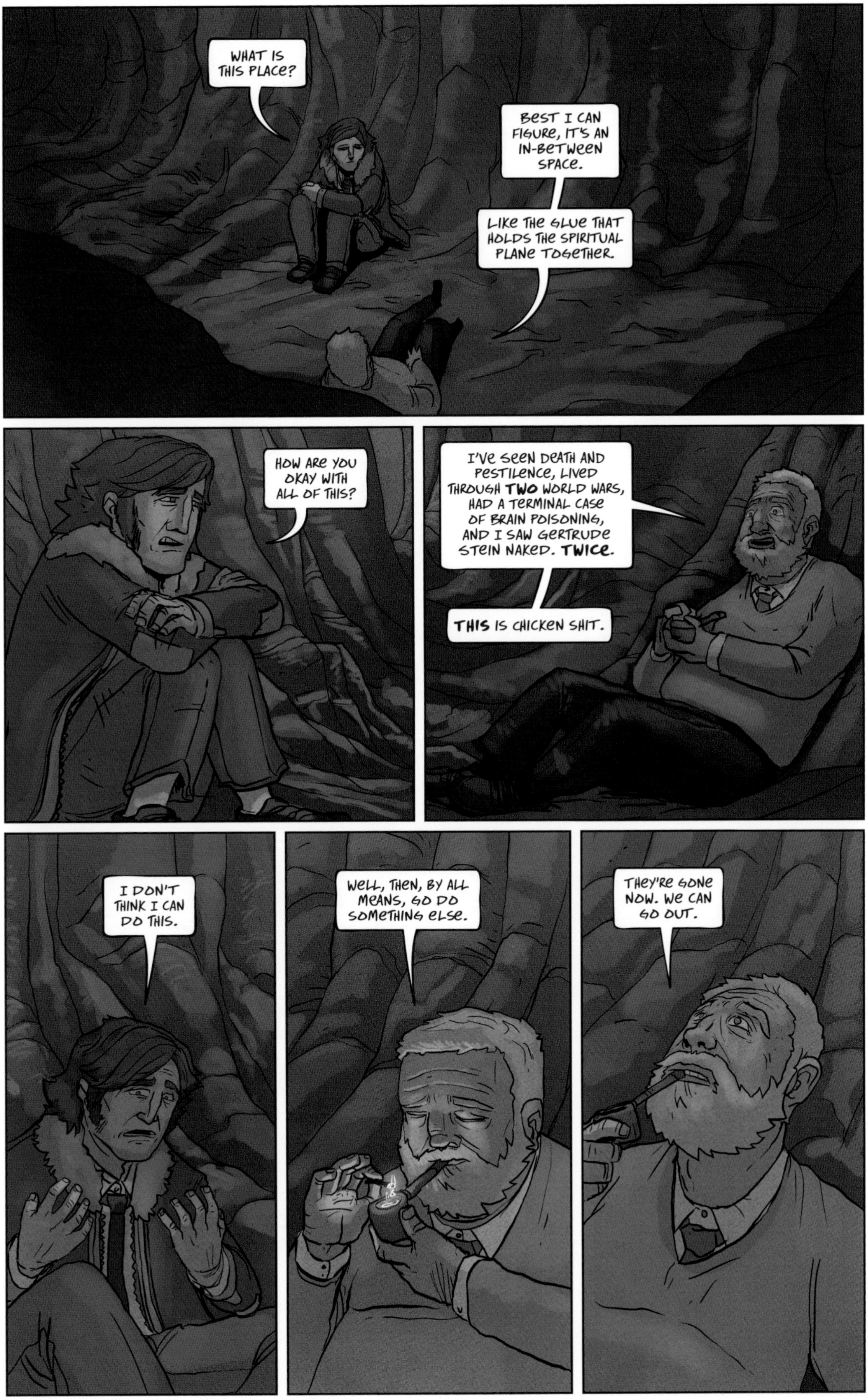
WHAT IS THIS PLACE?
BEST I CAN FIGURE, IT'S AN IN-BETWEEN SPACE.
LIKE THE GLUE THAT HOLDS THE SPIRITUAL PLANE TOGETHER.
HOW ARE YOU OKAY WITH ALL OF THIS?
I'VE SEEN DEATH AND PESTILENCE, LIVED THROUGH TWO WORLD WARS, HAD A TERMINAL CASE OF BRAIN POISONING, AND I SAW GERTRUDE STEIN NAKED. TWICE.
THIS IS CHICKEN SHIT.
I DON'T THINK I CAN DO THIS.
WELL, THEN, BY ALL MEANS, GO DO SOMETHING ELSE.
THEY'RE GONE NOW. WE CAN GO OUT.

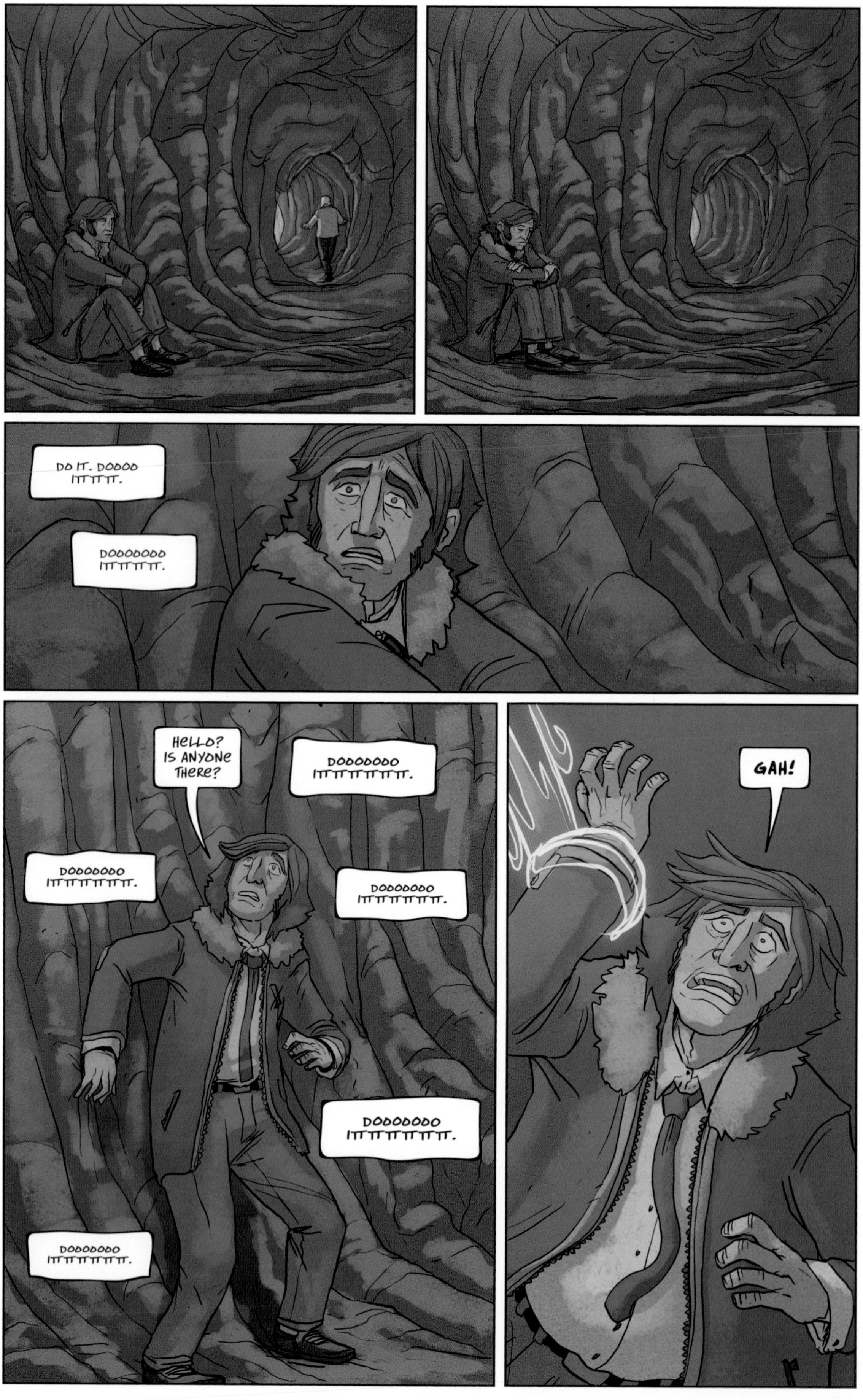
DO IT. DOOOO ITTTTT.
DOOOOOOO ITTTTTTT.
HELLO? IS ANYONE THERE?
DOOOOOOO ITTTTTTTTTT.
DOOOOOOO ITTTTTTTTT.
DOOOOOOO ITTTTTTTTT.
DOOOOOOO ITTTTTTTTT.
DOOOOOOO ITTTTTTTT.
GAH!

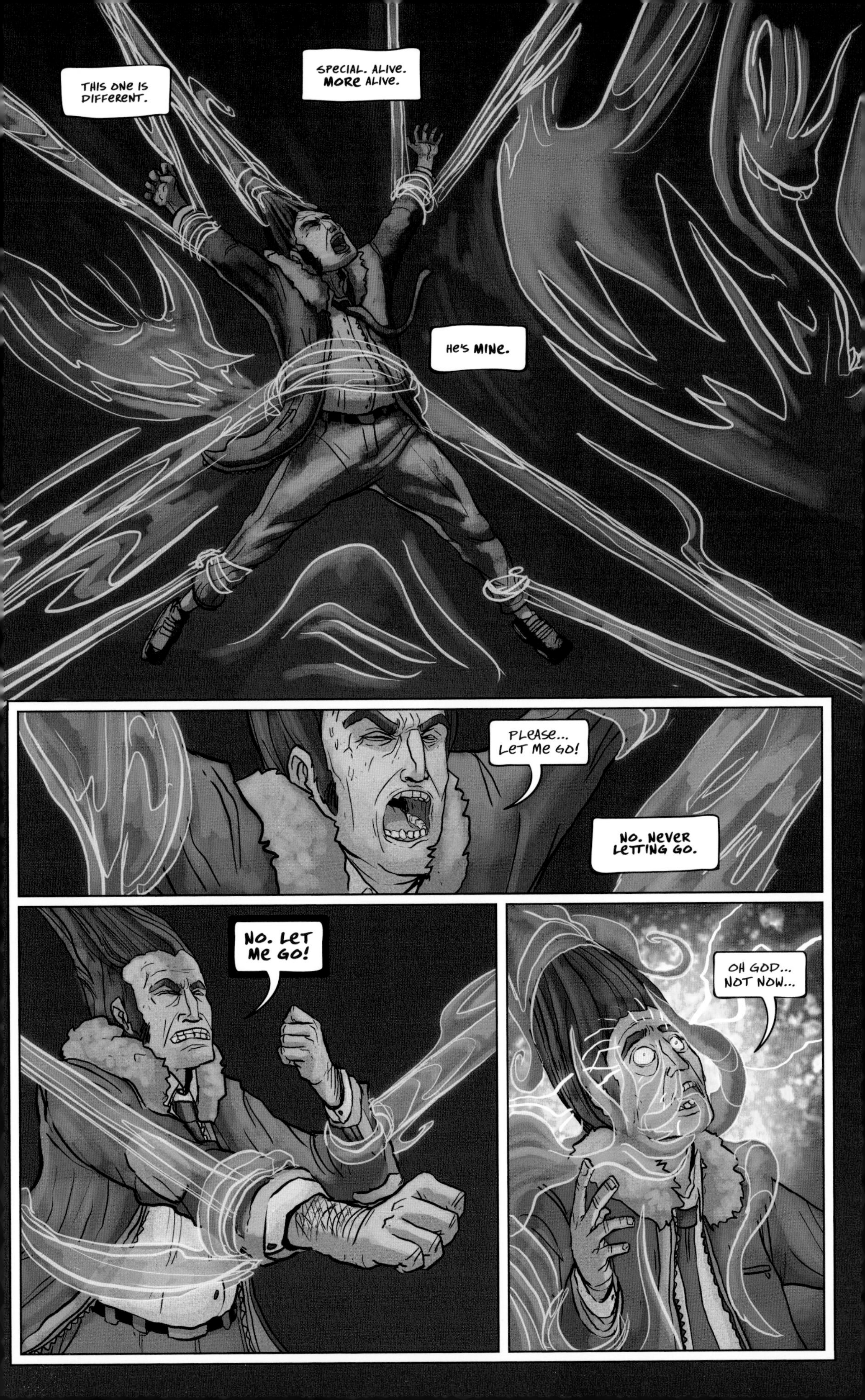
THIS ONE IS DIFFERENT.
SPECIAL. ALIVE. MORE ALIVE.
HE'S MINE.
PLEASE... LET ME GO!
NO. NEVER LETTING GO.
NO. LET ME GO!
OH GOD... NOT NOW...

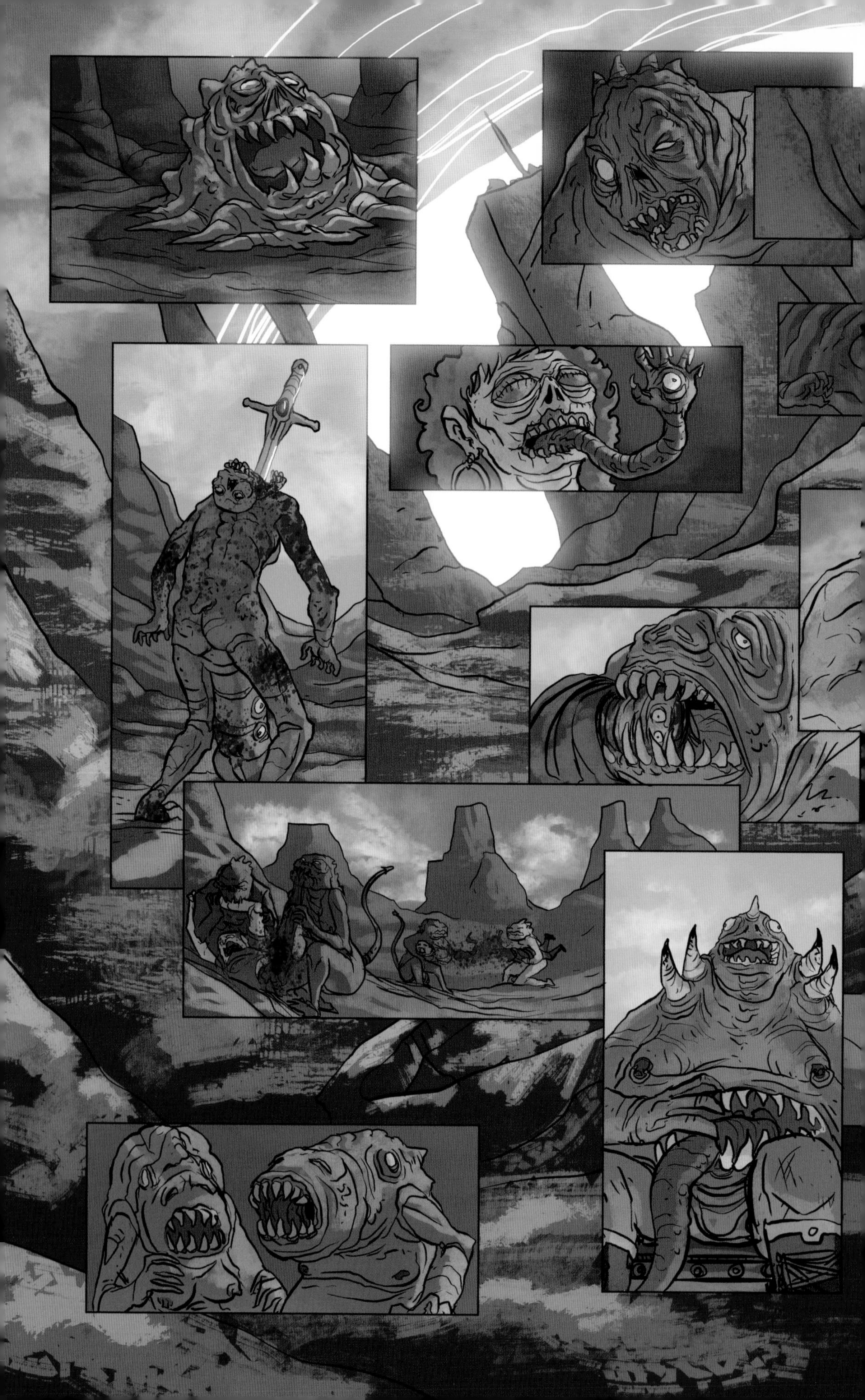

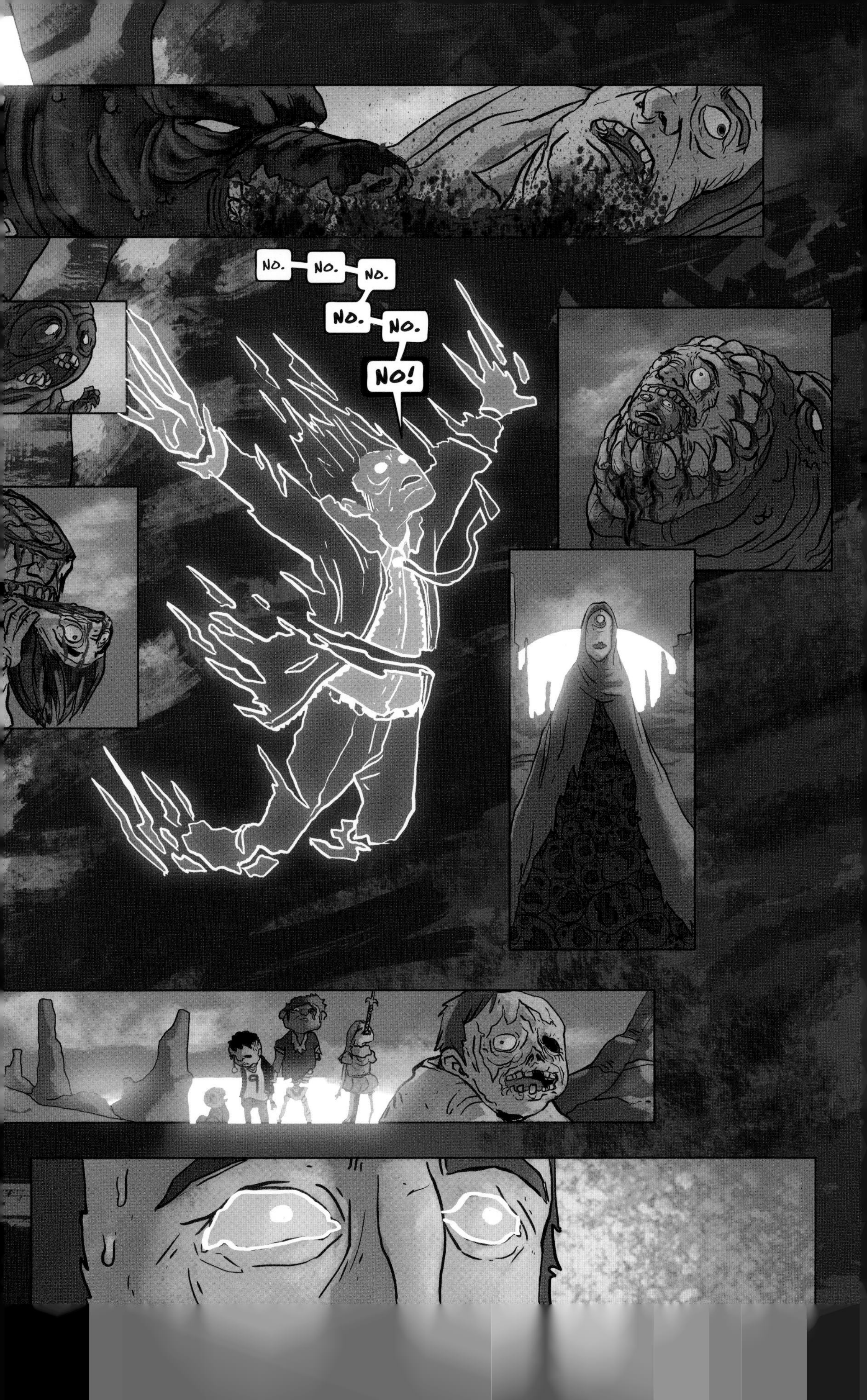
NO.
NO.
NO.
NO.
NO.
NO!

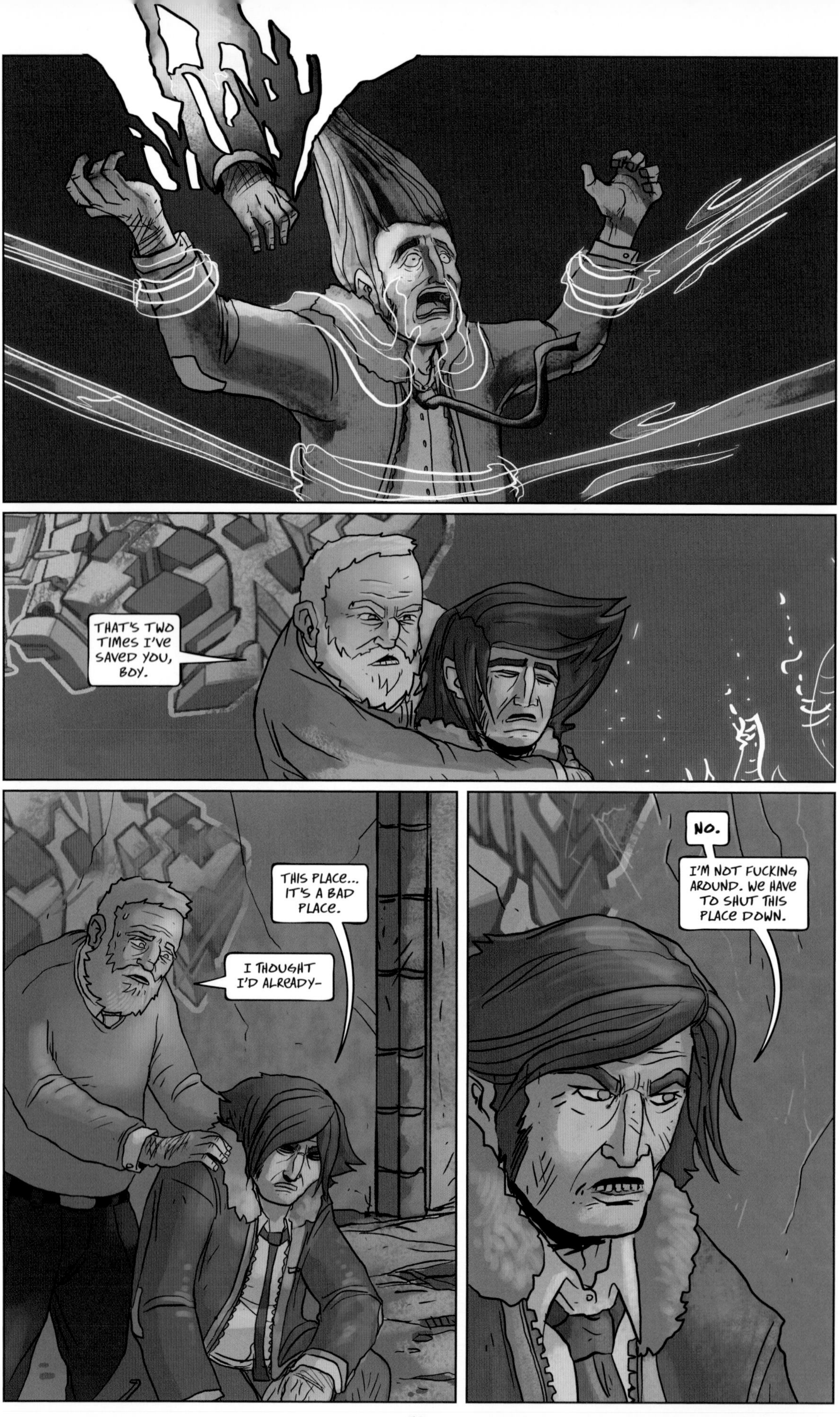
THAT'S TWO TIMES I'VE SAVED YOU, BOY.
THIS PLACE... IT'S A BAD PLACE.
I THOUGHT I'D ALREADY-
NO.
I'M NOT FUCKING AROUND. WE HAVE TO SHUT THIS PLACE DOWN.

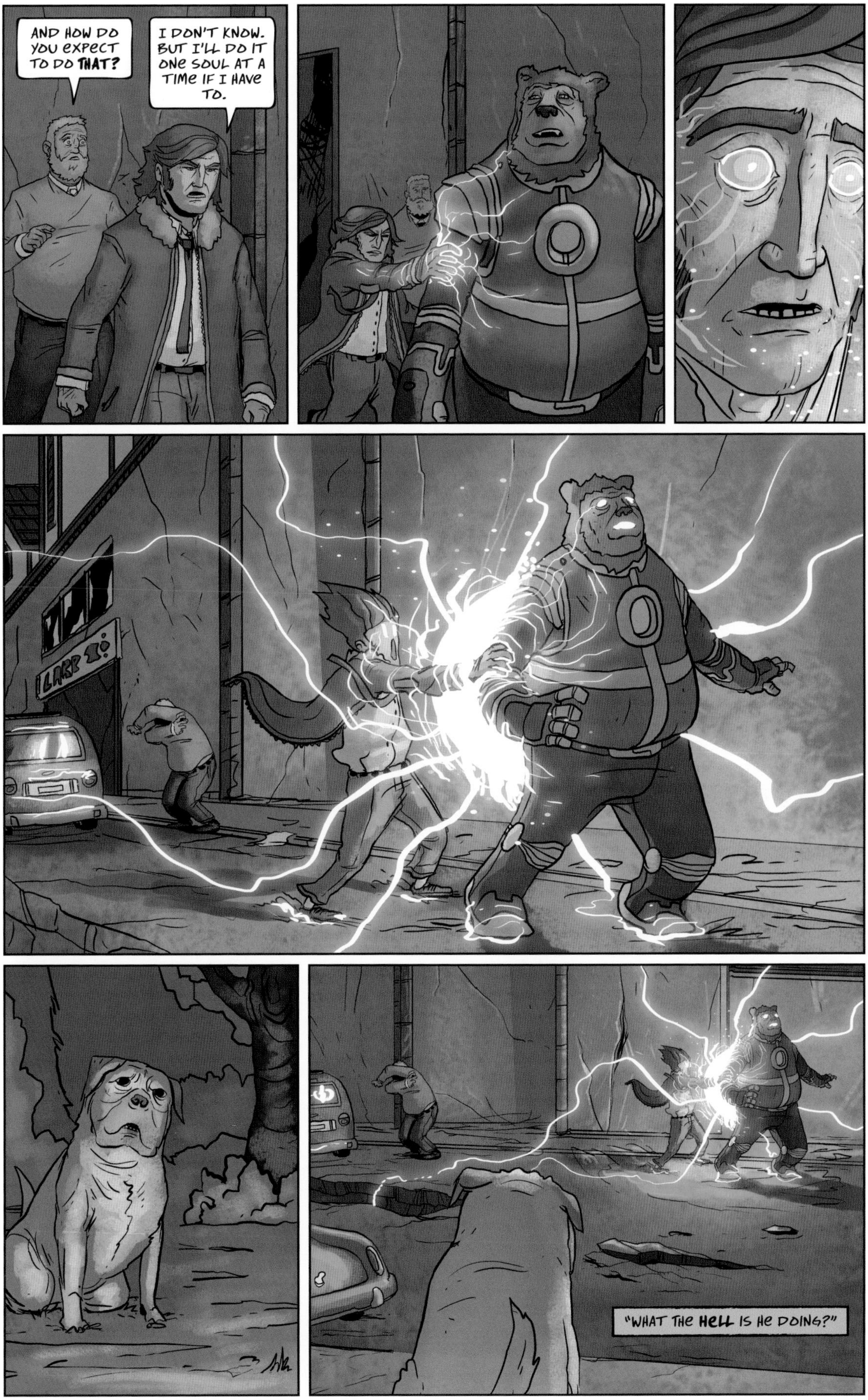
AND HOW DO YOU EXPECT TO DO **THAT?**
I DON'T KNOW. BUT I'LL DO IT ONE SOUL AT A TIME IF I HAVE TO.
"WHAT THE **HELL** IS HE DOING?"

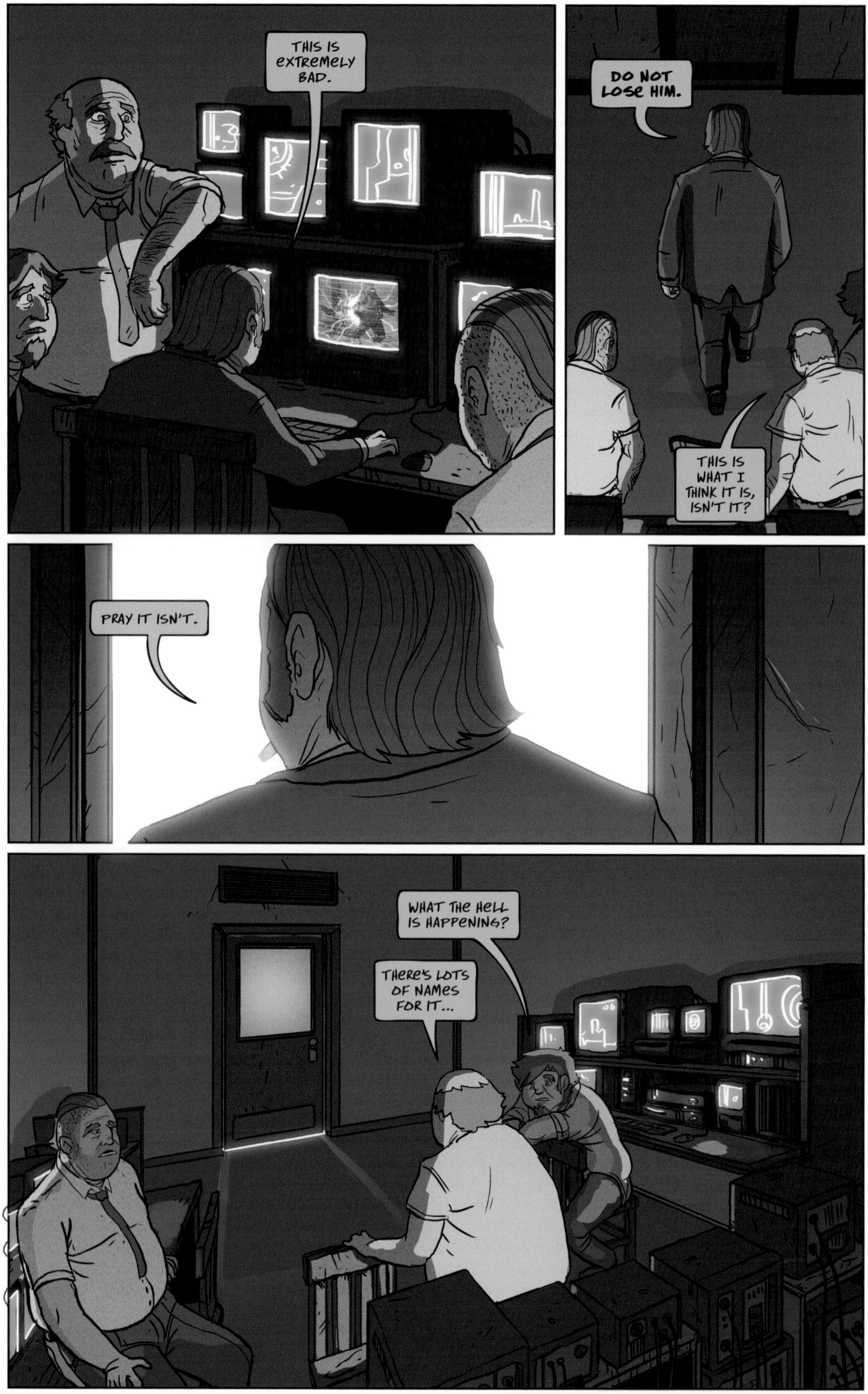
THIS IS EXTREMELY BAD.
DO NOT LOSE HIM.
THIS IS WHAT I THINK IT IS, ISN'T IT?
PRAY IT ISN'T.
WHAT THE HELL IS HAPPENING?
THERE'S LOTS OF NAMES FOR IT...

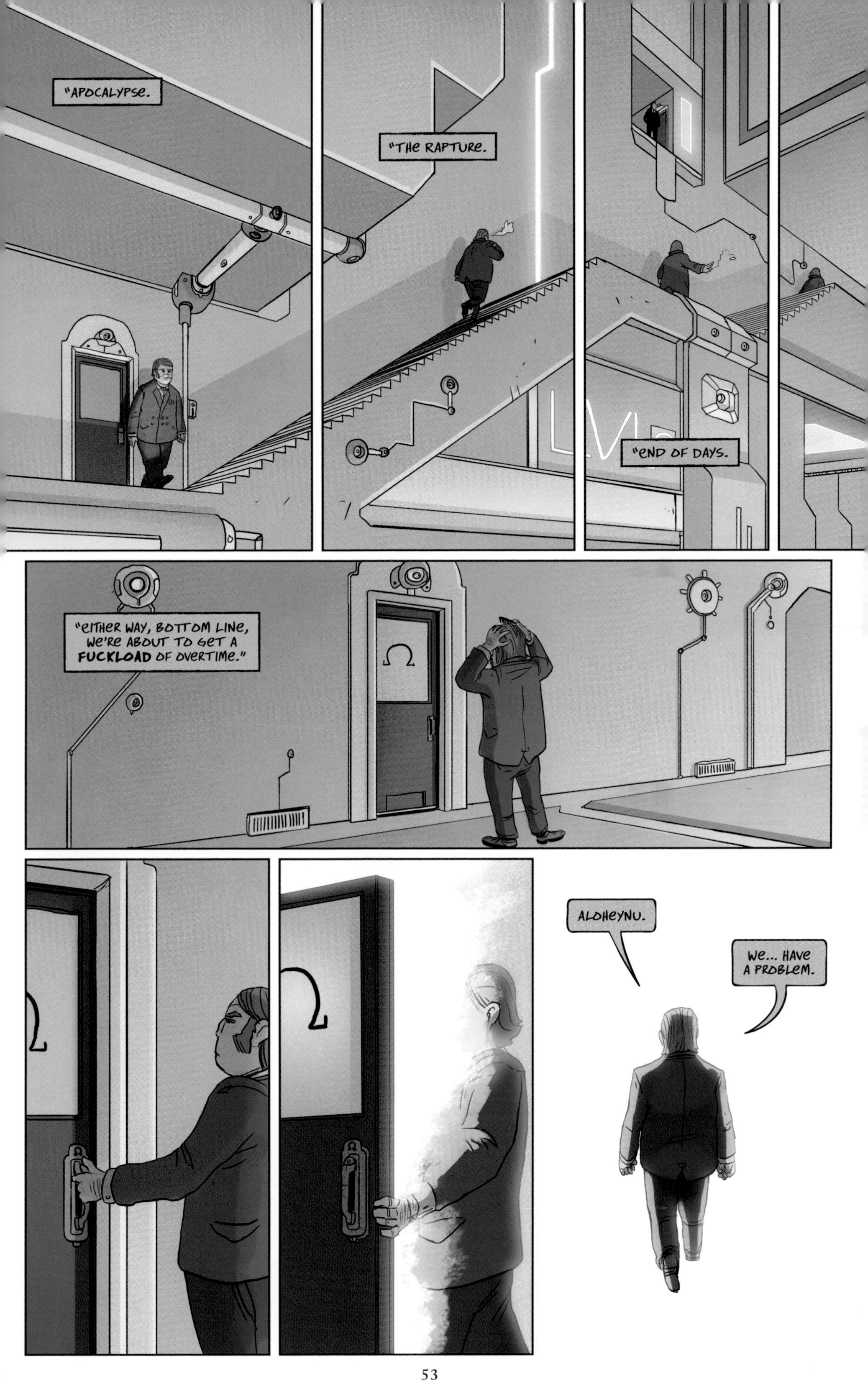
"APOCALYPSE.
"THE RAPTURE.
"END OF DAYS.
"EITHER WAY, BOTTOM LINE, WE'RE ABOUT TO GET A **FUCKLOAD** OF OVERTIME."
ALOHEYNU.
WE... HAVE A PROBLEM.

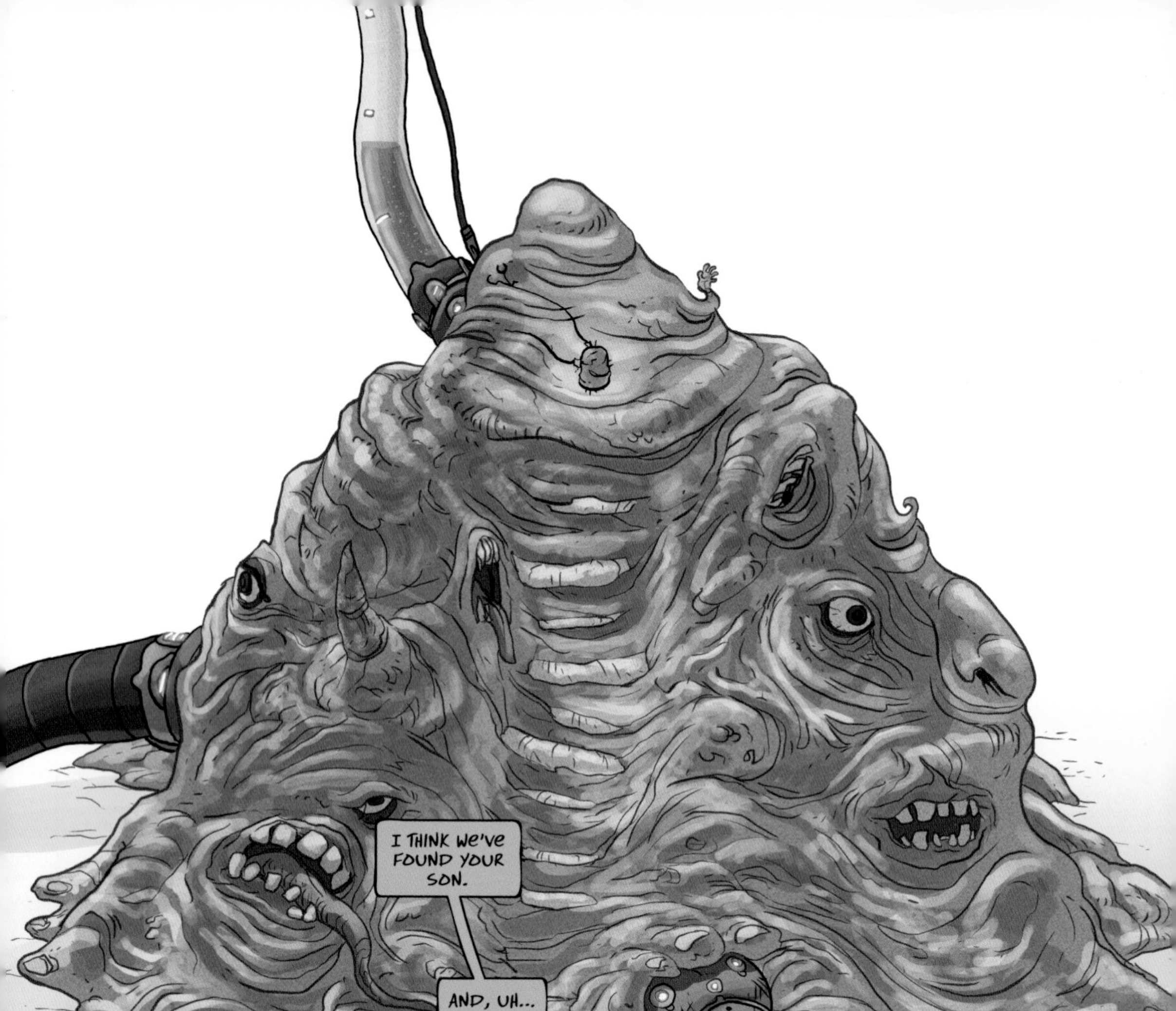
I THINK WE'VE FOUND YOUR SON.
AND, UH...

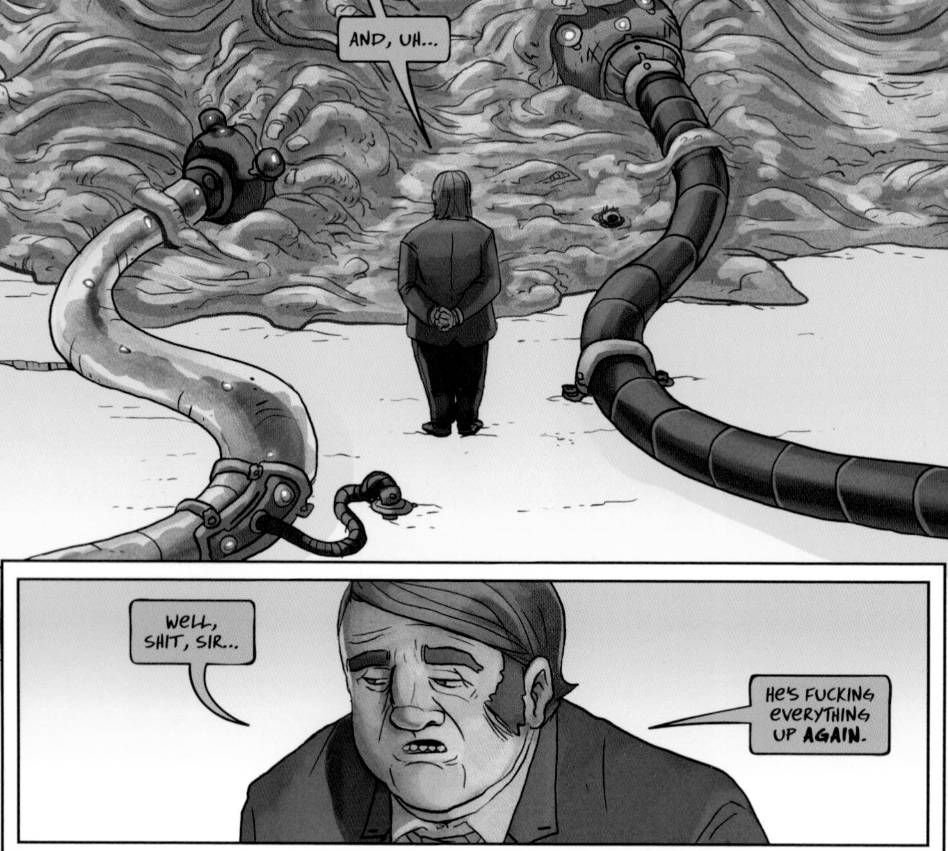
WELL, SHIT, SIR...
HE'S FUCKING EVERYTHING UP **AGAIN**.

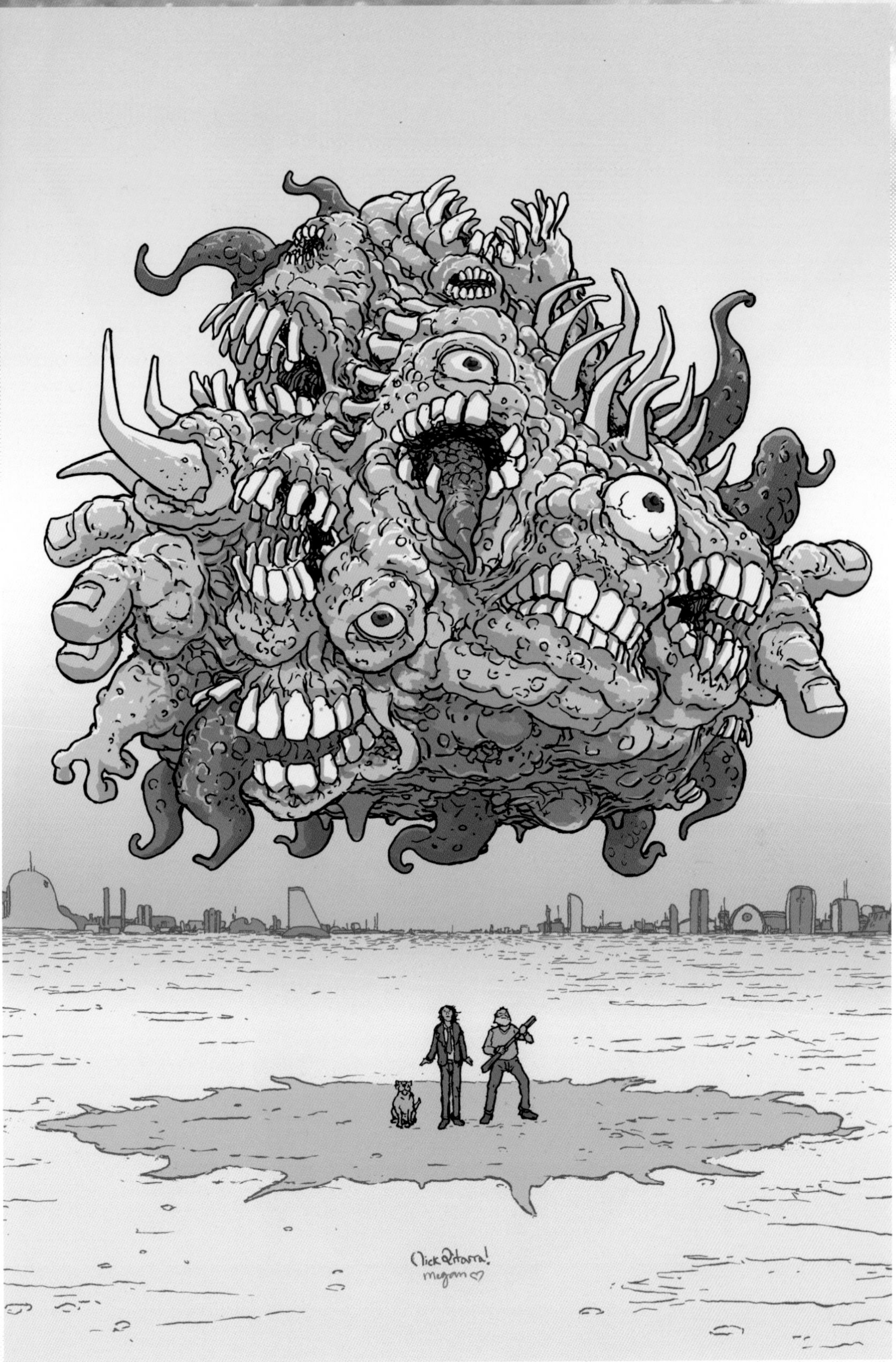

Chapter Three

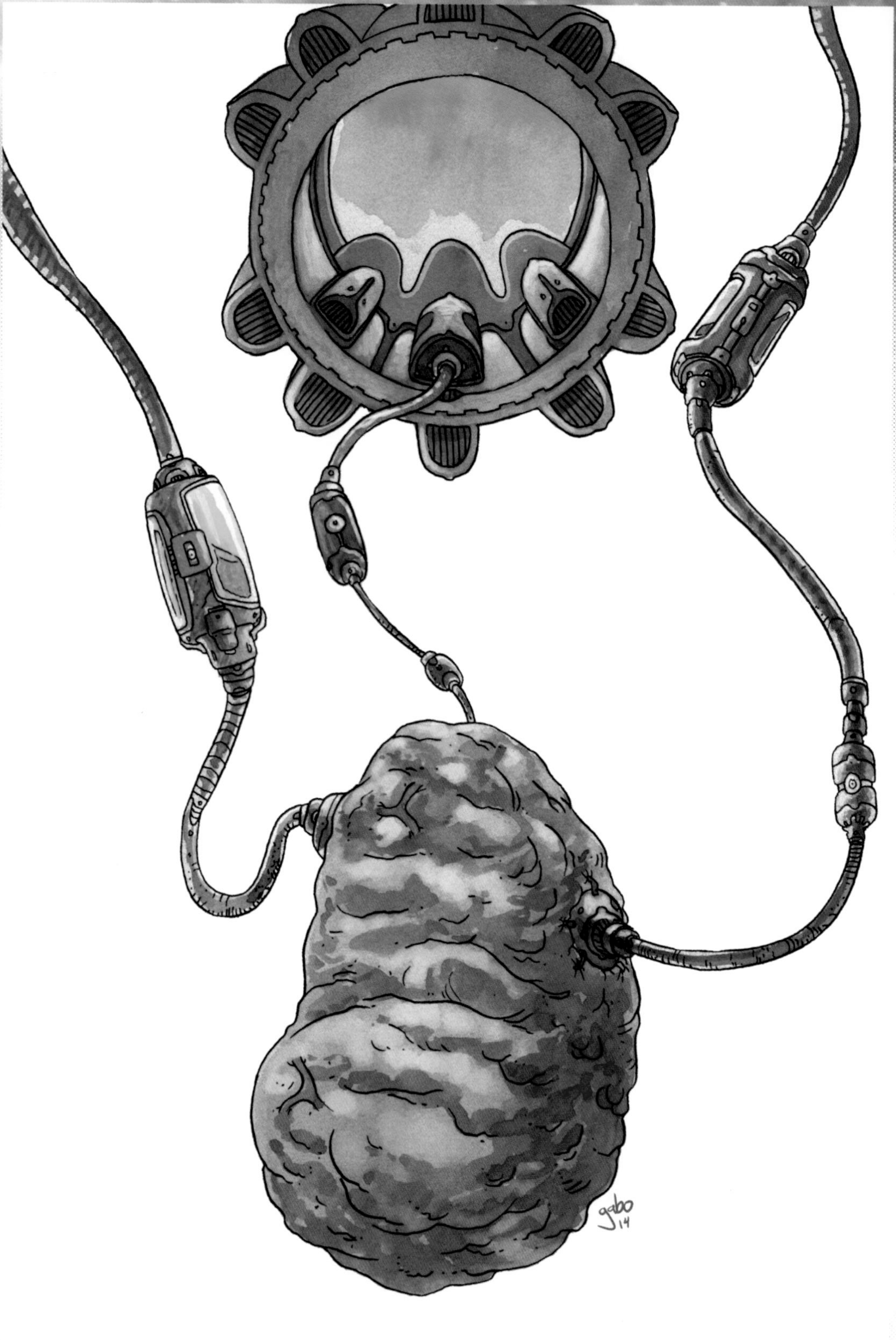
gabo
'14

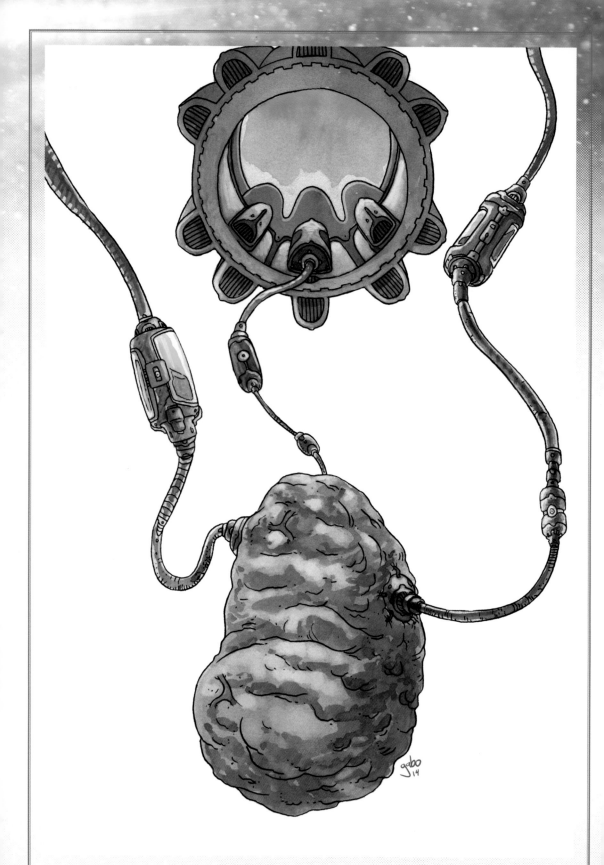

THE LIFE AFTER

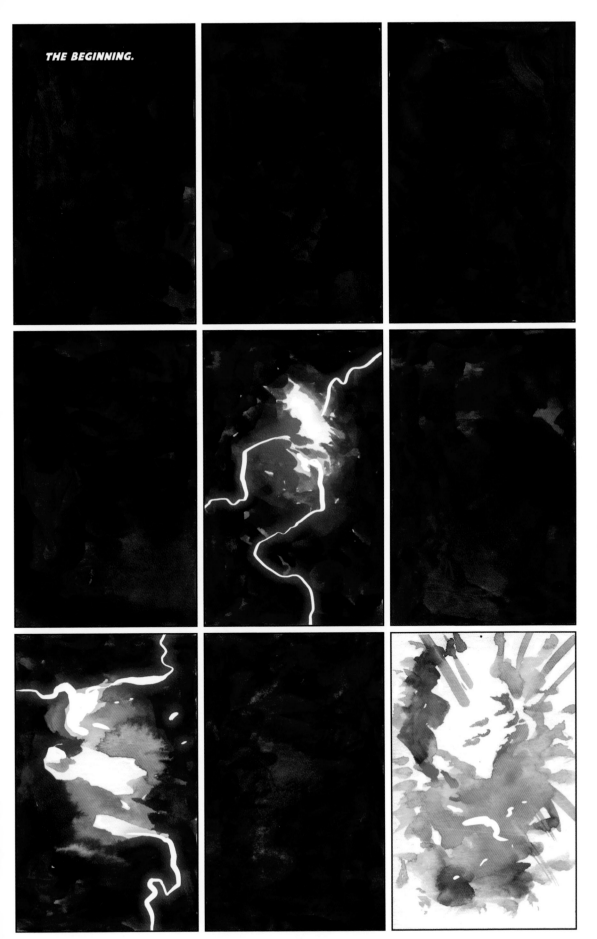

THE BEGINNING.

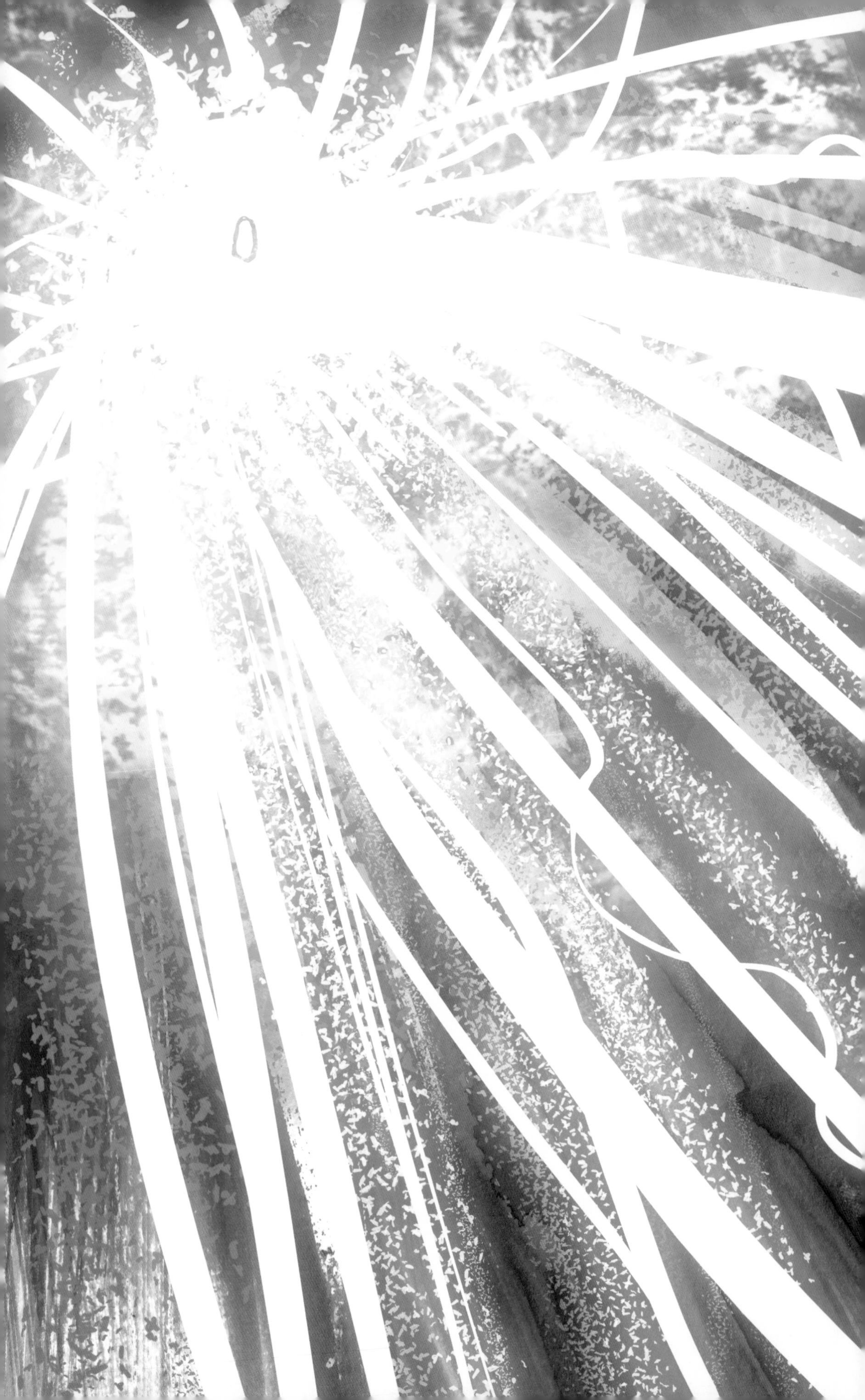

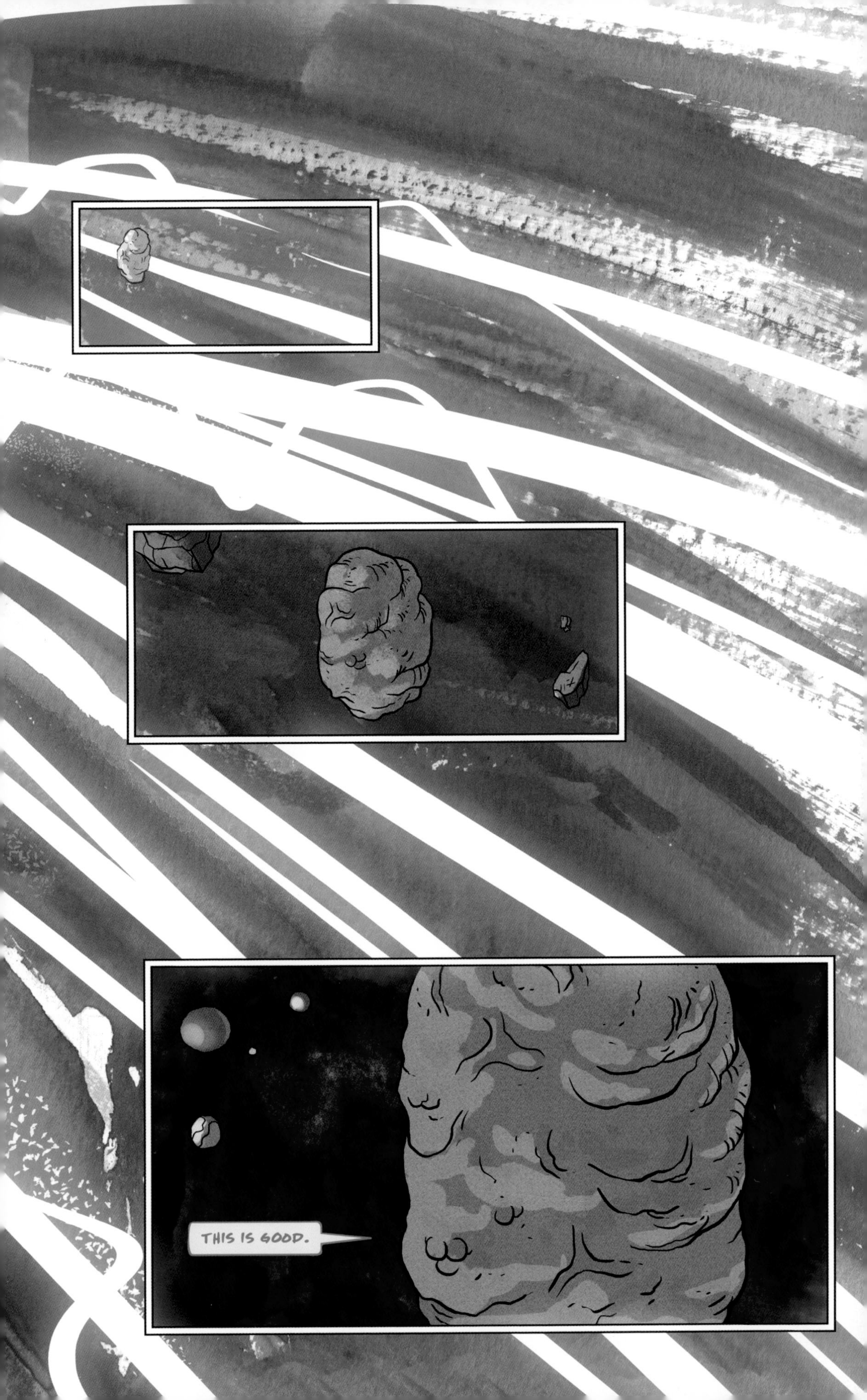
THIS IS GOOD.

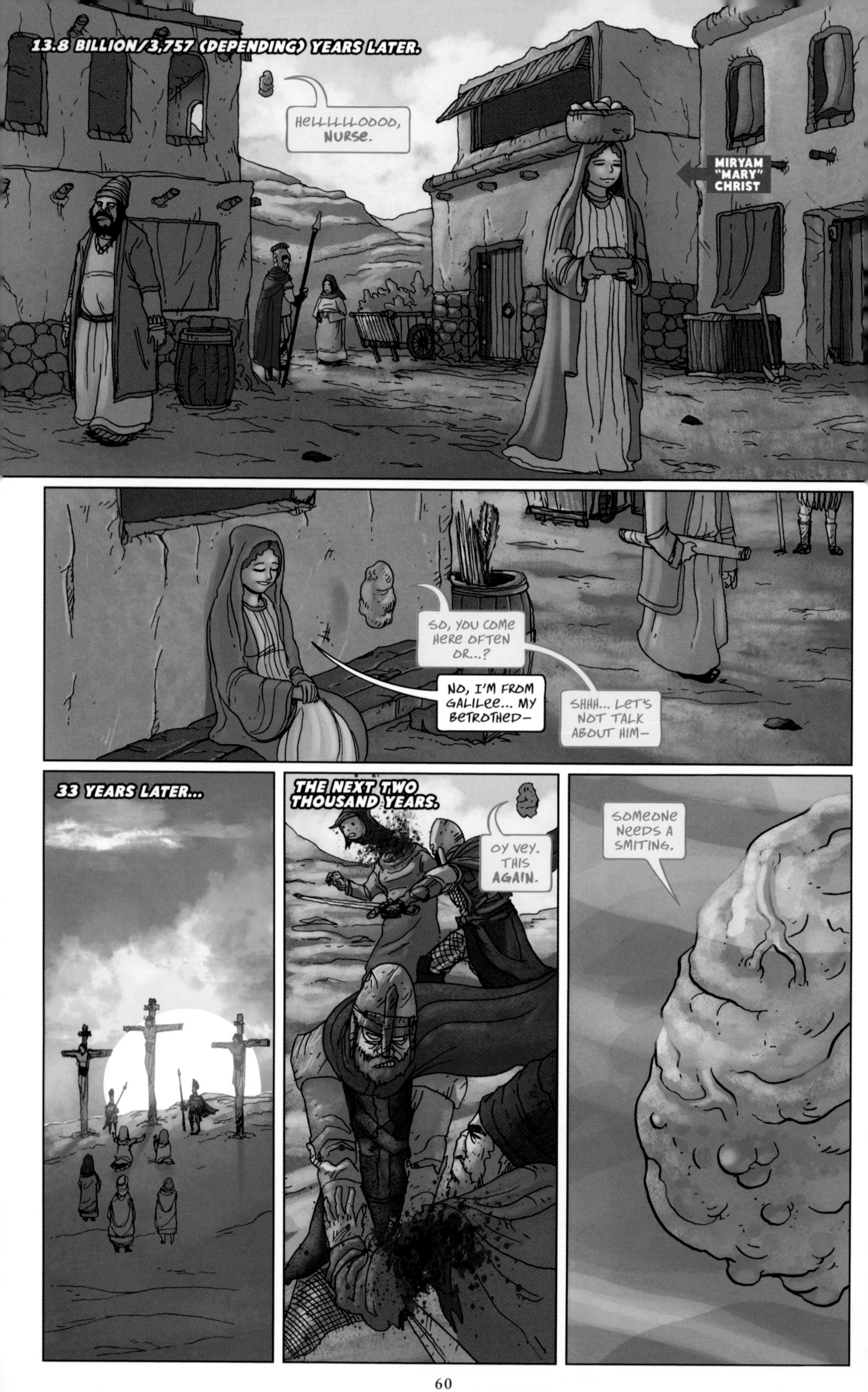
13.8 BILLION/3,757 (DEPENDING) YEARS LATER.
HELLLLLLOOOO, NURSE.
MIRYAM "MARY" CHRIST
SO, YOU COME HERE OFTEN OR...?
NO, I'M FROM GALILEE... MY BETROTHED—
SHHH... LET'S NOT TALK ABOUT HIM—
33 YEARS LATER...
THE NEXT TWO THOUSAND YEARS.
OY VEY. THIS AGAIN.
SOMEONE NEEDS A SMITING.

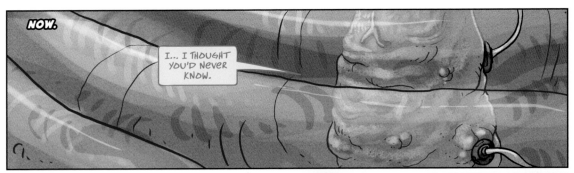

I... I THOUGHT YOU'D NEVER KNOW.

YOU... WORK IN MYSTERIOUS WAYS, SIR.

YEAH. ≷SIGH≷ I THOUGHT—

LAST TIME, IT DIDN'T GO GREAT. I HAD A KID, HE CAME TO SAVE THE WORLD, PEOPLE HATED HIM, MURDERED HIM...

YADA YADA YADA.

SO I FIGURED, LET'S TRY SOMETHING DIFFERENT. LET'S NOT LET ANOTHER GODLET RUN AROUND AND MAKE THEM ALL HATE EACH OTHER, SO I HID HIM HERE—

WHAT DO YOU WANT US TO DO...?

BRING HIM HERE, PLEASE.

NO. WAIT. CAN WE SOMEHOW GET HIM BACK IN LINE? ERASE HIS MEMORY OR SOMETHING—

SIR, WITH YOUR PERMISSION, I'D LIKE TO HANDLE THE SITUATION MYSELF, FOR YOU.

OF COURSE, OF COURSE.

JUST WHATEVER YOU DO, DON'T TELL THE OTHER SECTION LEADERS ABOUT IT. AND NO DEALS.

ESPECIALLY NOT WITH HIM.

ANGELS AND DEVILS AREN'T MY THING, SIR. I'M A BUREAUCRAT.

WE'RE MUCH, MUCH WORSE.

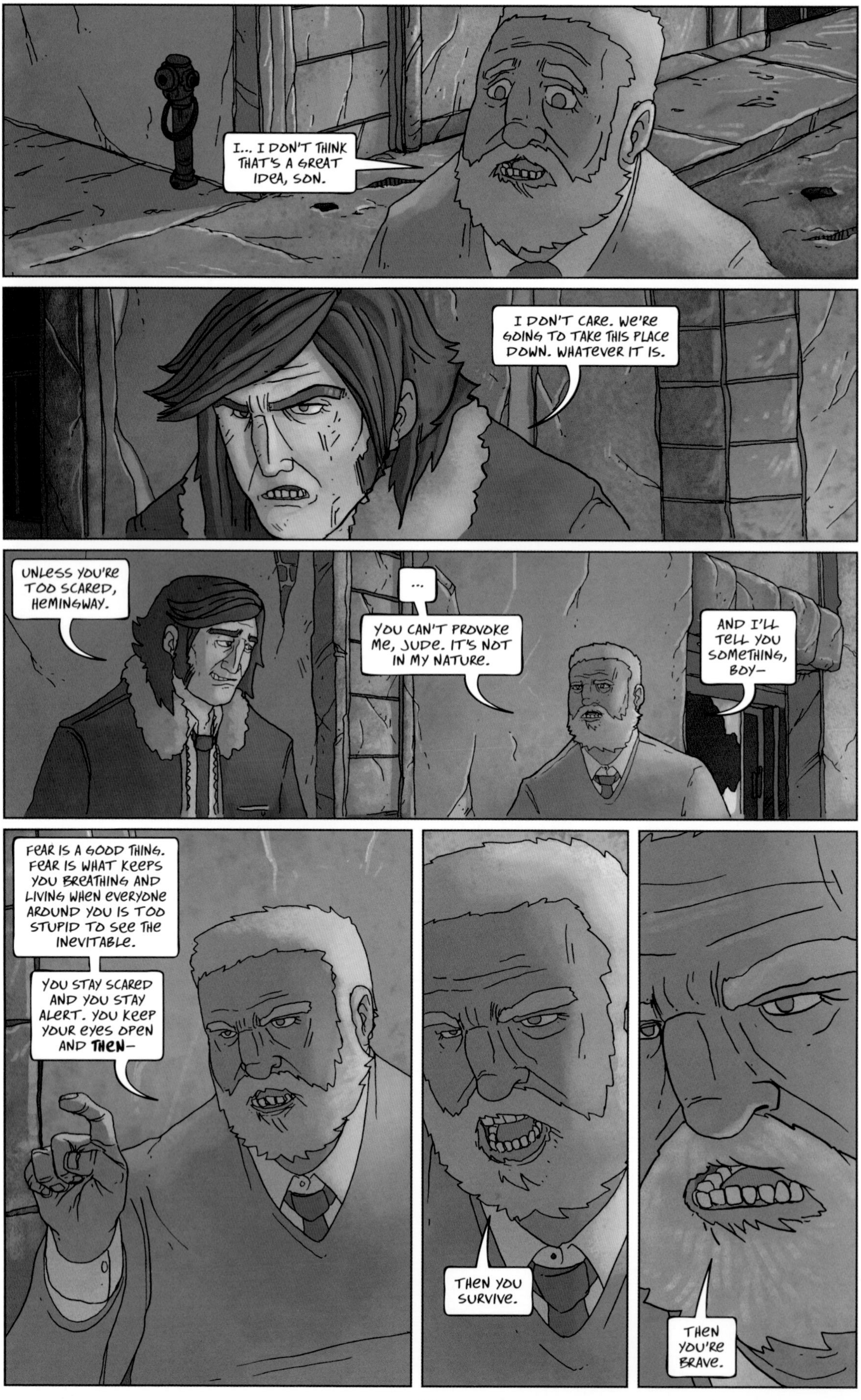
I... I DON'T THINK THAT'S A GREAT IDEA, SON.
I DON'T CARE. WE'RE GOING TO TAKE THIS PLACE DOWN. WHATEVER IT IS.
UNLESS YOU'RE TOO SCARED, HEMINGWAY.
...
YOU CAN'T PROVOKE ME, JUDE. IT'S NOT IN MY NATURE.
AND I'LL TELL YOU SOMETHING, BOY—
FEAR IS A GOOD THING. FEAR IS WHAT KEEPS YOU BREATHING AND LIVING WHEN EVERYONE AROUND YOU IS TOO STUPID TO SEE THE INEVITABLE.
YOU STAY SCARED AND YOU STAY ALERT. YOU KEEP YOUR EYES OPEN AND **THEN**—
THEN YOU SURVIVE.
THEN YOU'RE BRAVE.

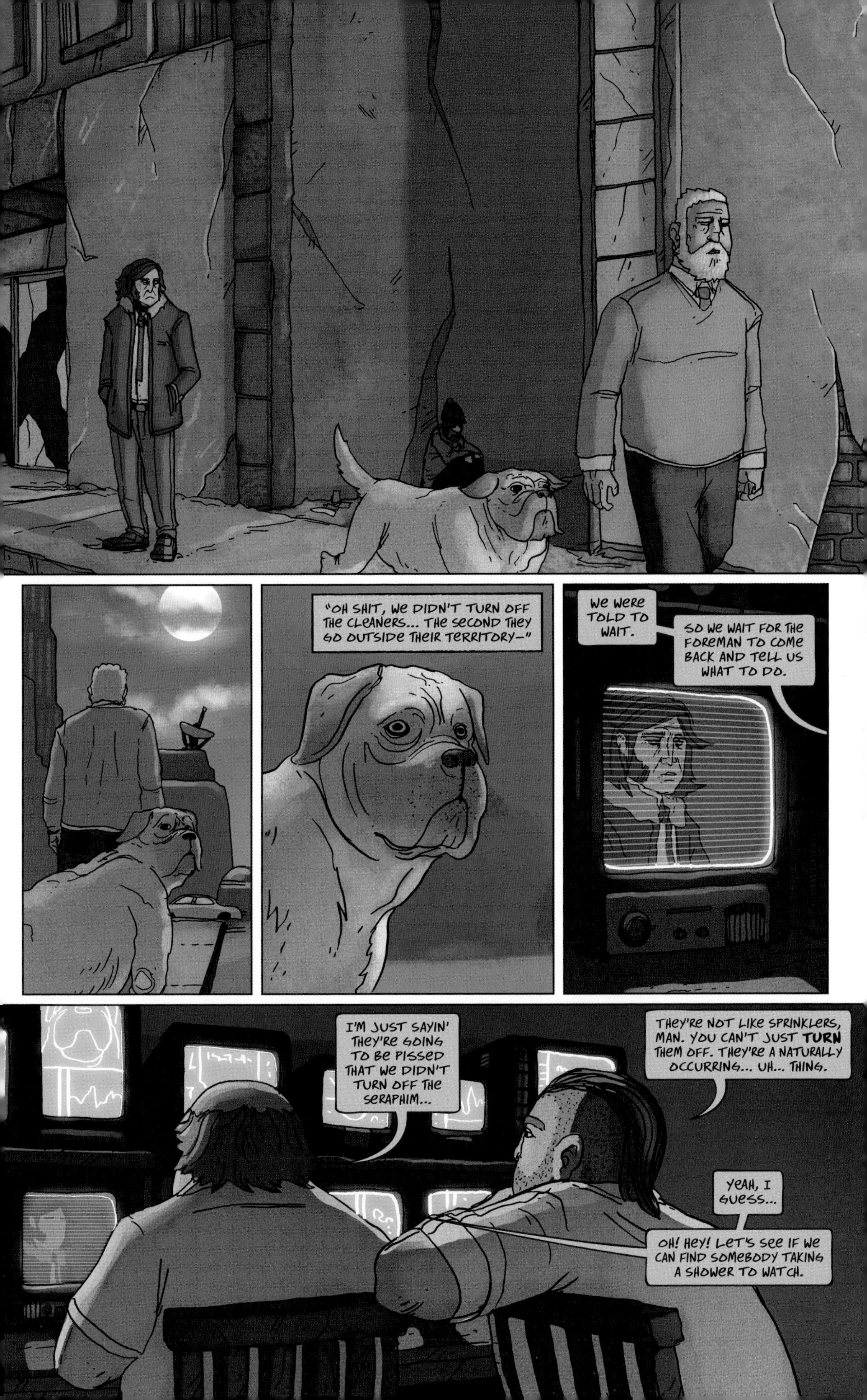
"OH SHIT, WE DIDN'T TURN OFF THE CLEANERS... THE SECOND THEY GO OUTSIDE THEIR TERRITORY—"
WE WERE TOLD TO WAIT.
SO WE WAIT FOR THE FOREMAN TO COME BACK AND TELL US WHAT TO DO.
I'M JUST SAYIN' THEY'RE GOING TO BE PISSED THAT WE DIDN'T TURN OFF THE SERAPHIM...
THEY'RE NOT LIKE SPRINKLERS, MAN. YOU CAN'T JUST TURN THEM OFF. THEY'RE A NATURALLY OCCURRING... UH... THING.
YEAH, I GUESS...
OH! HEY! LET'S SEE IF WE CAN FIND SOMEBODY TAKING A SHOWER TO WATCH.

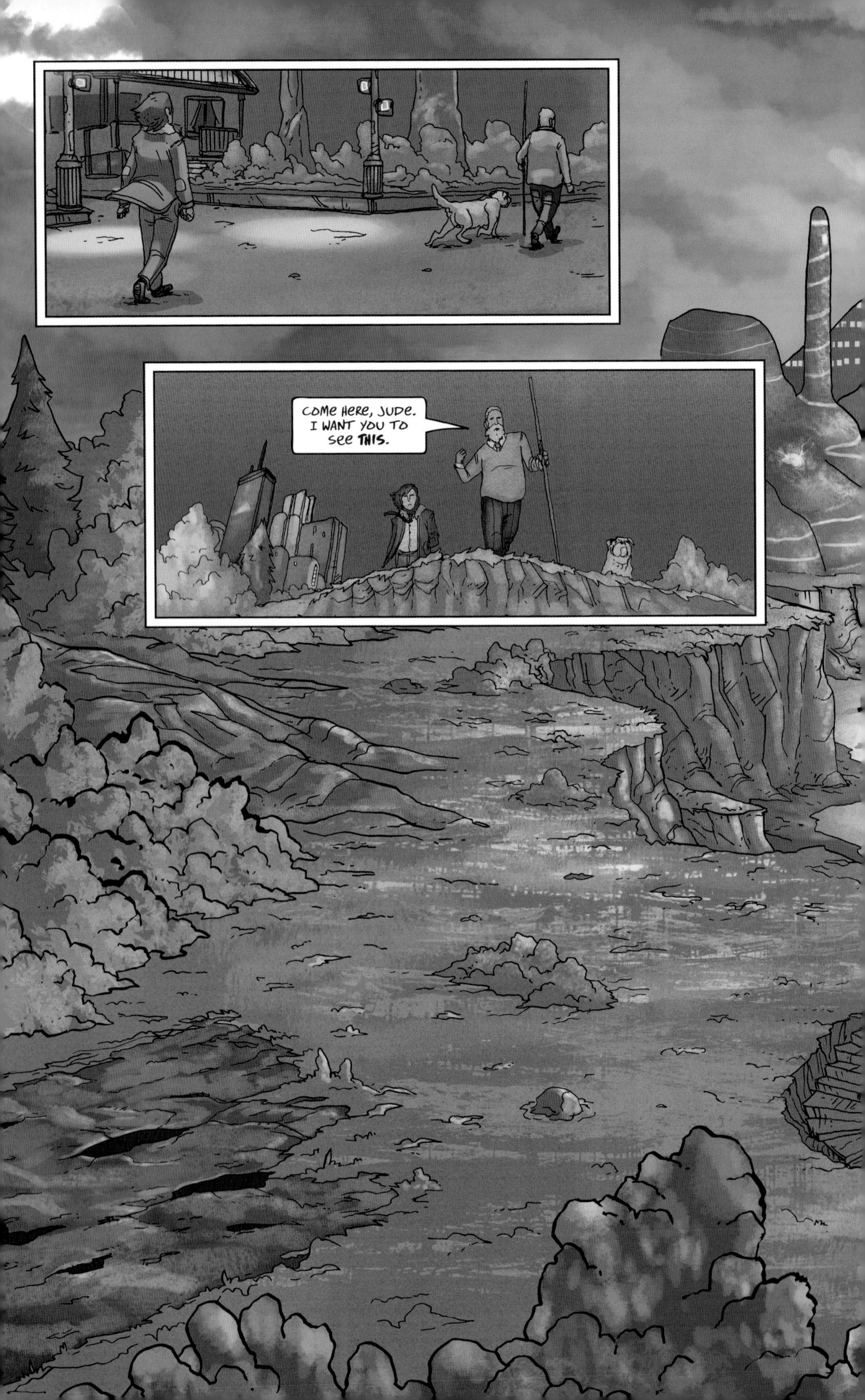
COME HERE, JUDE. I WANT YOU TO SEE **THIS**.

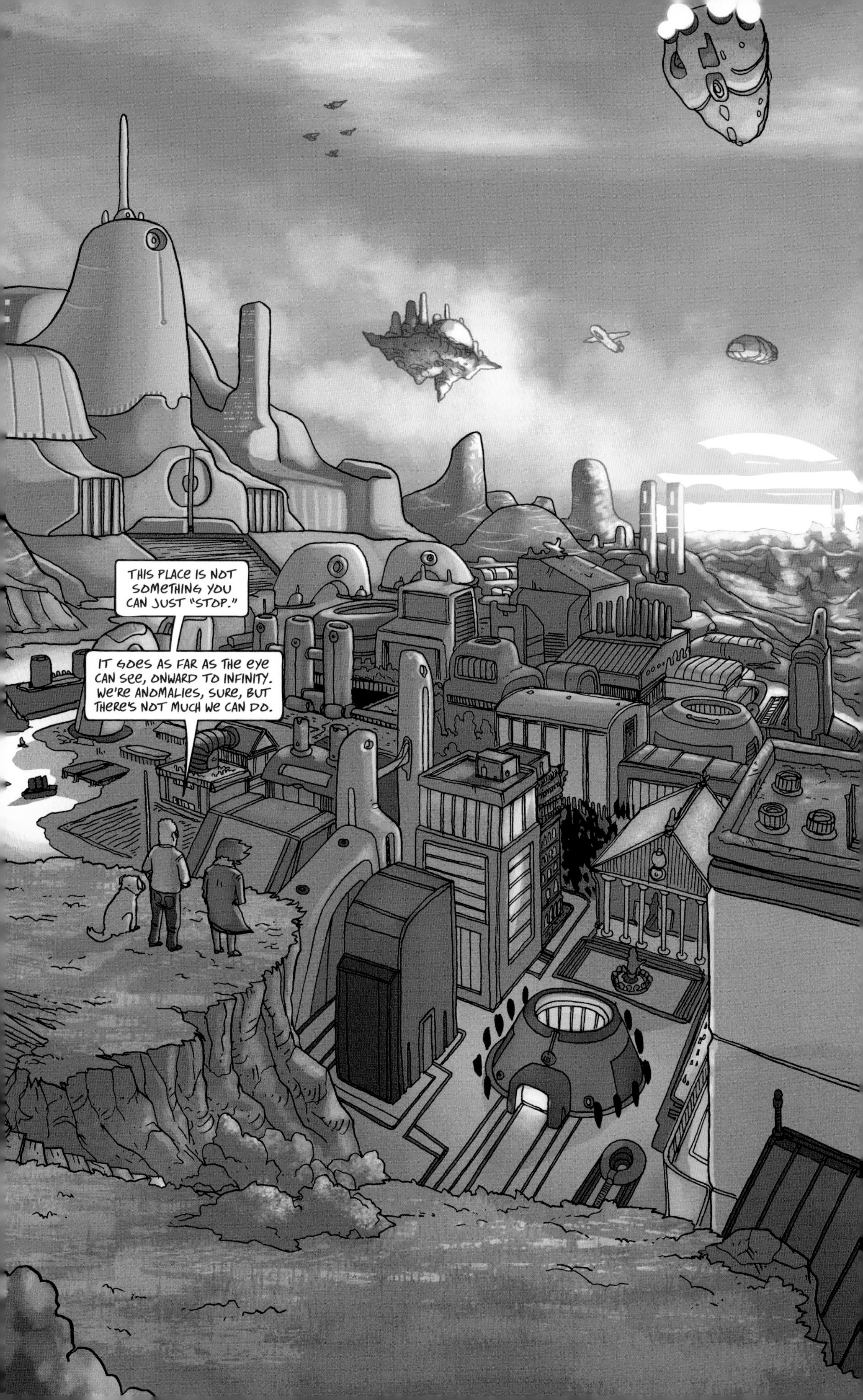
THIS PLACE IS NOT SOMETHING YOU CAN JUST "STOP."
IT GOES AS FAR AS THE EYE CAN SEE, ONWARD TO INFINITY. WE'RE ANOMALIES, SURE, BUT THERE'S NOT MUCH WE CAN DO.

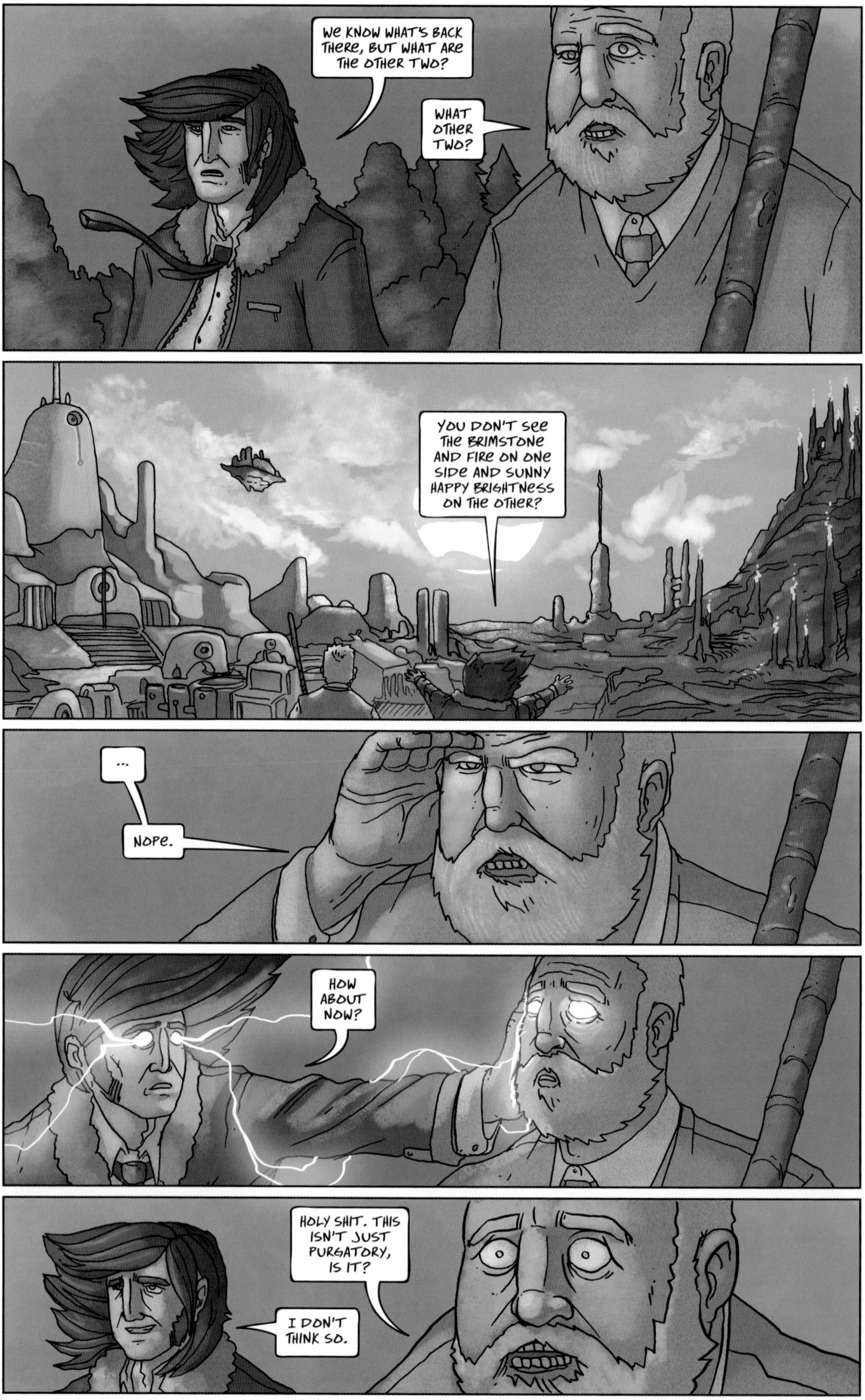
WE KNOW WHAT'S BACK THERE, BUT WHAT ARE THE OTHER TWO?
WHAT OTHER TWO?
YOU DON'T SEE THE BRIMSTONE AND FIRE ON ONE SIDE AND SUNNY HAPPY BRIGHTNESS ON THE OTHER?
...
NOPE.
HOW ABOUT NOW?
HOLY SHIT. THIS ISN'T JUST PURGATORY, IS IT?
I DON'T THINK SO.

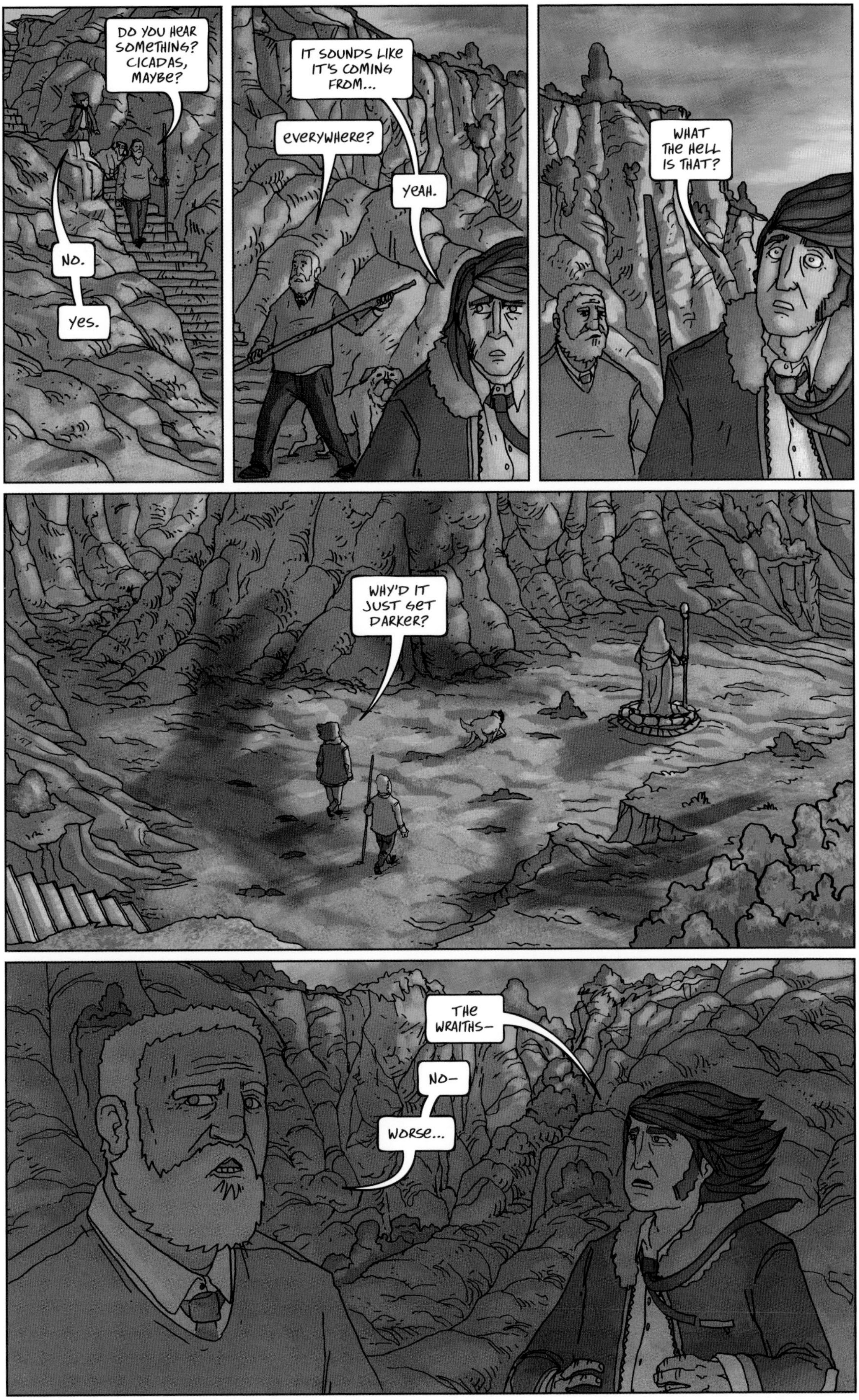
DO YOU HEAR SOMETHING? CICADAS, MAYBE?
NO.
YES.
IT SOUNDS LIKE IT'S COMING FROM...
EVERYWHERE?
YEAH.
WHAT THE HELL IS THAT?
WHY'D IT JUST GET DARKER?
THE WRAITHS-
NO-
WORSE...

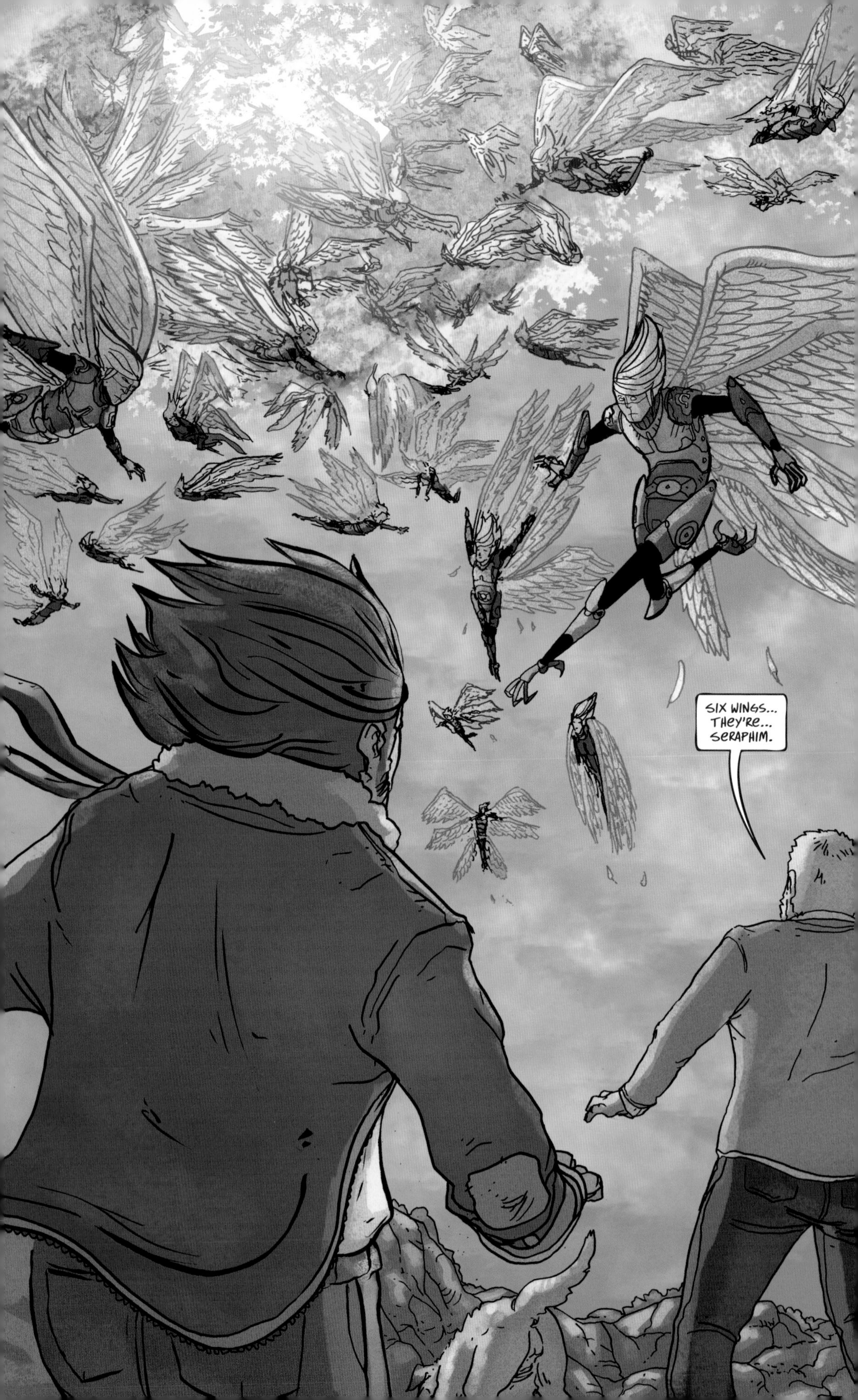
SIX WINGS... THEY'RE... SERAPHIM.

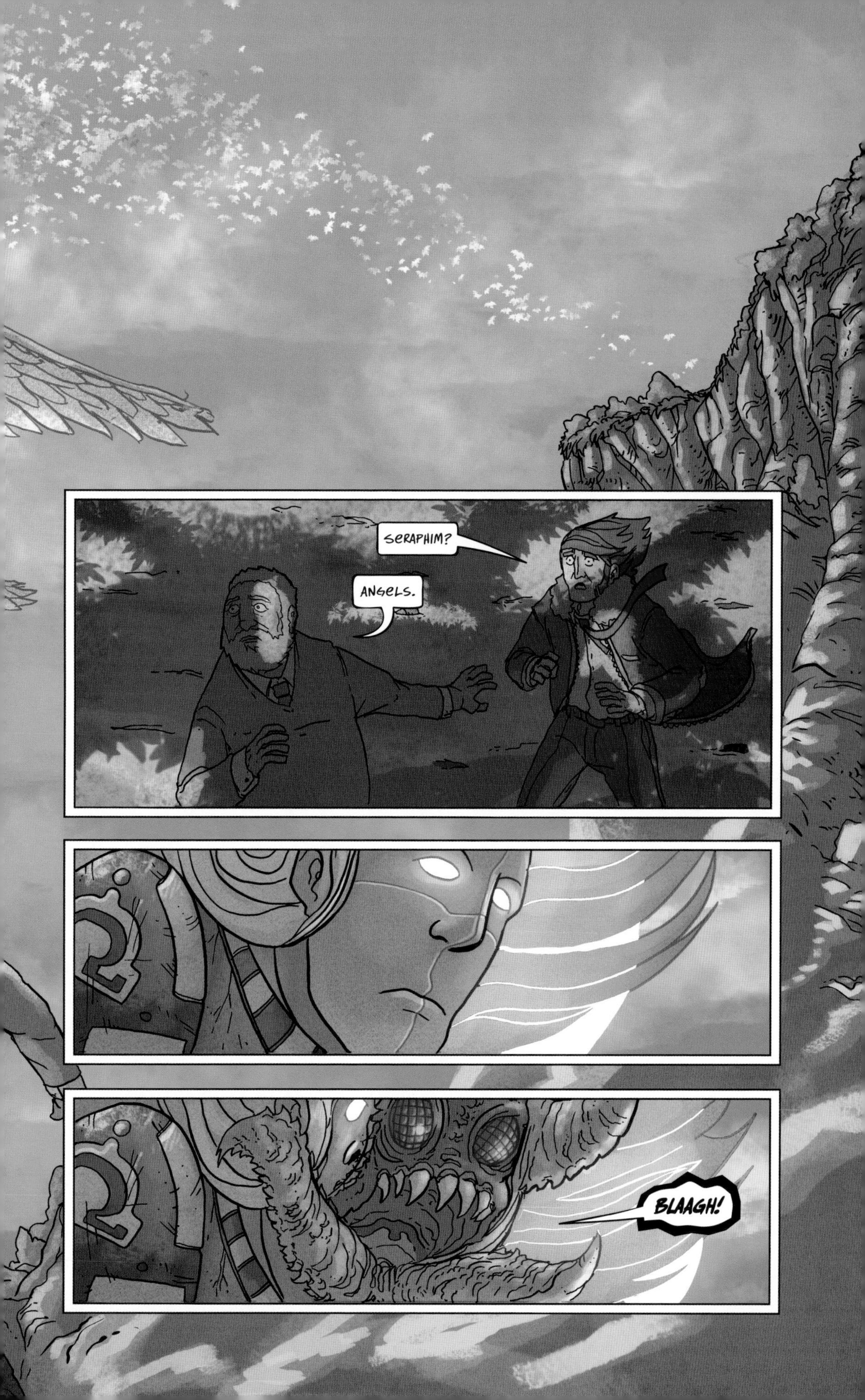
SERAPHIM?
ANGELS.
BLAAGH!

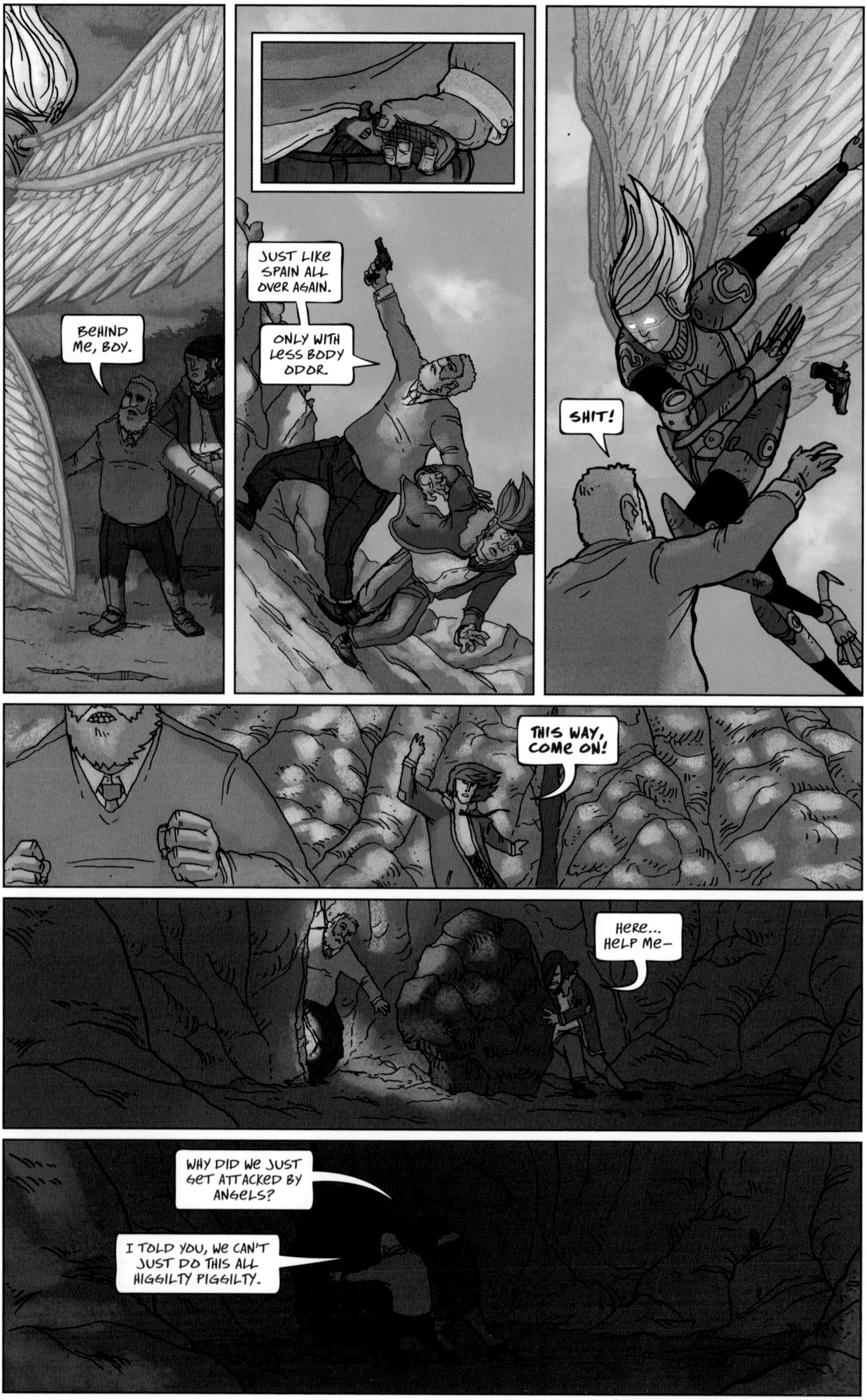
BEHIND ME, BOY.
JUST LIKE SPAIN ALL OVER AGAIN.
ONLY WITH LESS BODY ODOR.
SHIT!
THIS WAY, COME ON!
HERE... HELP ME–
WHY DID WE JUST GET ATTACKED BY ANGELS?
I TOLD YOU, WE CAN'T JUST DO THIS ALL HIGGILTY PIGGILTY.

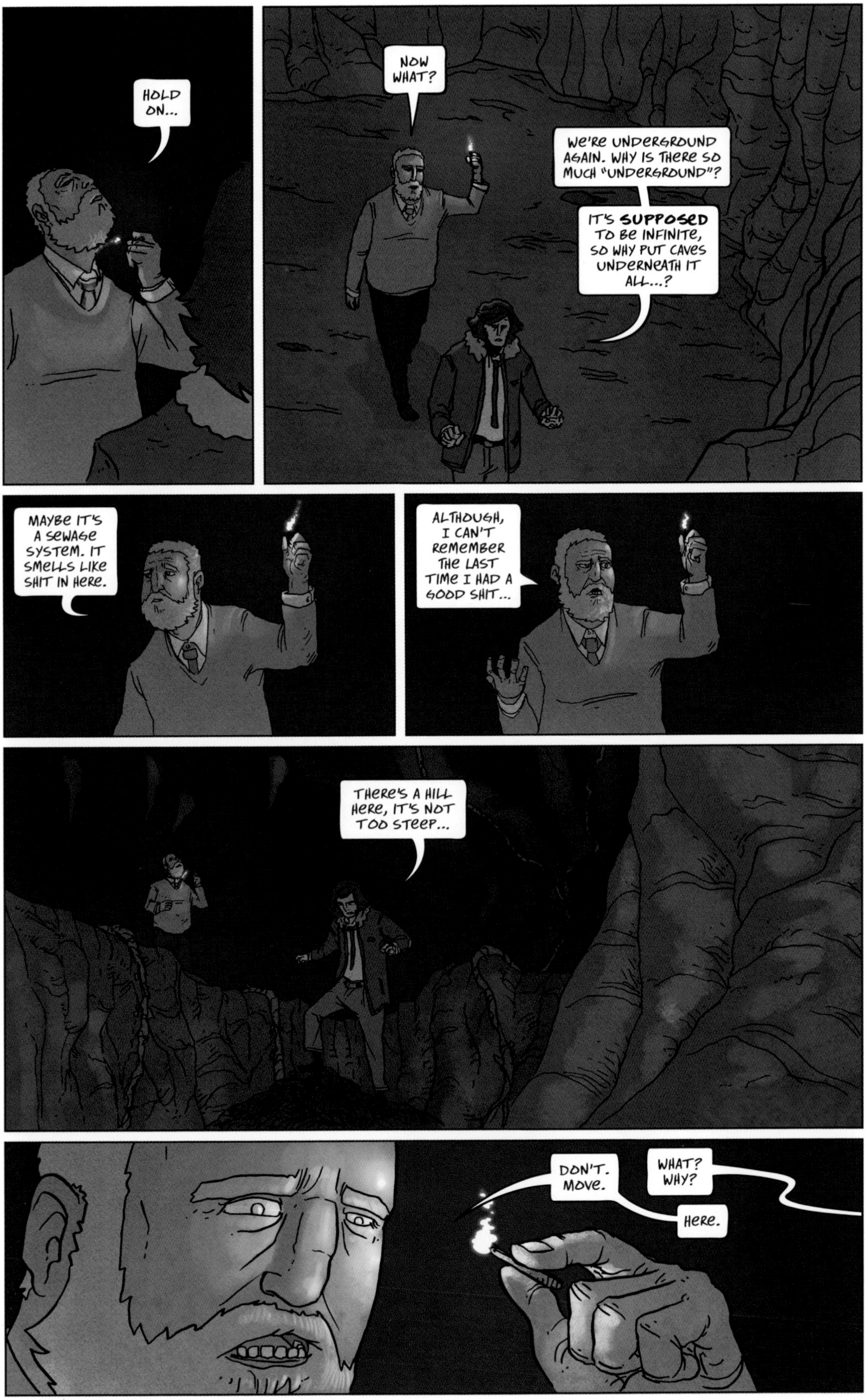
HOLD ON...
NOW WHAT?
WE'RE UNDERGROUND AGAIN. WHY IS THERE SO MUCH "UNDERGROUND"?
IT'S SUPPOSED TO BE INFINITE, SO WHY PUT CAVES UNDERNEATH IT ALL...?
MAYBE IT'S A SEWAGE SYSTEM. IT SMELLS LIKE SHIT IN HERE.
ALTHOUGH, I CAN'T REMEMBER THE LAST TIME I HAD A GOOD SHIT...
THERE'S A HILL HERE, IT'S NOT TOO STEEP...
DON'T. MOVE.
WHAT? WHY?
HERE.

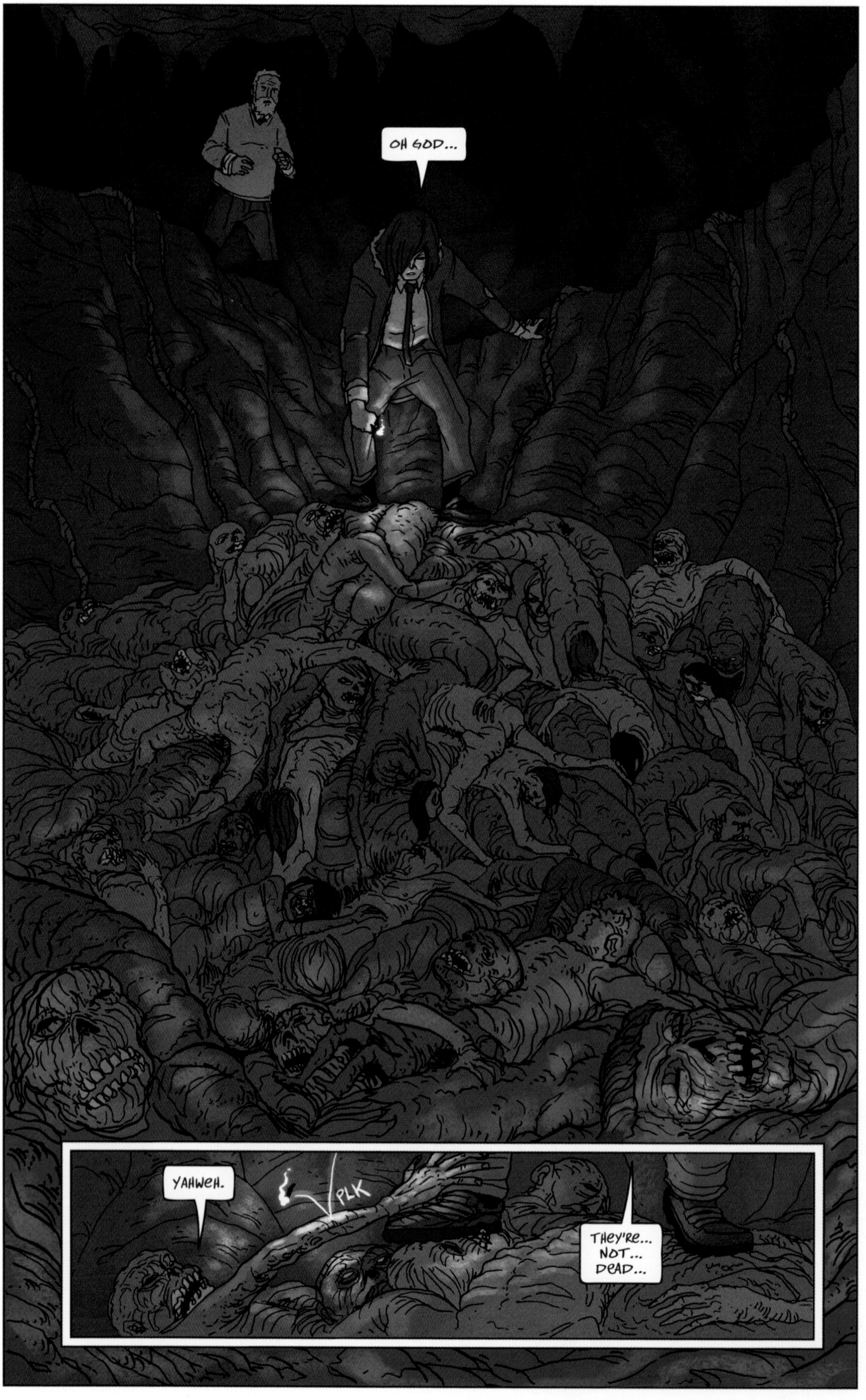
OH GOD...
YAHWEH.
PLK
THEY'RE... NOT... DEAD...

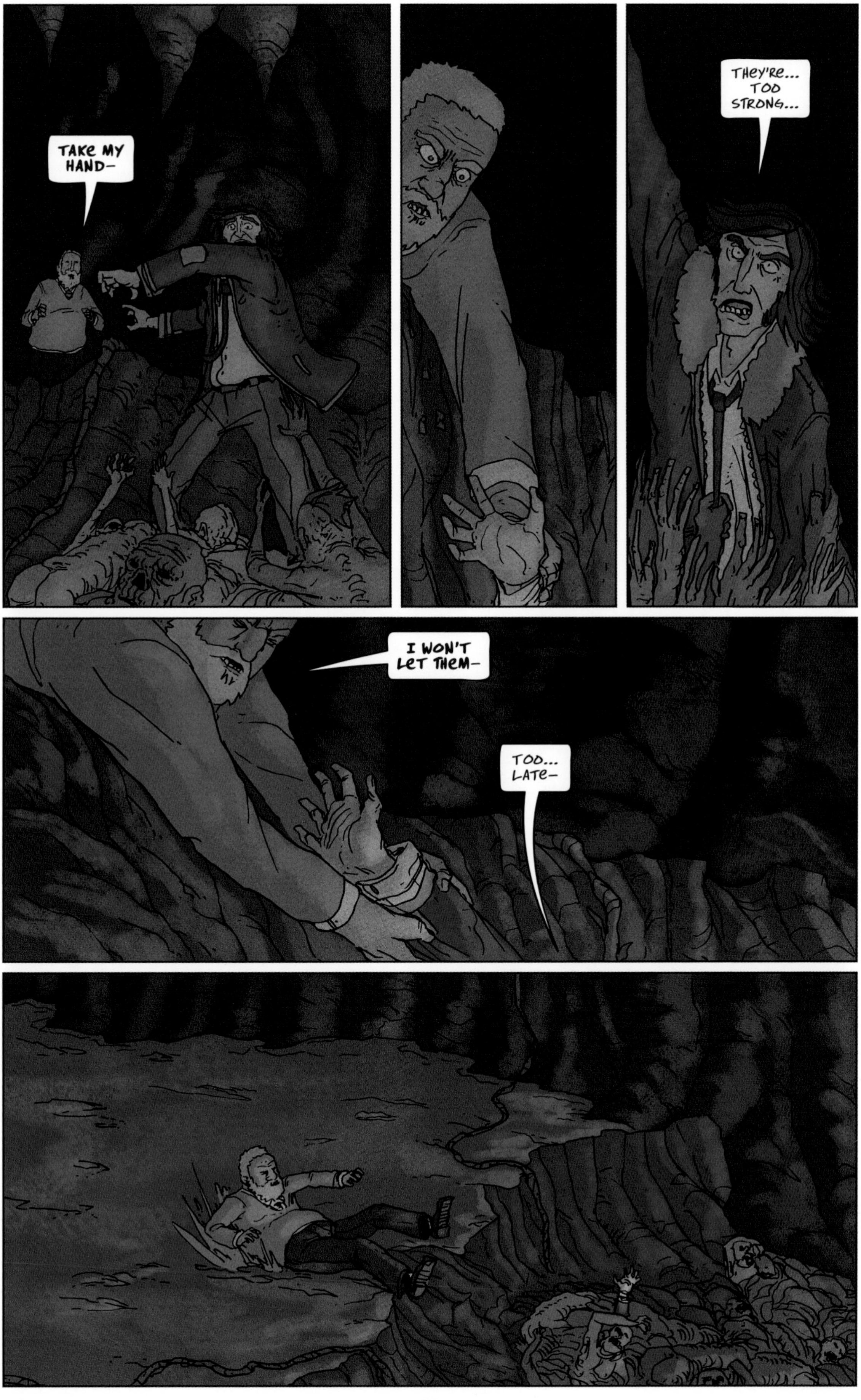
TAKE MY HAND—
THEY'RE... TOO STRONG...
I WON'T LET THEM—
TOO... LATE—

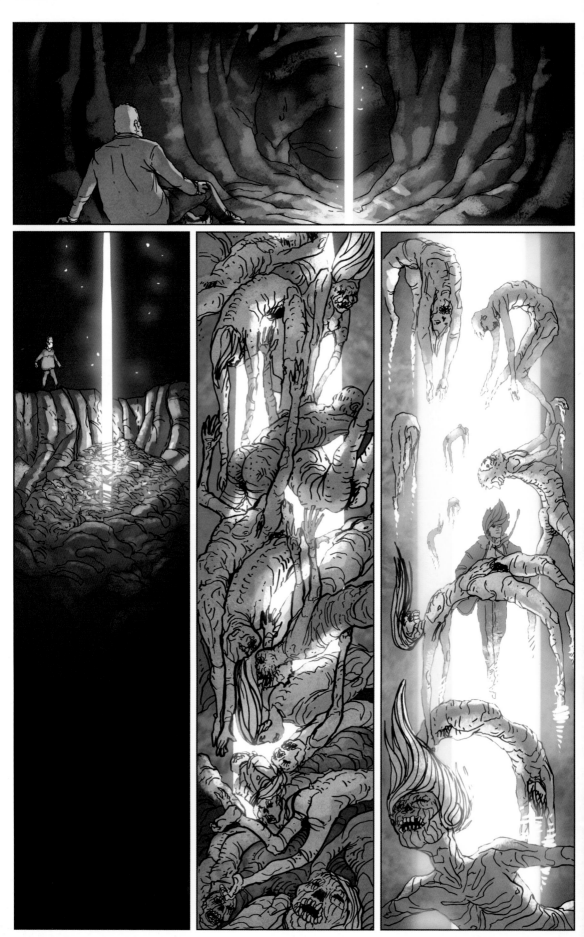

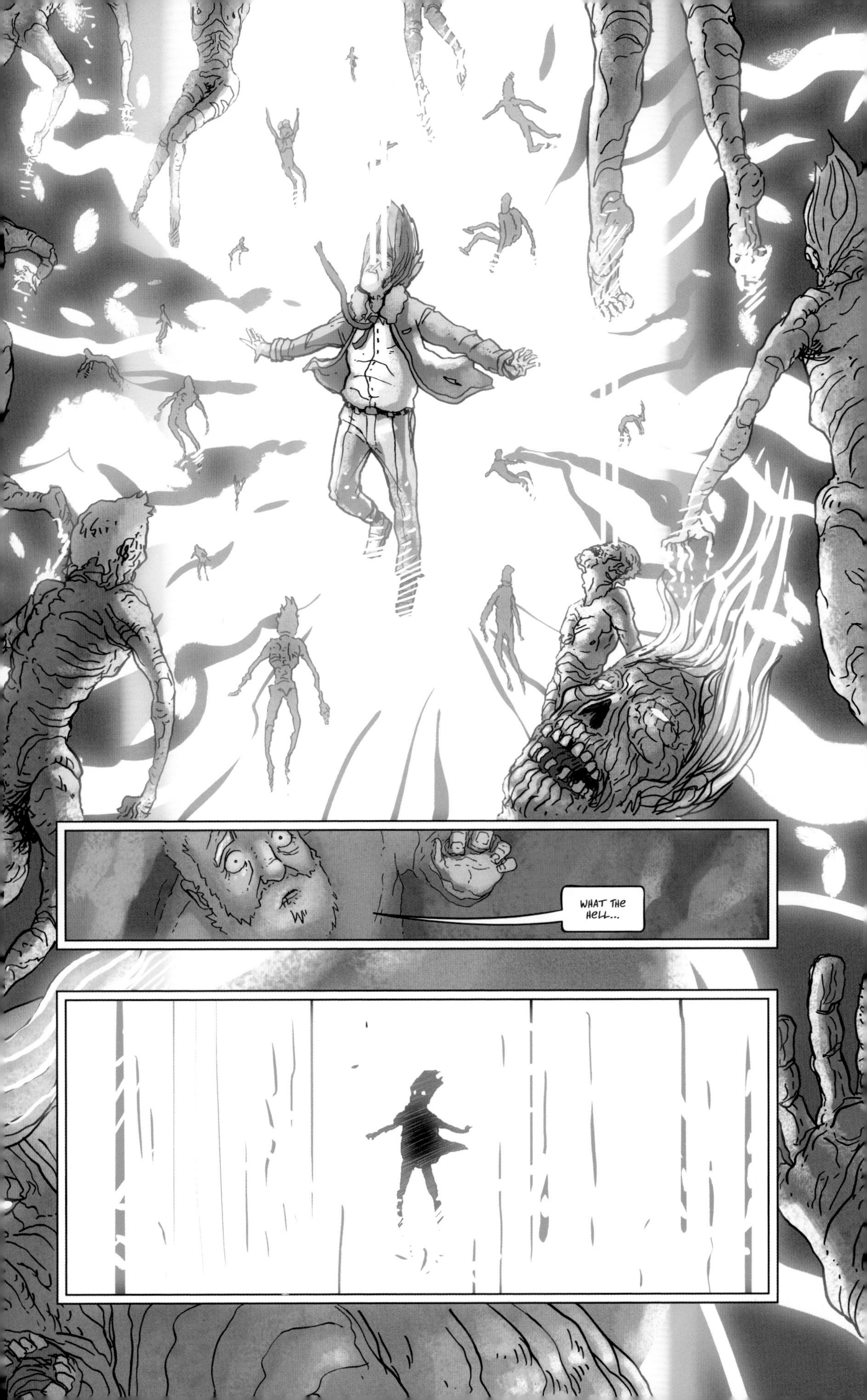
WHAT THE HELL...

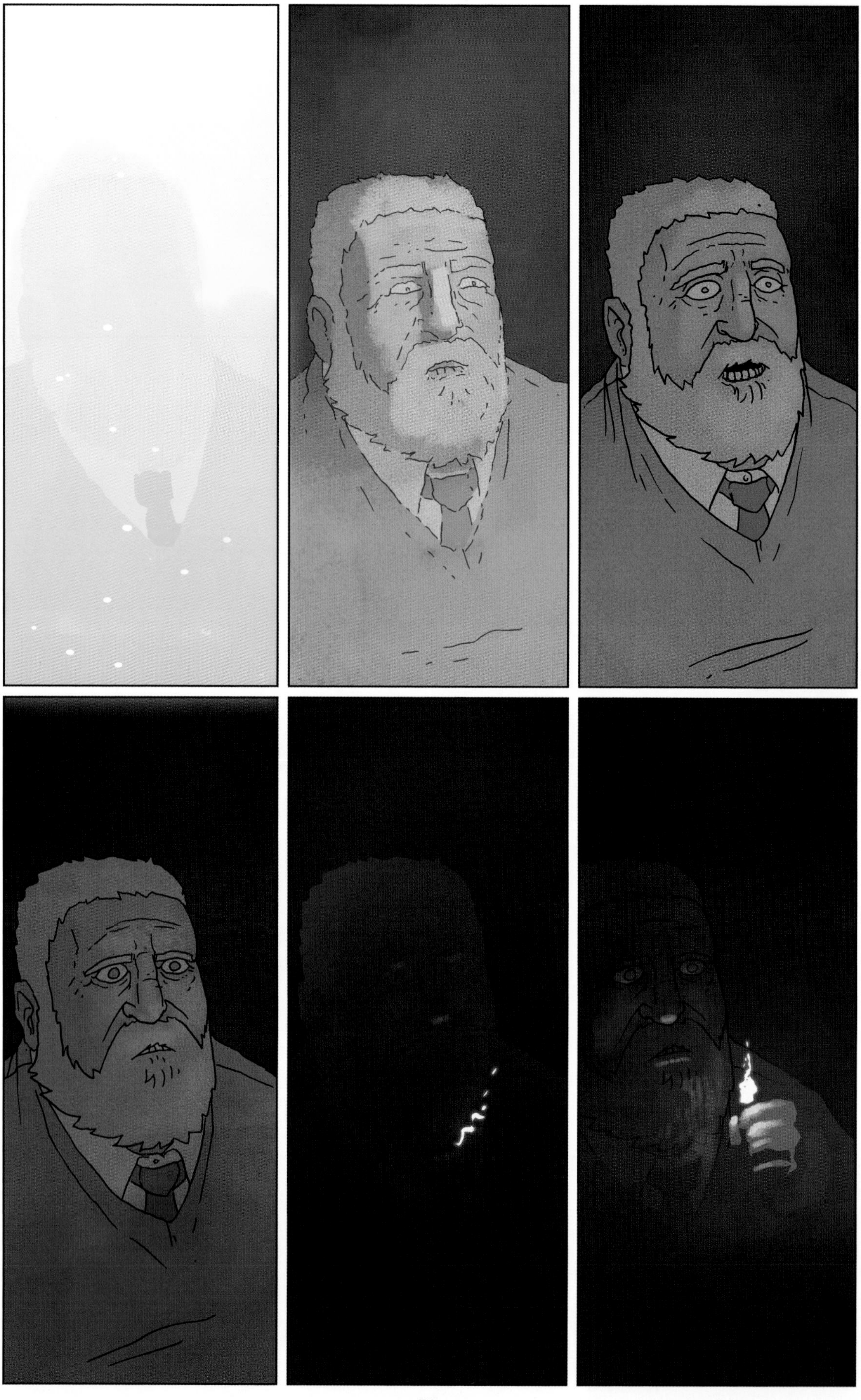

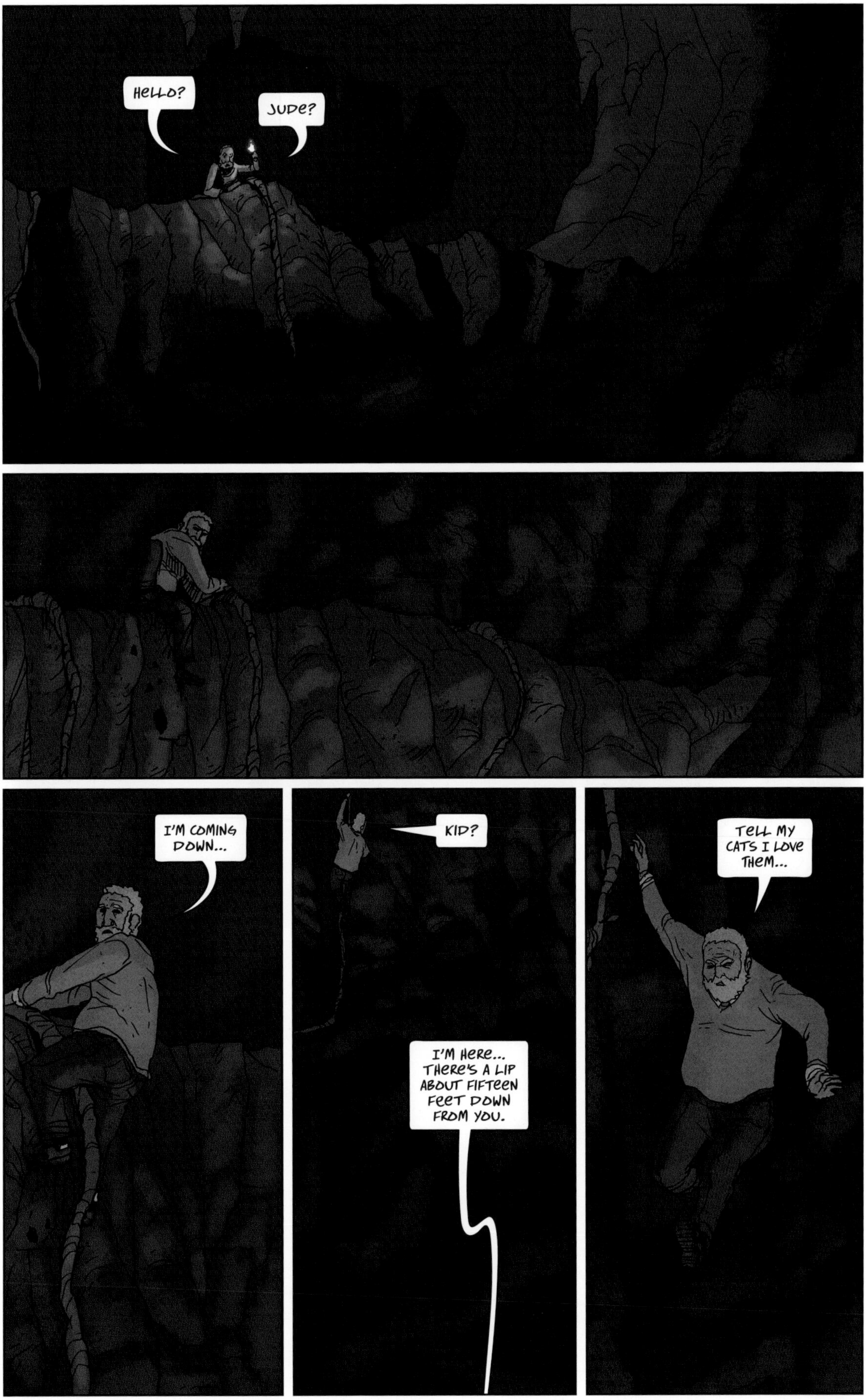
HELLO?
JUDE?
I'M COMING DOWN...
KID?
I'M HERE... THERE'S A LIP ABOUT FIFTEEN FEET DOWN FROM YOU.
TELL MY CATS I LOVE THEM...

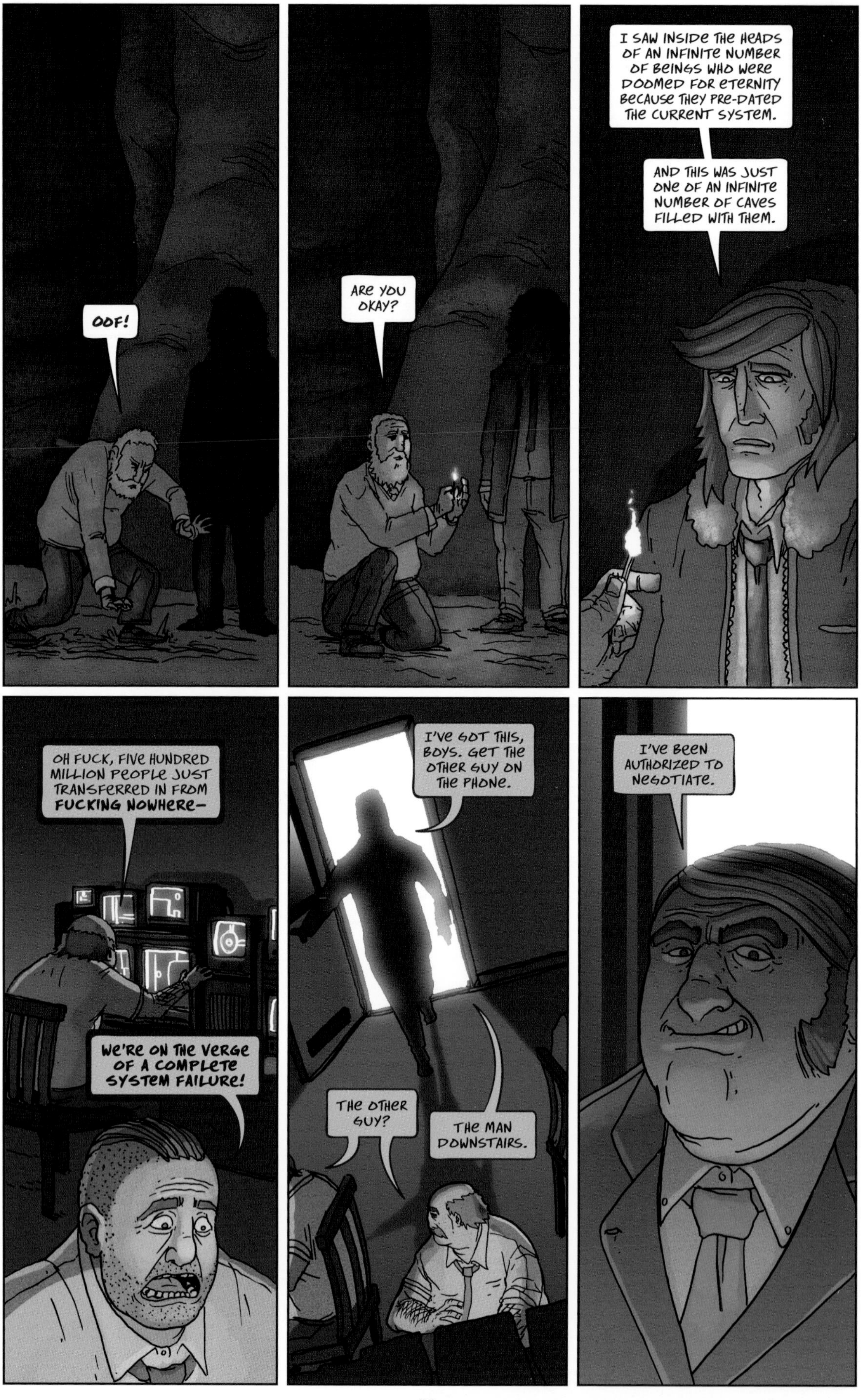
OOF!
ARE YOU OKAY?
I SAW INSIDE THE HEADS OF AN INFINITE NUMBER OF BEINGS WHO WERE DOOMED FOR ETERNITY BECAUSE THEY PRE-DATED THE CURRENT SYSTEM.
AND THIS WAS JUST ONE OF AN INFINITE NUMBER OF CAVES FILLED WITH THEM.
OH FUCK, FIVE HUNDRED MILLION PEOPLE JUST TRANSFERRED IN FROM FUCKING NOWHERE—
WE'RE ON THE VERGE OF A COMPLETE SYSTEM FAILURE!
I'VE GOT THIS, BOYS. GET THE OTHER GUY ON THE PHONE.
THE OTHER GUY?
THE MAN DOWNSTAIRS.
I'VE BEEN AUTHORIZED TO NEGOTIATE.

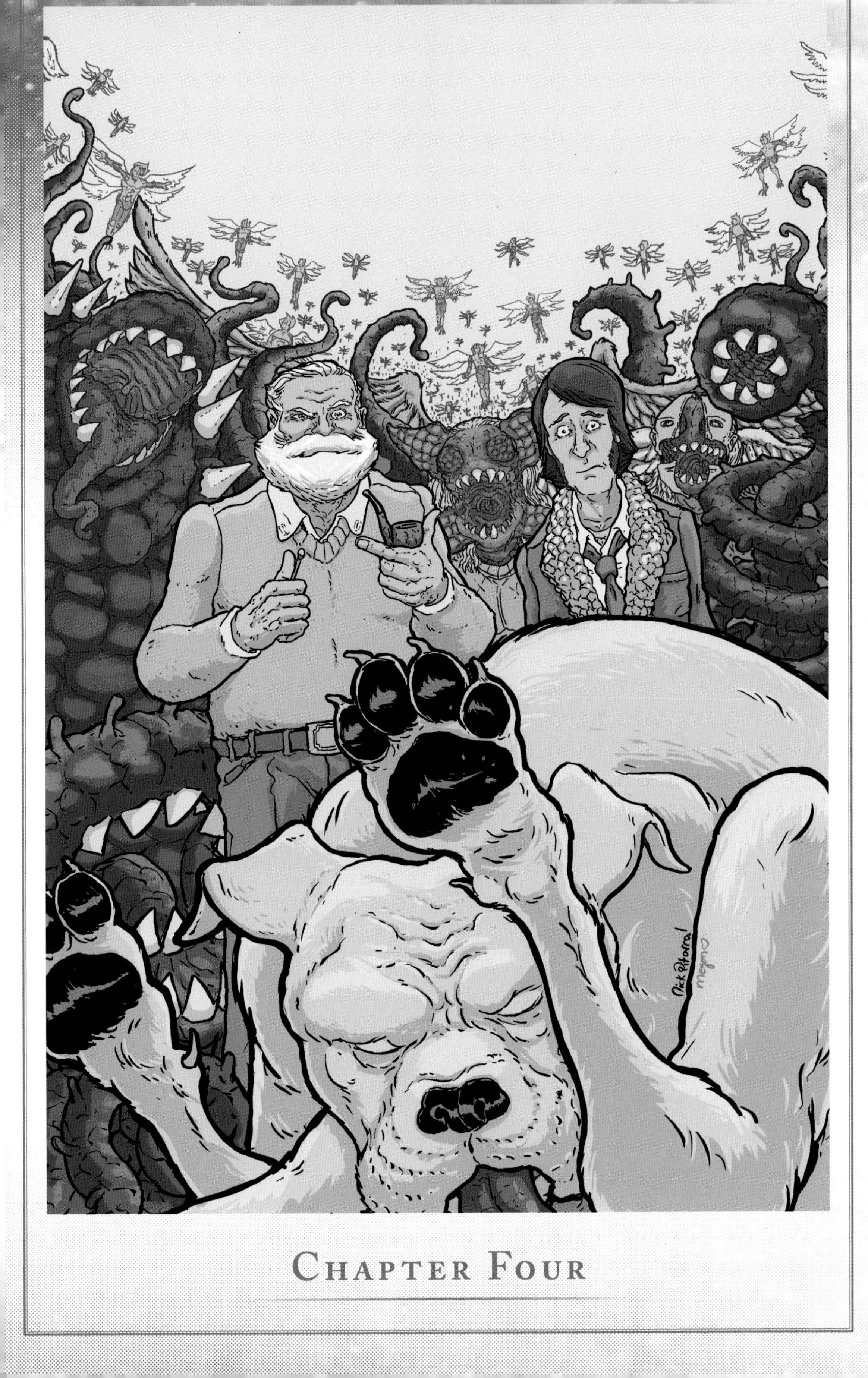

Chapter Four

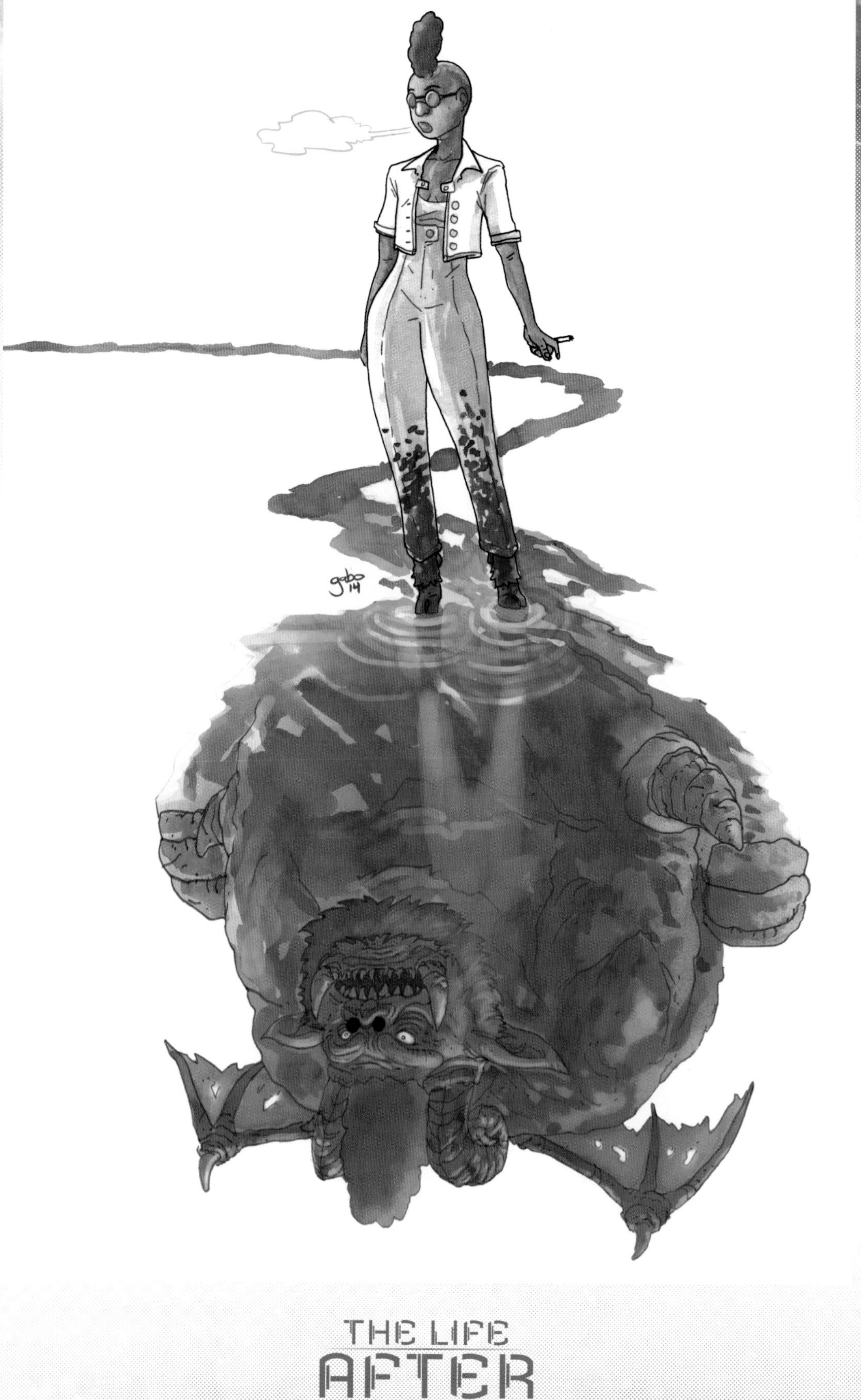

THE LIFE AFTER

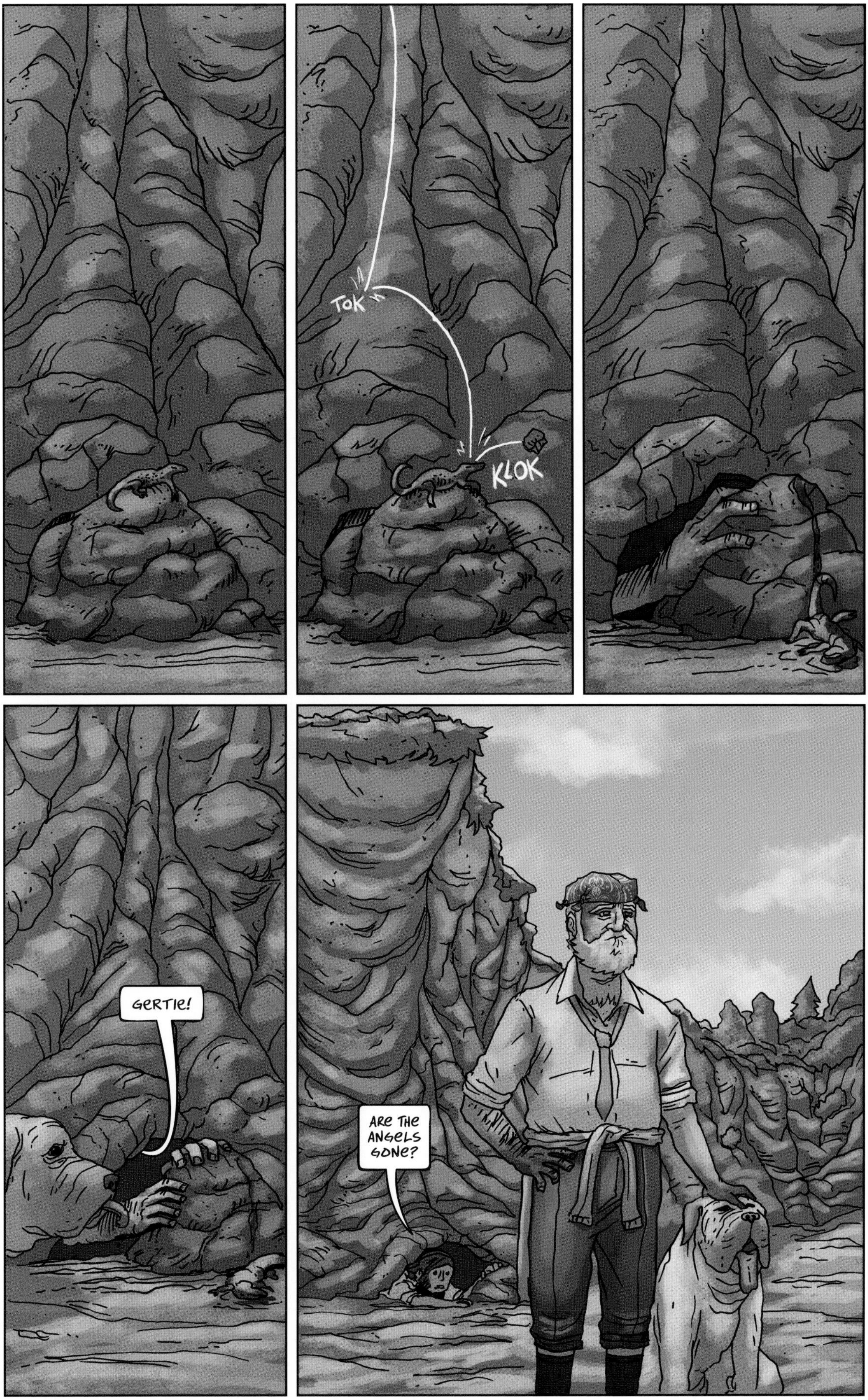
TOK
KLOK
GERTIE!
ARE THE ANGELS GONE?

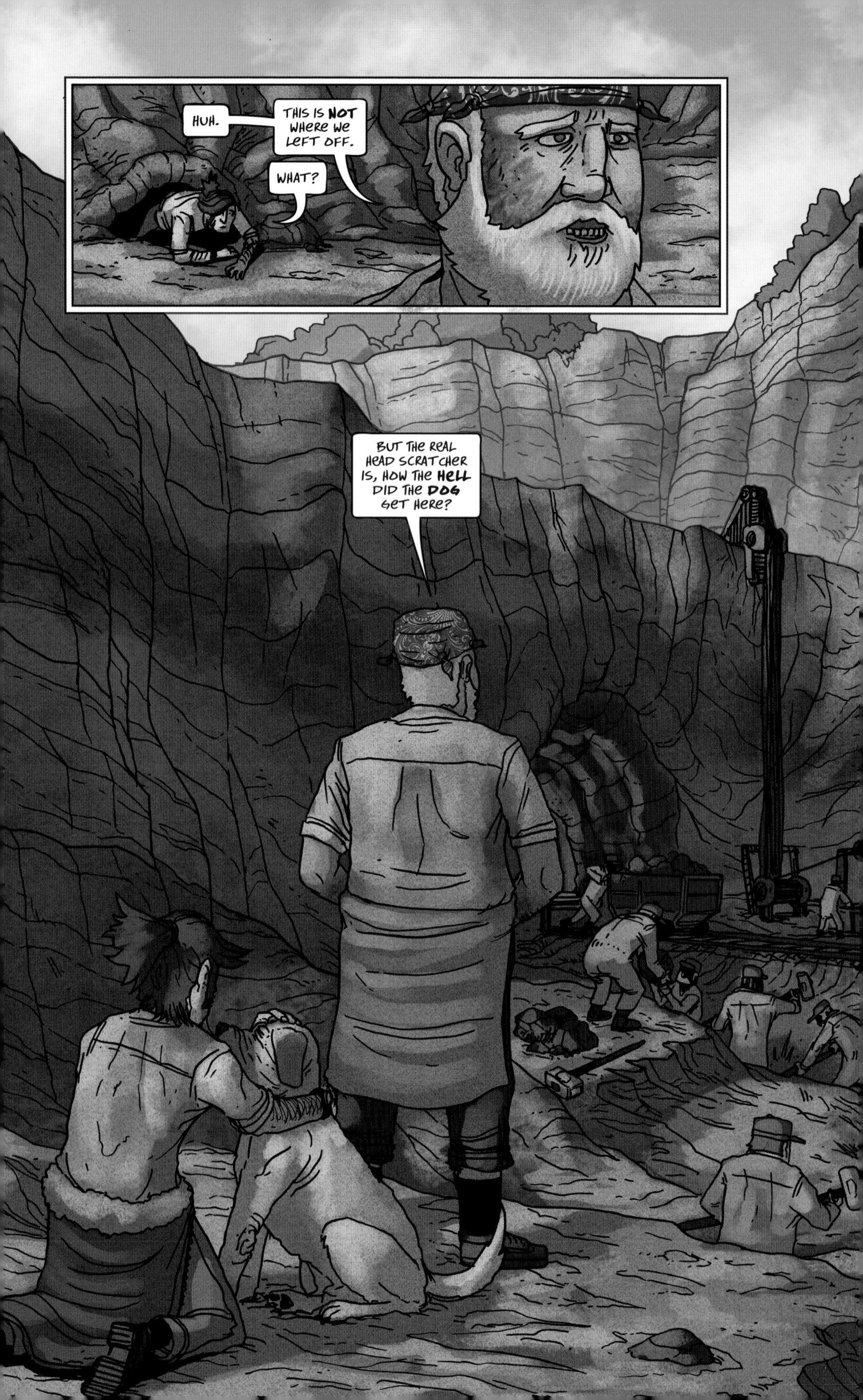
HUH.
THIS IS **NOT** WHERE WE LEFT OFF.
WHAT?
BUT THE REAL HEAD SCRATCHER IS, HOW THE **HELL** DID THE **DOG** GET HERE?

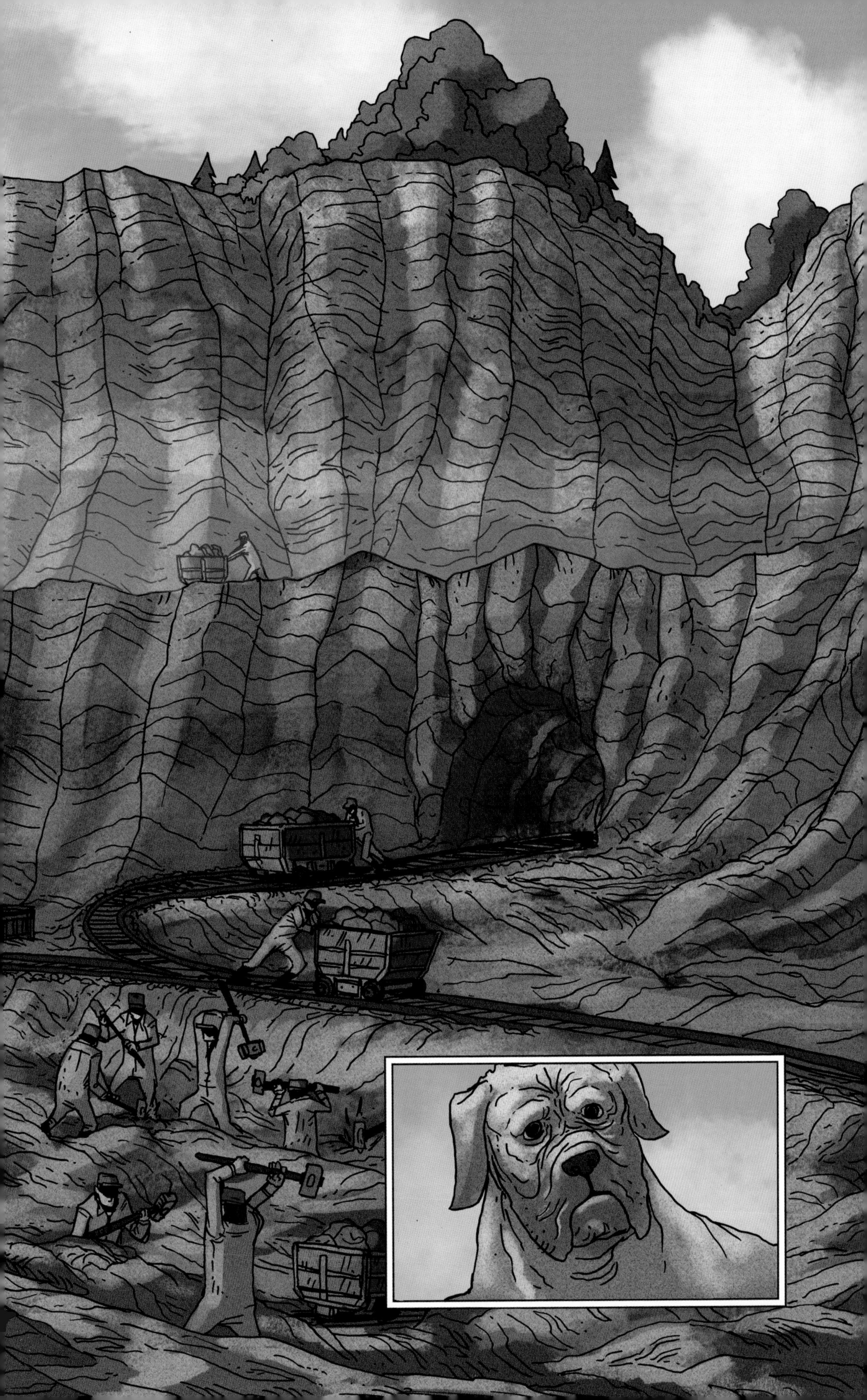

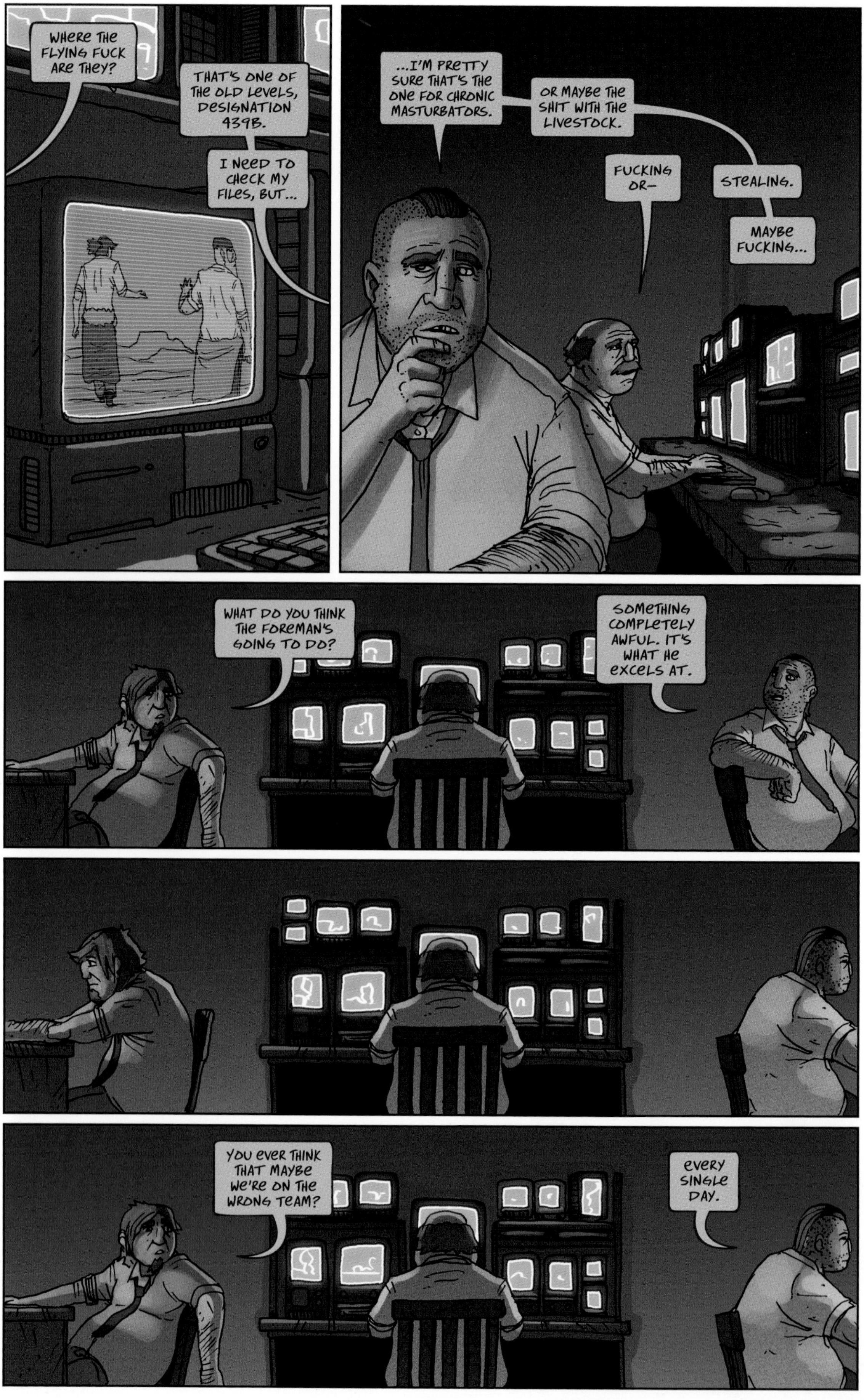
WHERE THE FLYING FUCK ARE THEY?
THAT'S ONE OF THE OLD LEVELS, DESIGNATION 439B.
I NEED TO CHECK MY FILES, BUT...
...I'M PRETTY SURE THAT'S THE ONE FOR CHRONIC MASTURBATORS.
OR MAYBE THE SHIT WITH THE LIVESTOCK.
FUCKING OR—
STEALING.
MAYBE FUCKING...
WHAT DO YOU THINK THE FOREMAN'S GOING TO DO?
SOMETHING COMPLETELY AWFUL. IT'S WHAT HE EXCELS AT.
YOU EVER THINK THAT MAYBE WE'RE ON THE WRONG TEAM?
EVERY SINGLE DAY.

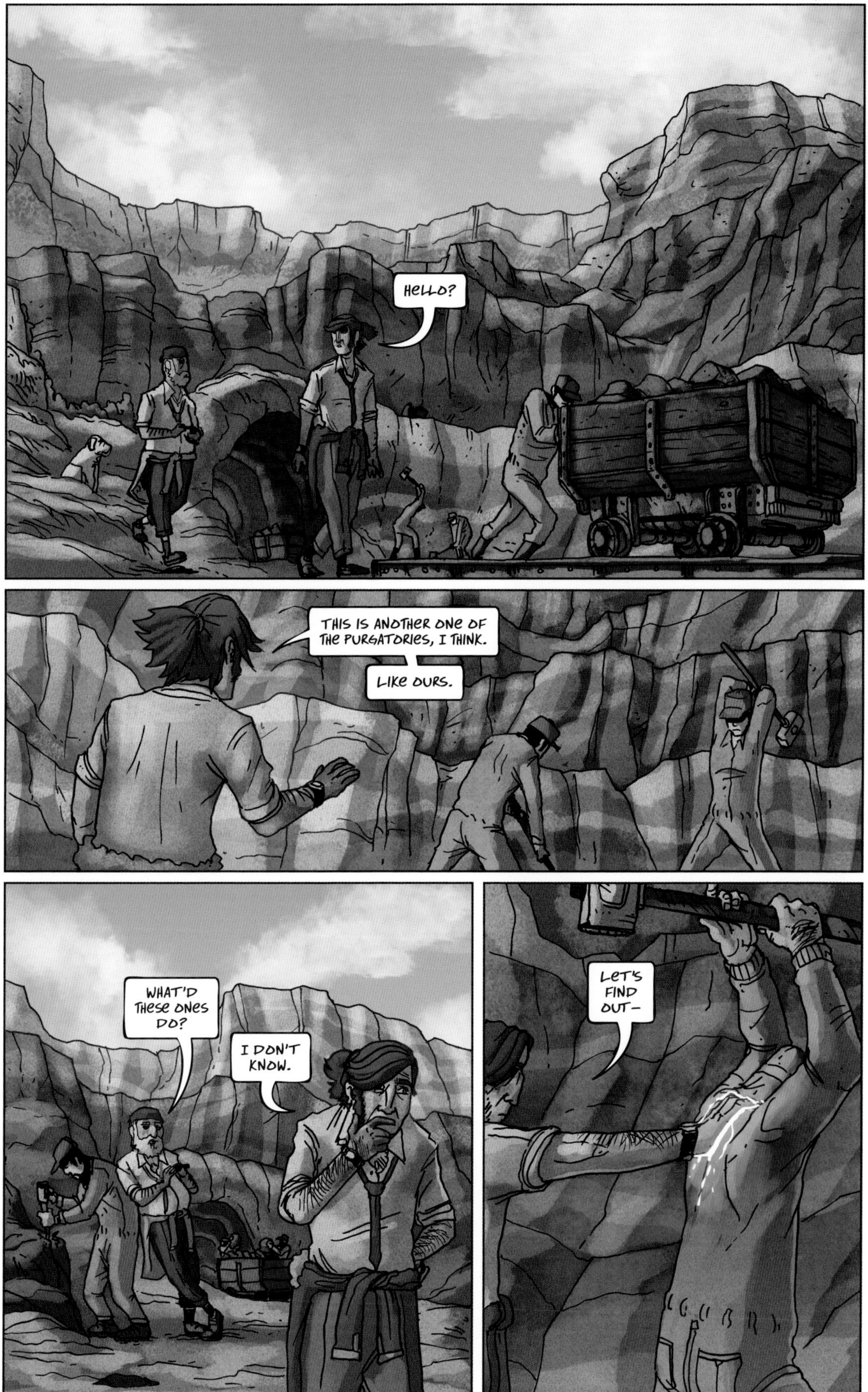
HELLO?
THIS IS ANOTHER ONE OF THE PURGATORIES, I THINK.
LIKE OURS.
WHAT'D THESE ONES DO?
I DON'T KNOW.
LET'S FIND OUT–

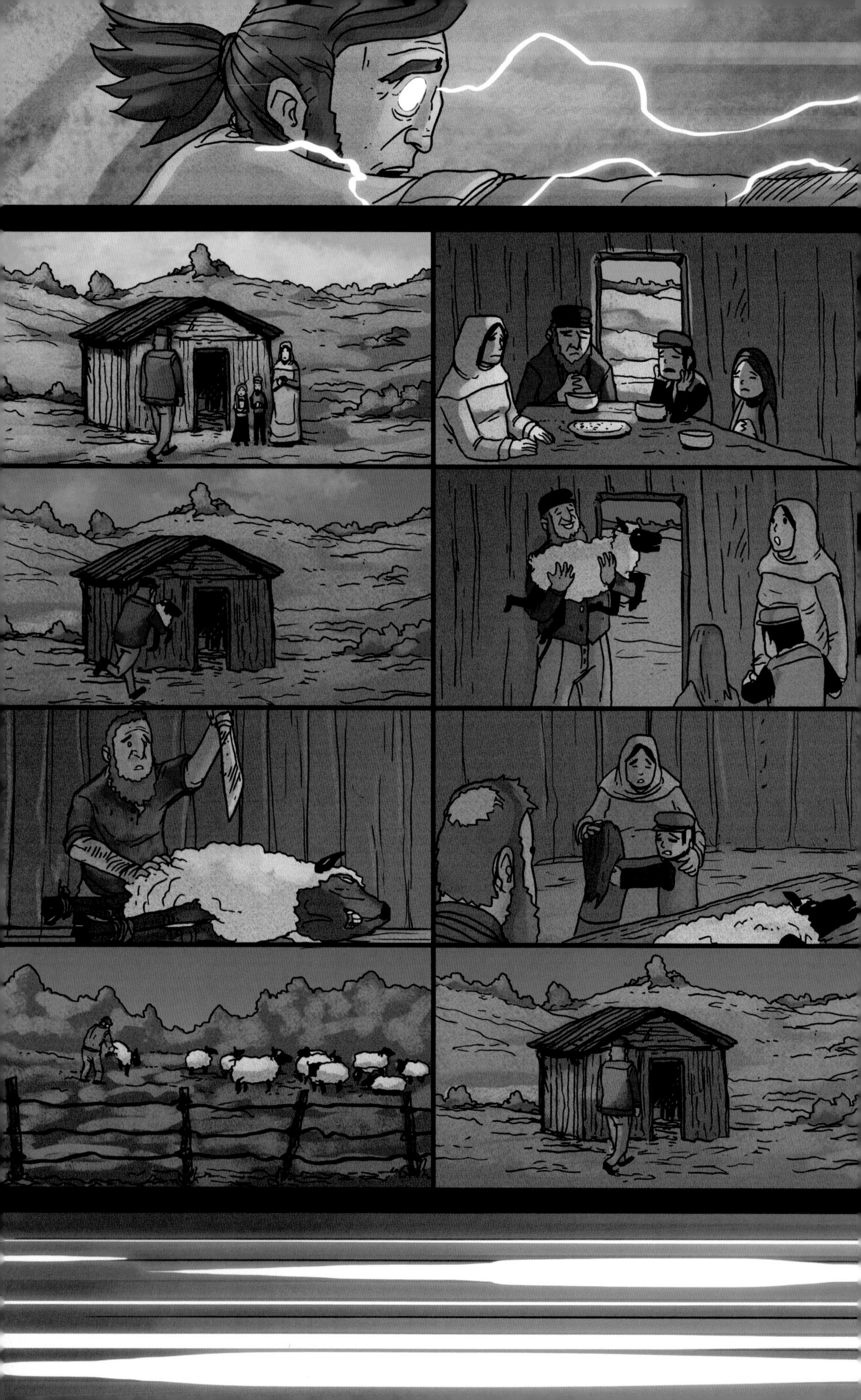

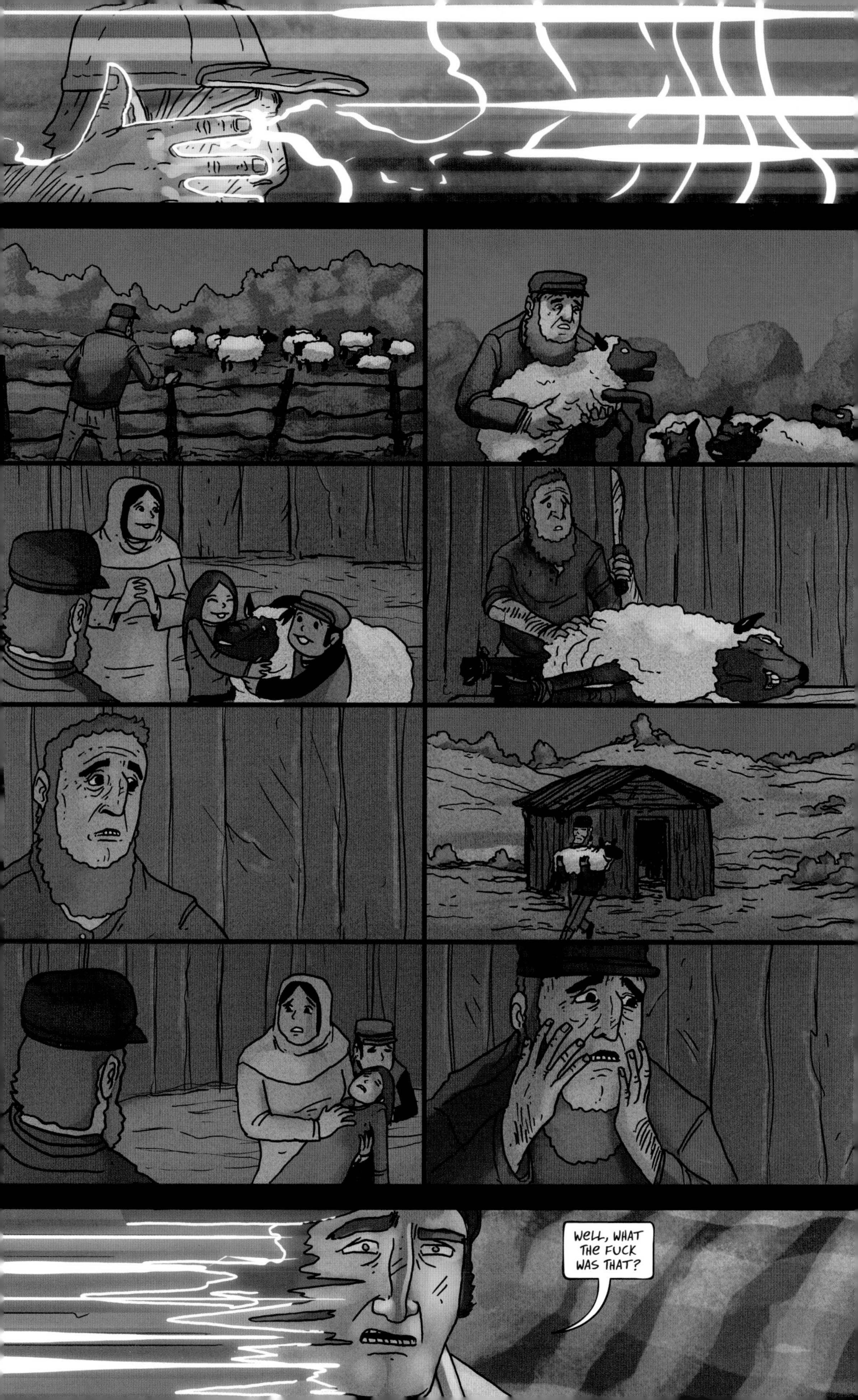
WELL, WHAT THE FUCK WAS THAT?

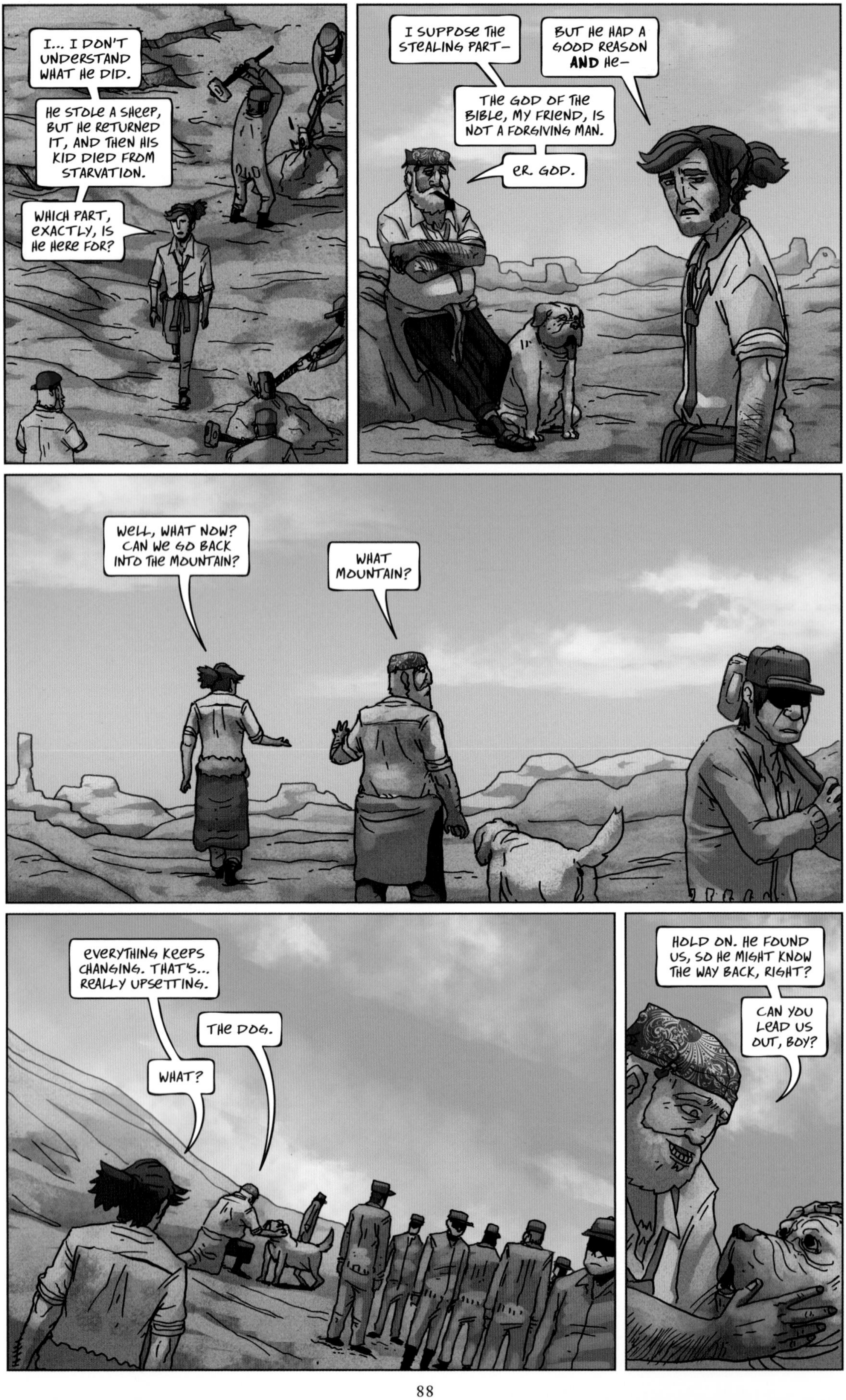
I... I DON'T UNDERSTAND WHAT HE DID.
HE STOLE A SHEEP, BUT HE RETURNED IT, AND THEN HIS KID DIED FROM STARVATION.
WHICH PART, EXACTLY, IS HE HERE FOR?
I SUPPOSE THE STEALING PART—
BUT HE HAD A GOOD REASON **AND** HE—
THE GOD OF THE BIBLE, MY FRIEND, IS NOT A FORGIVING MAN.
ER. GOD.
WELL, WHAT NOW? CAN WE GO BACK INTO THE MOUNTAIN?
WHAT MOUNTAIN?
EVERYTHING KEEPS CHANGING. THAT'S... REALLY UPSETTING.
THE DOG.
WHAT?
HOLD ON. HE FOUND US, SO HE MIGHT KNOW THE WAY BACK, RIGHT?
CAN YOU LEAD US OUT, BOY?

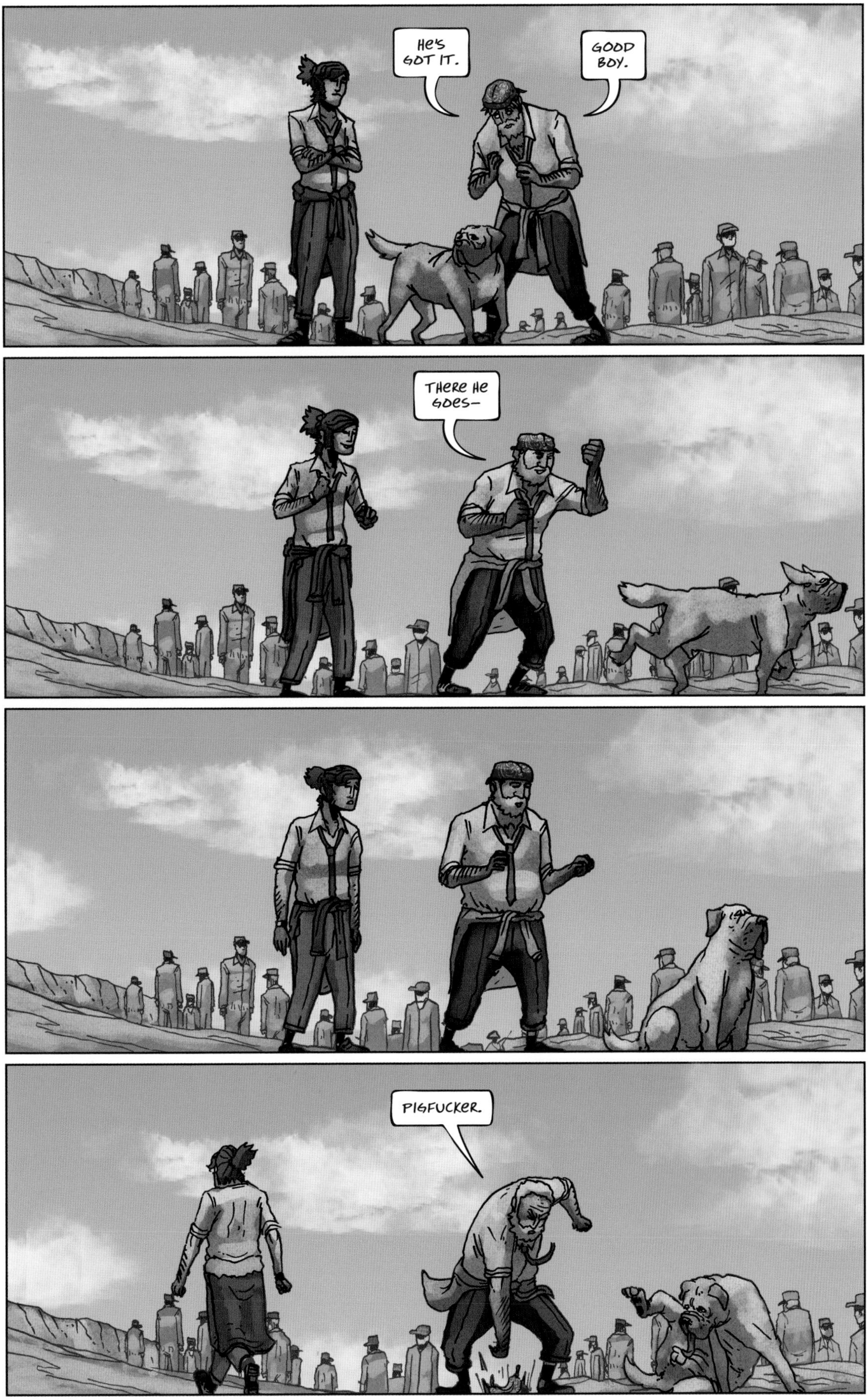
He's got it.
Good boy.
There he goes—
Pigfucker.

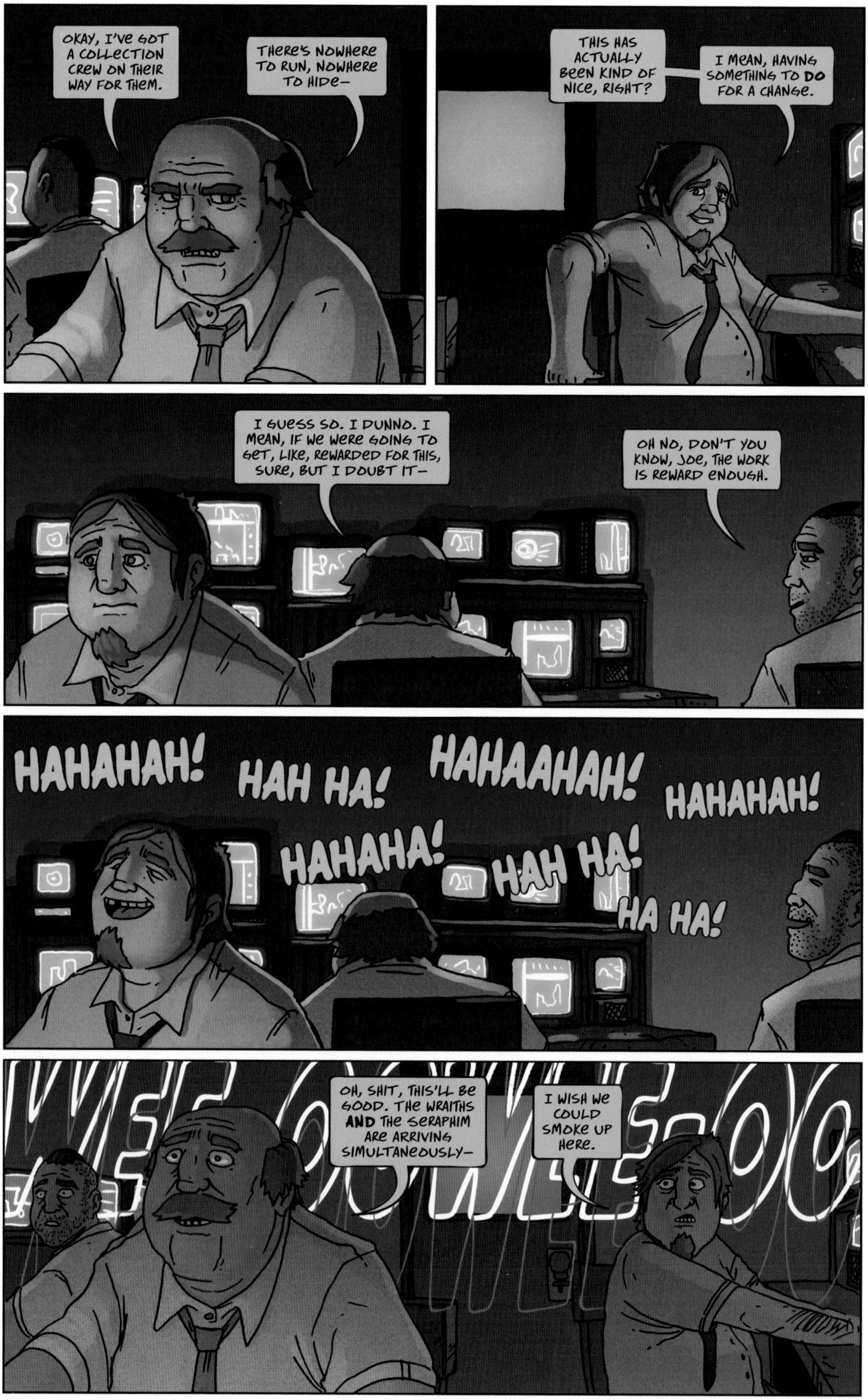
OKAY, I'VE GOT A COLLECTION CREW ON THEIR WAY FOR THEM.
THERE'S NOWHERE TO RUN, NOWHERE TO HIDE—
THIS HAS ACTUALLY BEEN KIND OF NICE, RIGHT?
I MEAN, HAVING SOMETHING TO **DO** FOR A CHANGE.
I GUESS SO. I DUNNO. I MEAN, IF WE WERE GOING TO GET, LIKE, REWARDED FOR THIS, SURE, BUT I DOUBT IT—
OH NO, DON'T YOU KNOW, JOE, THE WORK IS REWARD ENOUGH.
HAHAHAH!
HAH HA!
HAHAAAHAH!
HAHAHAH!
HAHAHA!
HAH HA!
HA HA!
OH, SHIT, THIS'LL BE GOOD. THE WRAITHS **AND** THE SERAPHIM ARE ARRIVING SIMULTANEOUSLY—
I WISH WE COULD SMOKE UP HERE.

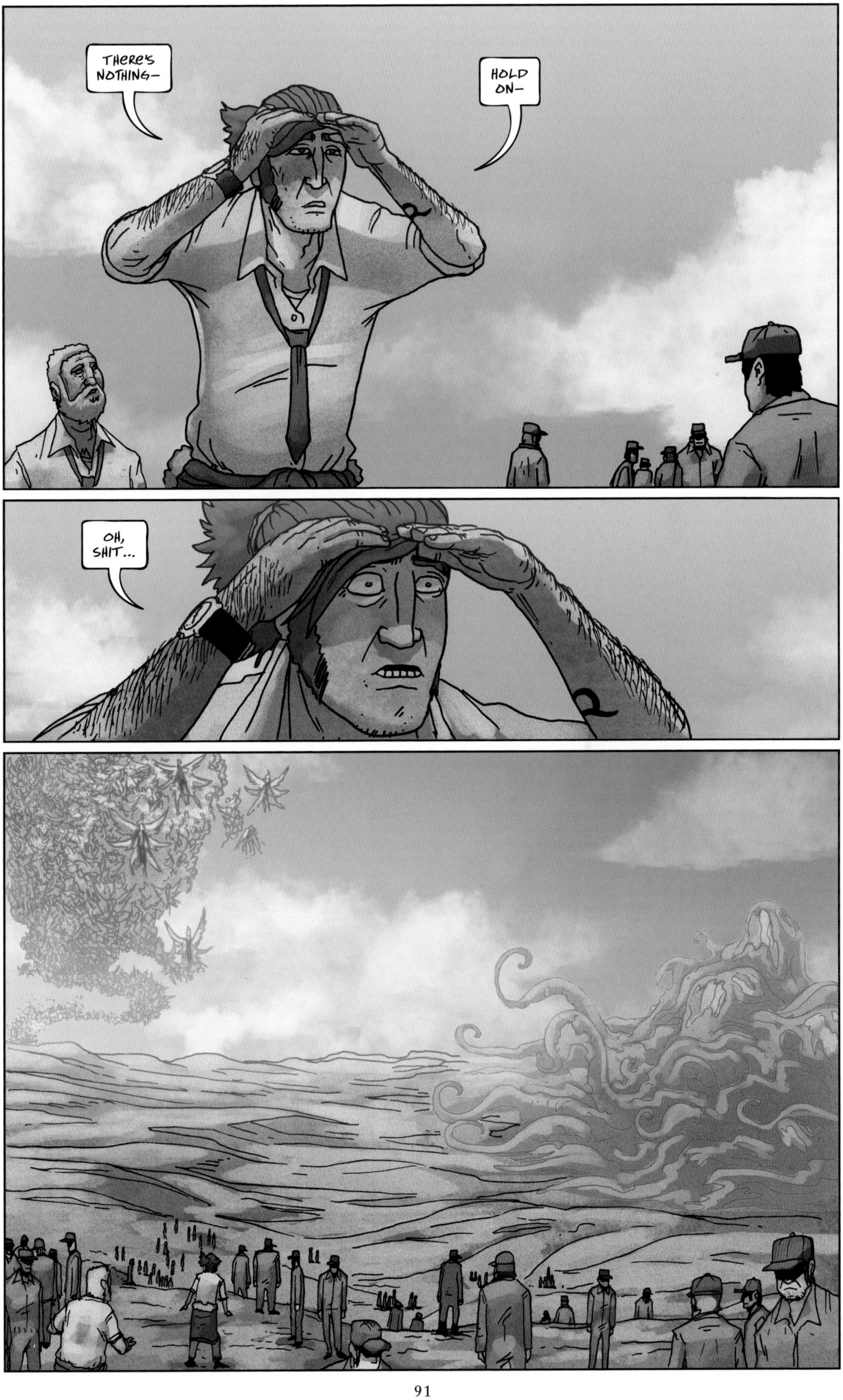
THERE'S NOTHING—
HOLD ON—
OH, SHIT...

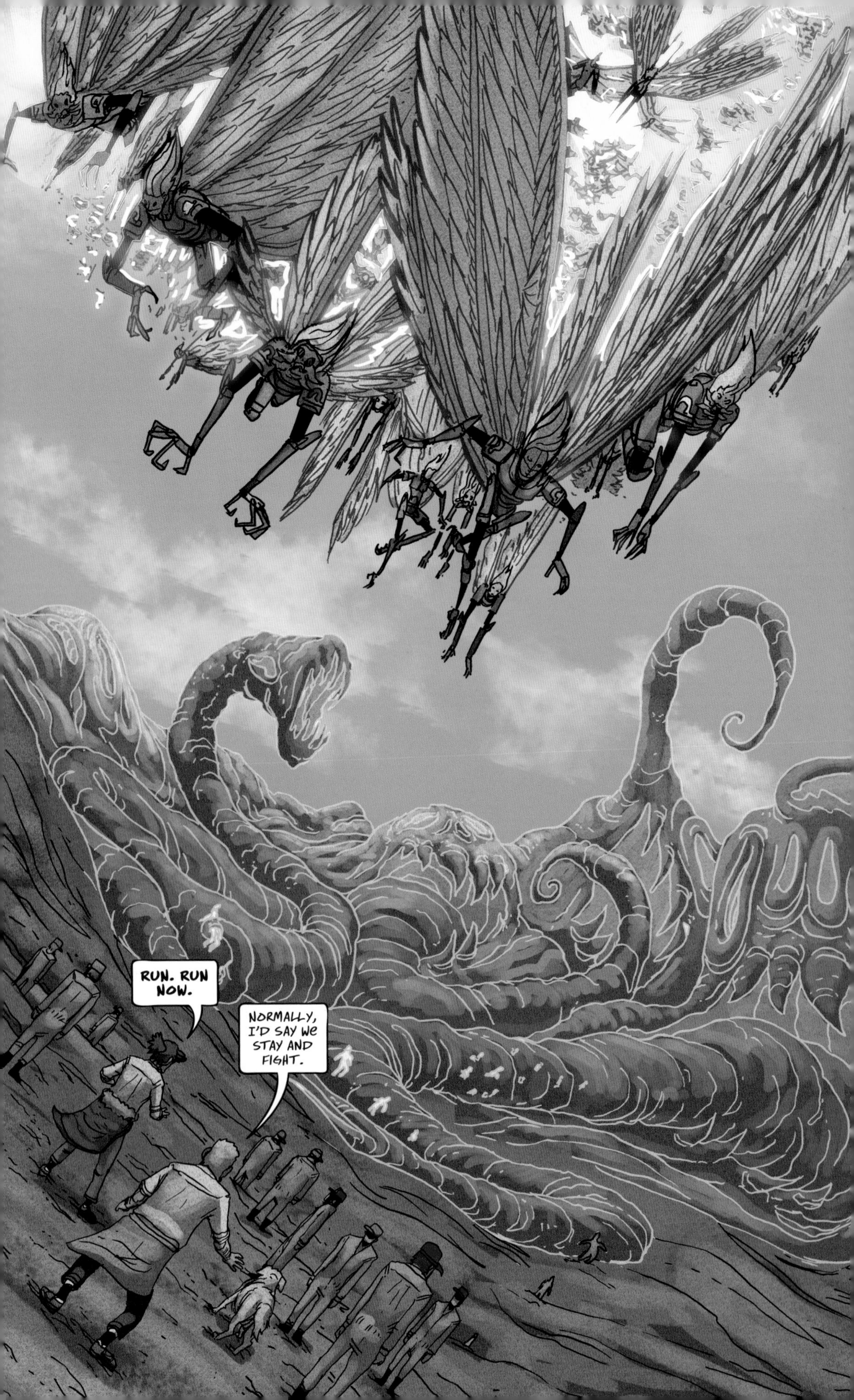
RUN. RUN NOW.
NORMALLY, I'D SAY WE STAY AND FIGHT.

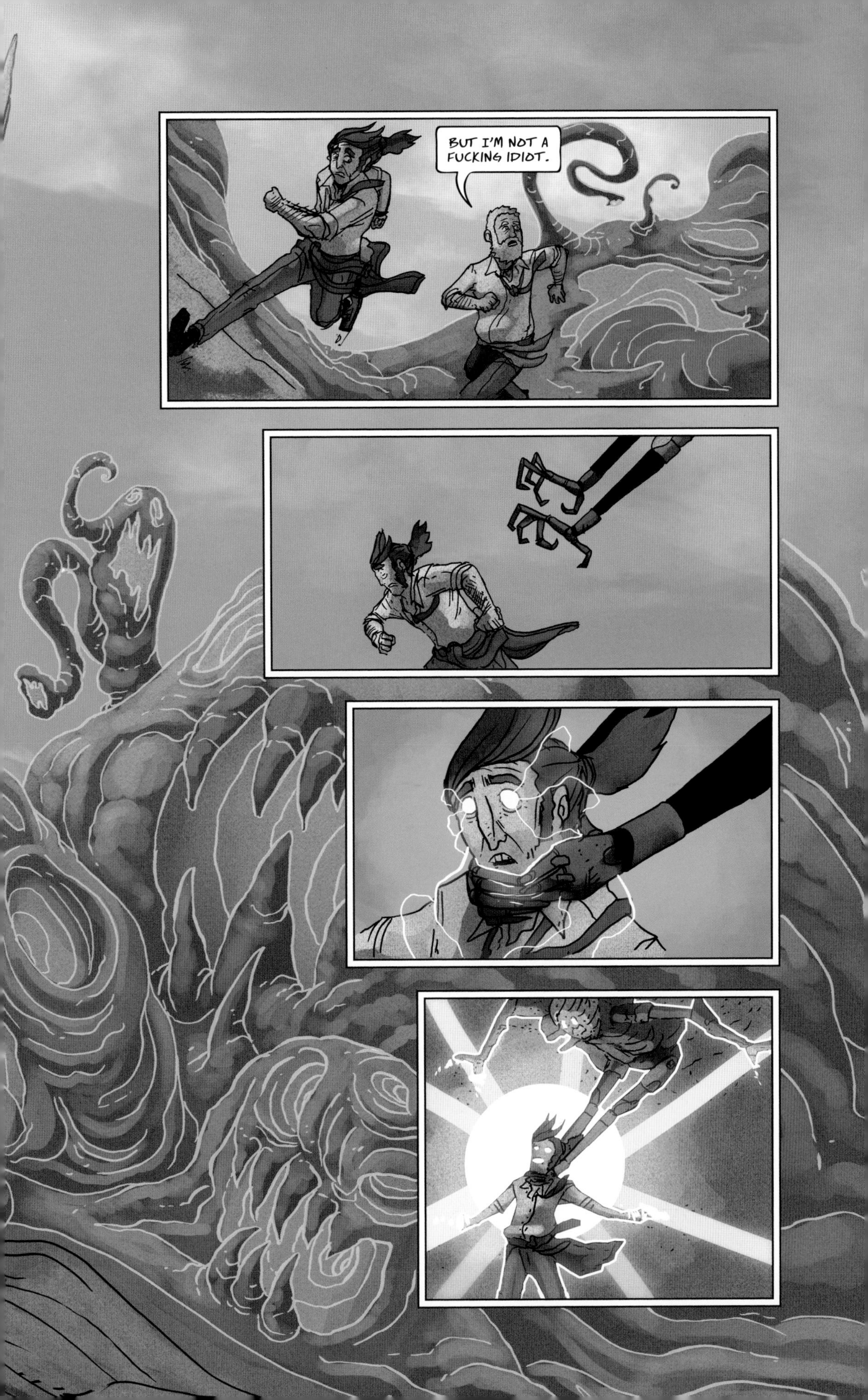
BUT I'M NOT A FUCKING IDIOT.

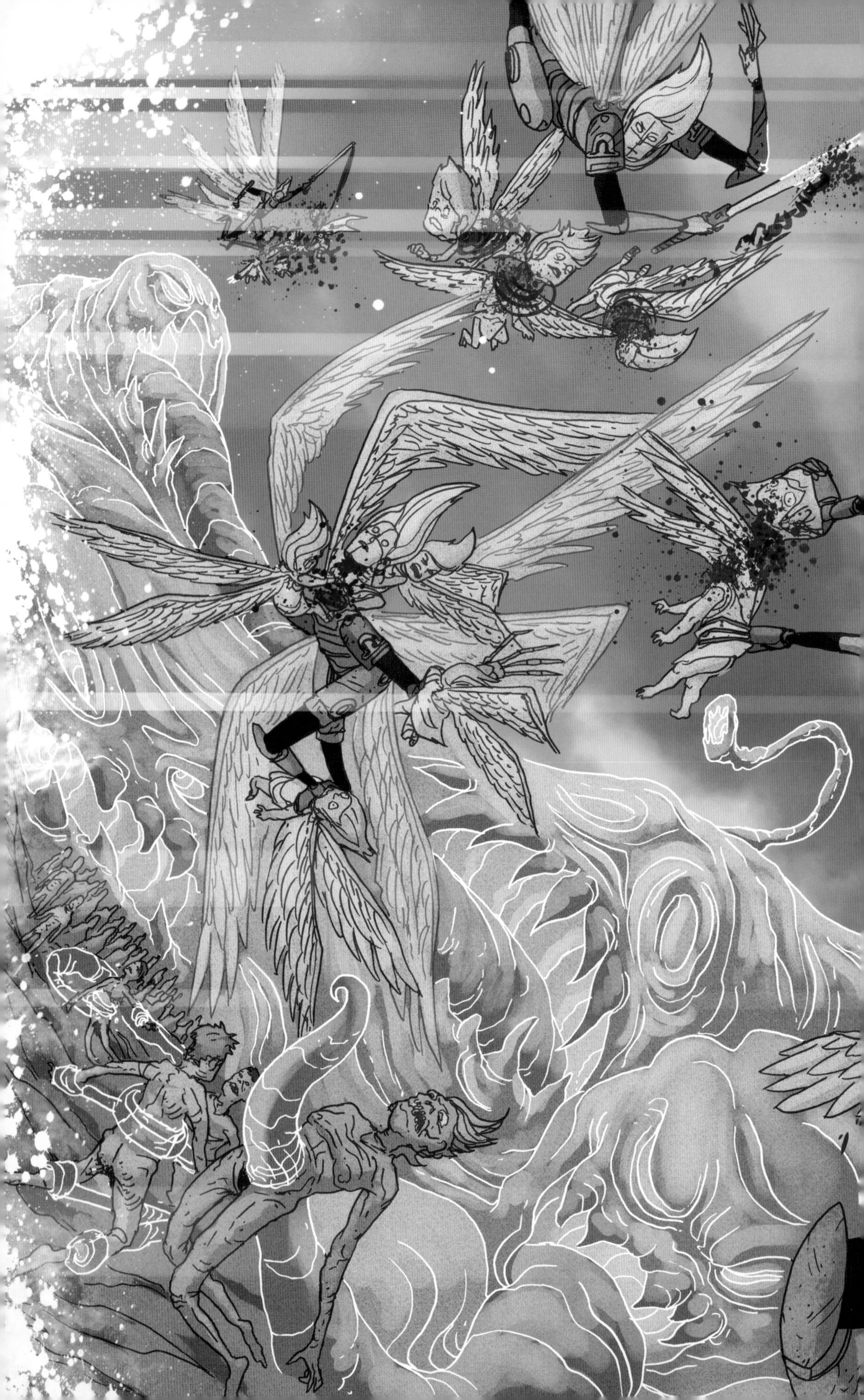

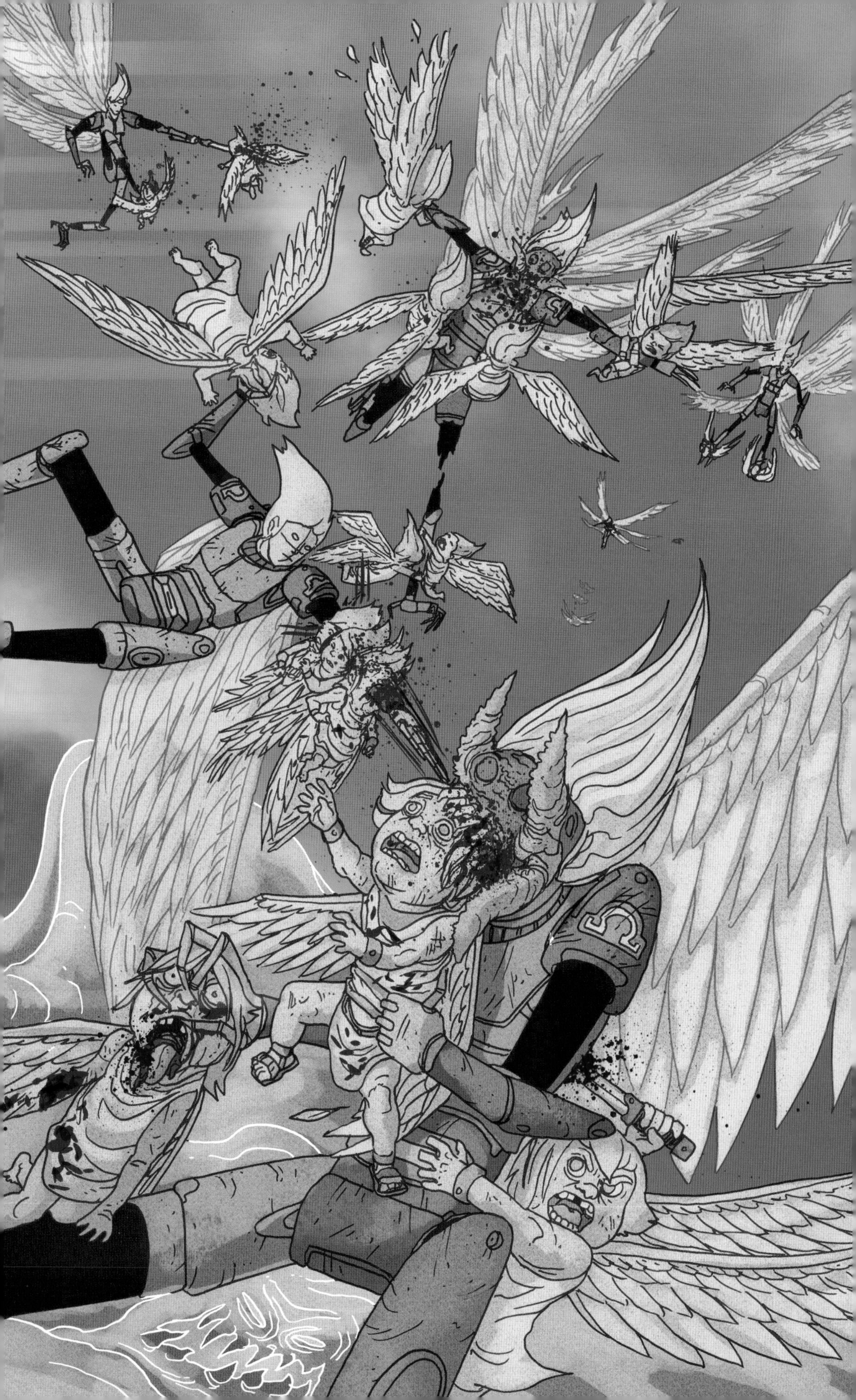

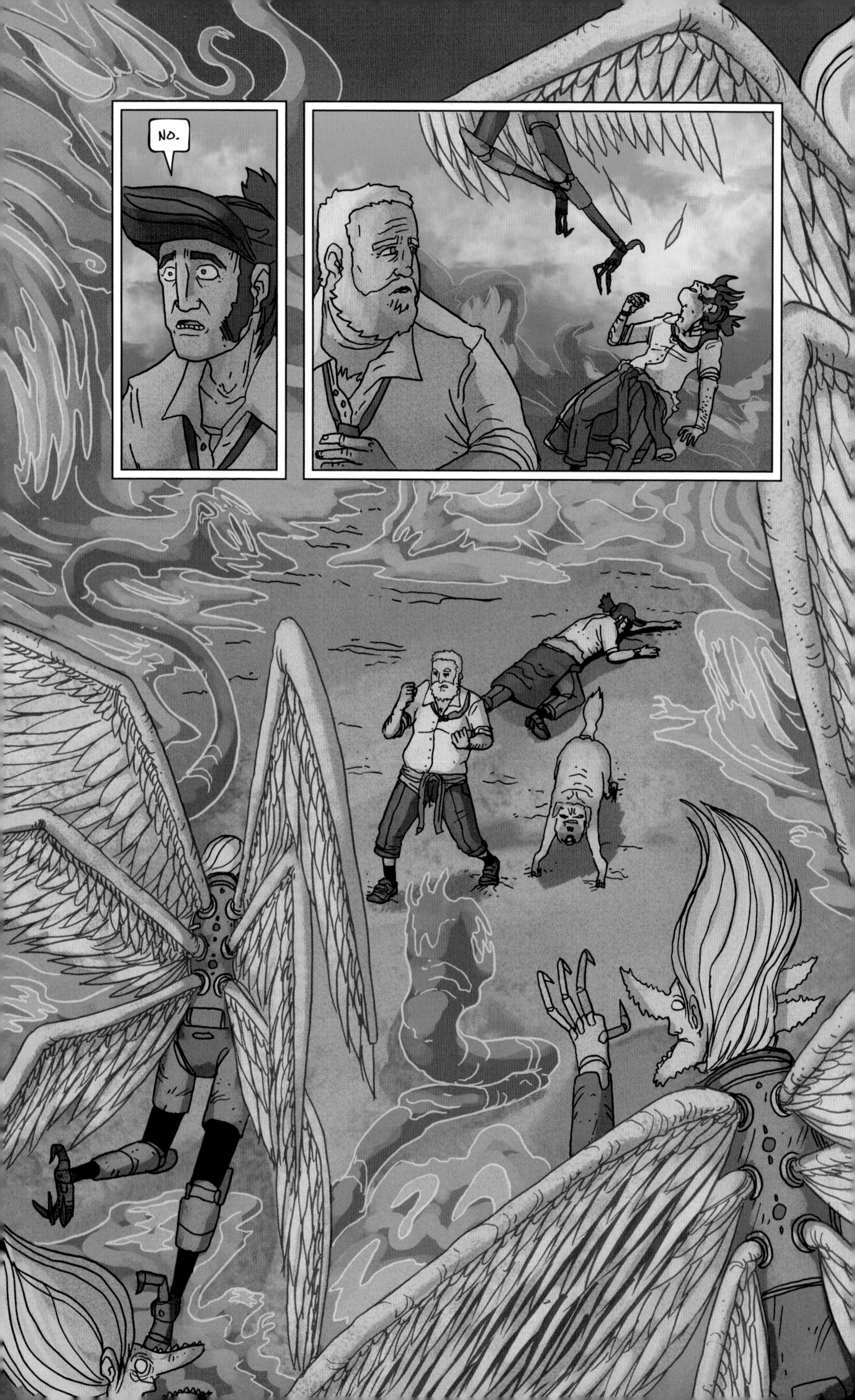
NO.

VRRRRRRRRRRR
SIR?
YES?
RRRRRRRRRRRR
RRRRRRRRRRR—
SORRY TO BOTHER YOU, SIR, TWO THINGS. FIRST, THE ROGUES ARE SURROUNDED, AND SHOULD BE IN CUSTODY SOON.
THAT'S... THAT'S TERRIFIC.
AND, ALSO, YOUR...
...GUEST IS HERE.
SEND THEM AWAY! SERVICES NO LONGER REQUIRED—

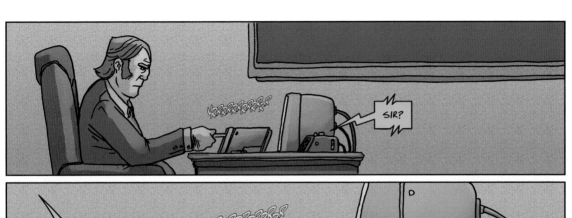

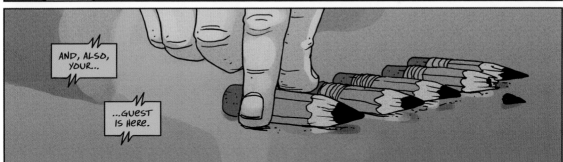

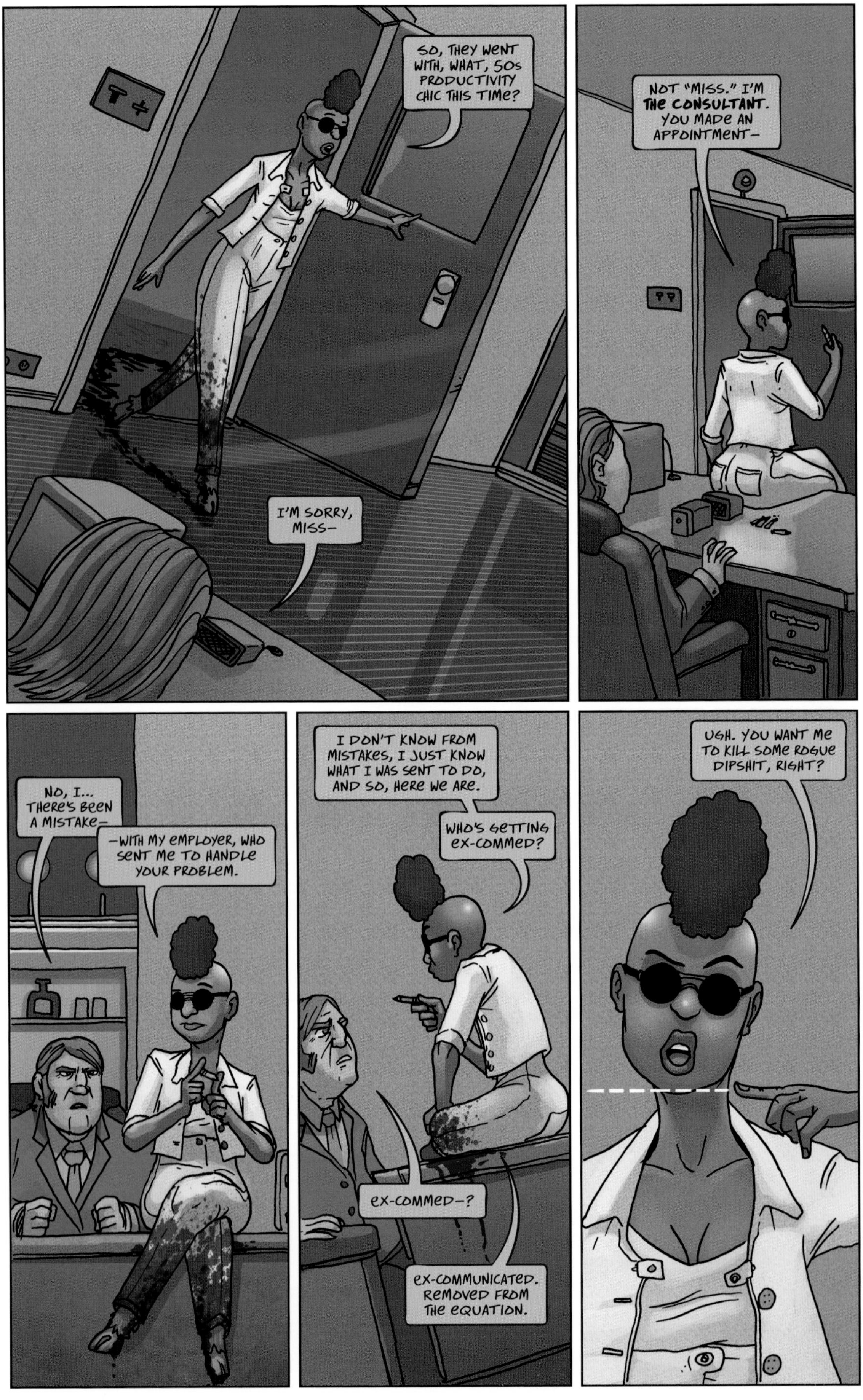
SO, THEY WENT WITH, WHAT, 50s PRODUCTIVITY CHIC THIS TIME?
I'M SORRY, MISS—
NOT "MISS." I'M THE CONSULTANT. YOU MADE AN APPOINTMENT—
NO, I... THERE'S BEEN A MISTAKE—
—WITH MY EMPLOYER, WHO SENT ME TO HANDLE YOUR PROBLEM.
I DON'T KNOW FROM MISTAKES, I JUST KNOW WHAT I WAS SENT TO DO, AND SO, HERE WE ARE.
WHO'S GETTING EX-COMMED?
EX-COMMED—?
EX-COMMUNICATED. REMOVED FROM THE EQUATION.
UGH. YOU WANT ME TO KILL SOME ROGUE DIPSHIT, RIGHT?

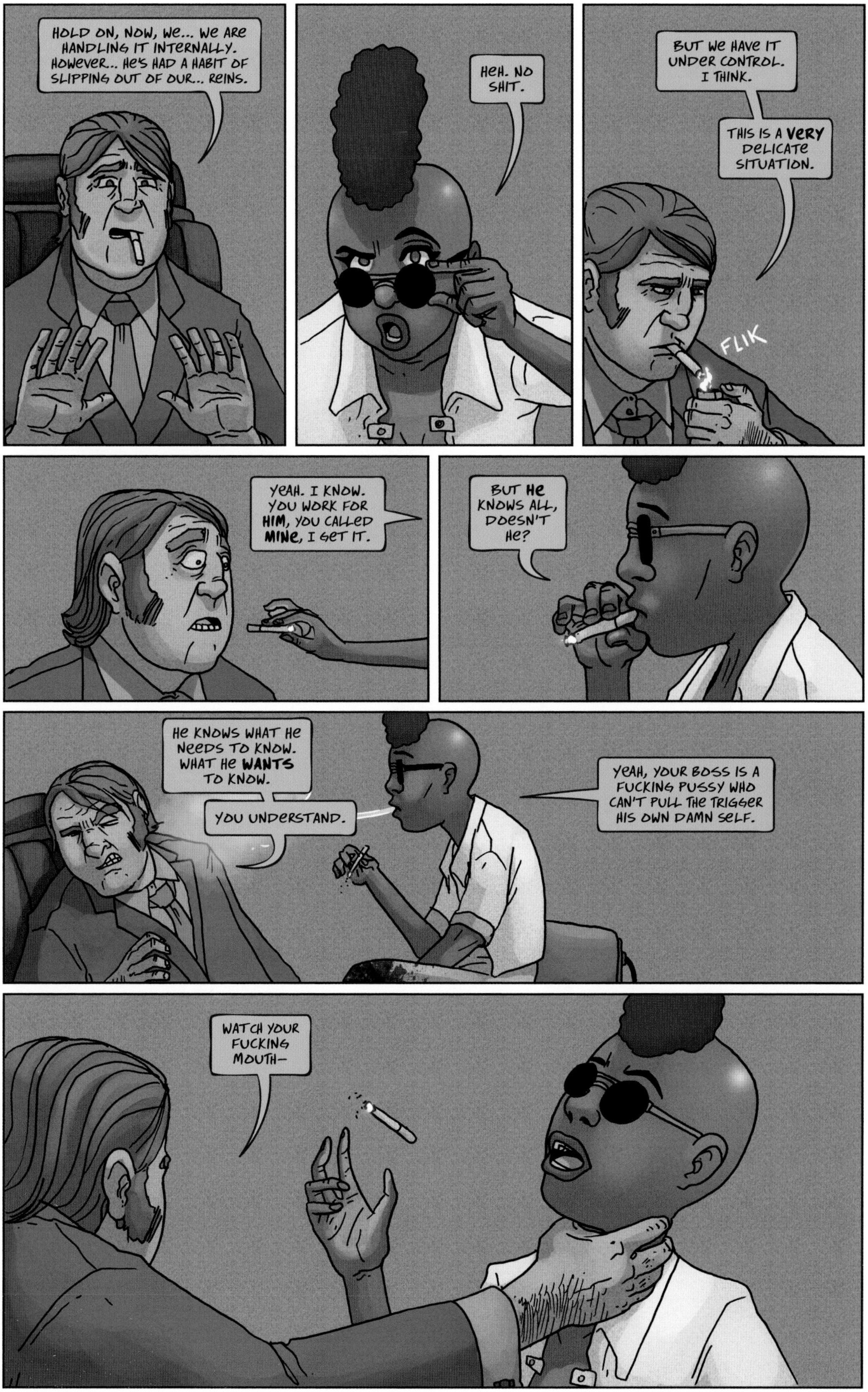
HOLD ON, NOW, WE... WE ARE HANDLING IT INTERNALLY. HOWEVER... HE'S HAD A HABIT OF SLIPPING OUT OF OUR... REINS.
HEH. NO SHIT.
BUT WE HAVE IT UNDER CONTROL. I THINK.
THIS IS A **VERY** DELICATE SITUATION.
FLIK
YEAH. I KNOW. YOU WORK FOR **HIM**, YOU CALLED **MINE**, I GET IT.
BUT **HE** KNOWS ALL, DOESN'T HE?
HE KNOWS WHAT HE NEEDS TO KNOW. WHAT HE **WANTS** TO KNOW.
YOU UNDERSTAND.
YEAH, YOUR BOSS IS A FUCKING PUSSY WHO CAN'T PULL THE TRIGGER HIS OWN DAMN SELF.
WATCH YOUR FUCKING MOUTH—

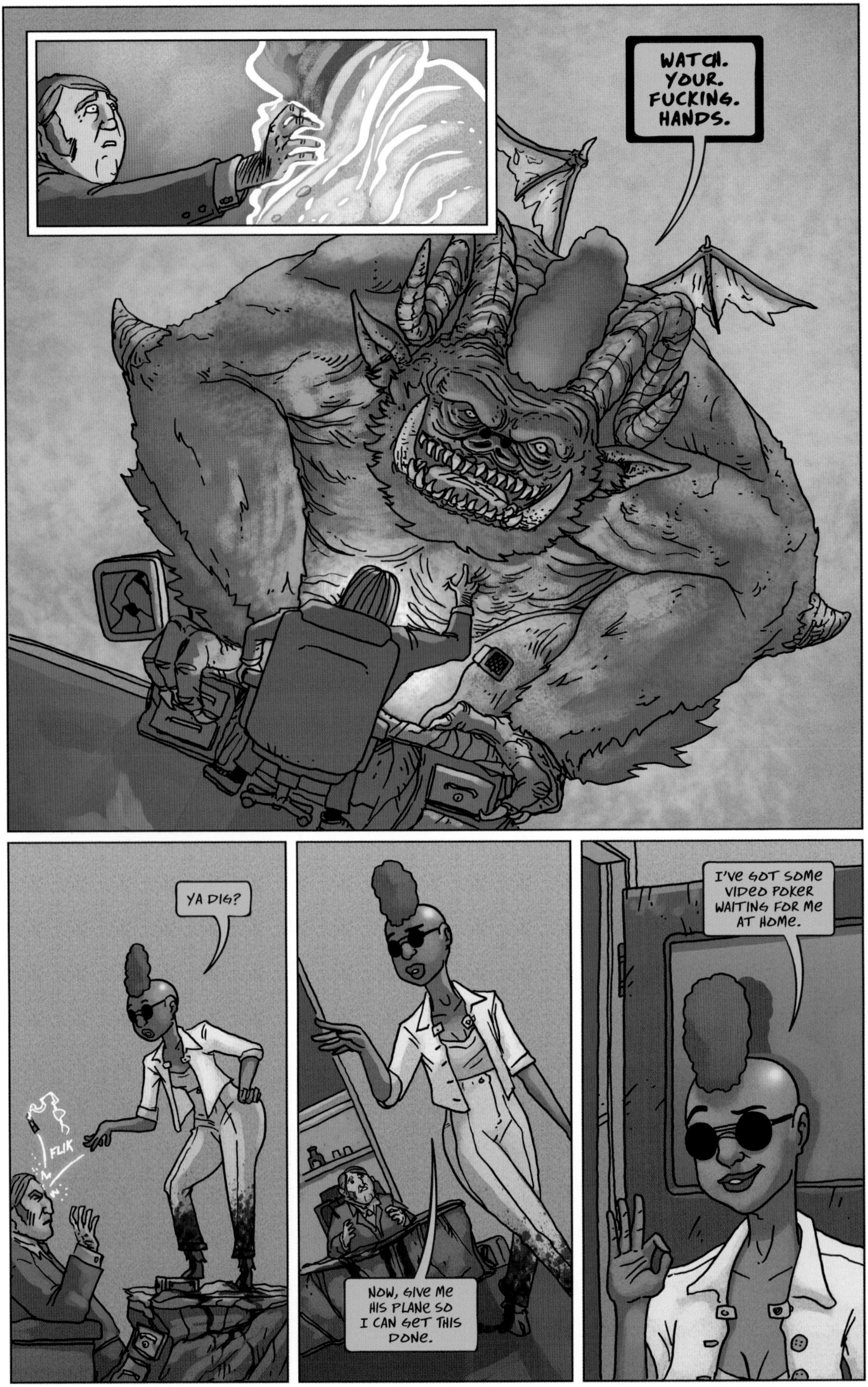
WATCH. YOUR. FUCKING. HANDS.
YA DIG?
FLIK
NOW, GIVE ME HIS PLANE SO I CAN GET THIS DONE.
I'VE GOT SOME VIDEO POKER WAITING FOR ME AT HOME.

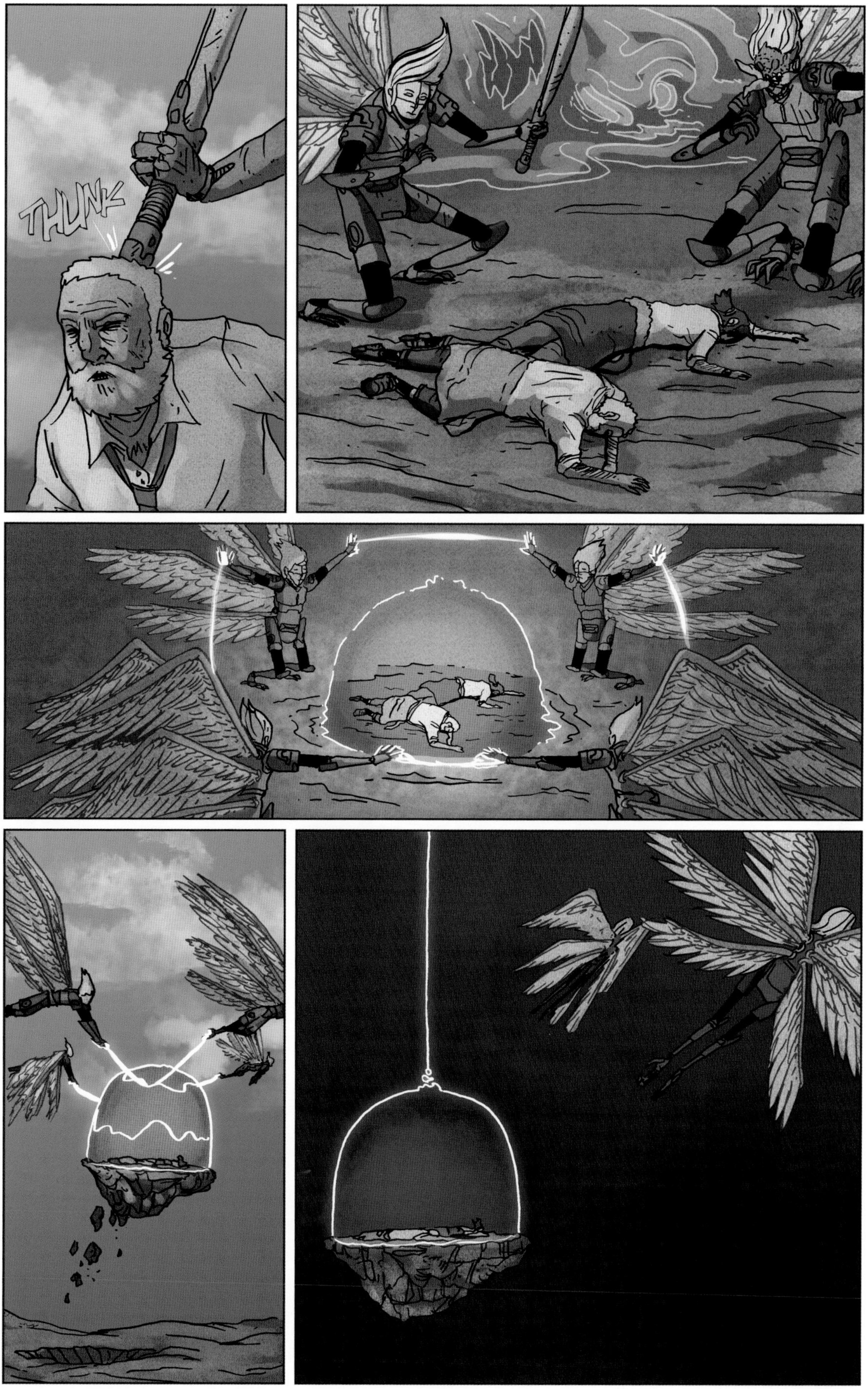
THUNK

C'MON, JUDE, WAKE UP, MY BOY.

I'M GOING TO NEED SOME HELP—

I DON'T THINK THAT'LL WORK.

I CAN'T SEE YOU, COME INTO THE LIGHT.

NO. I'M FINE, THANKS.

WHAT... WHAT IS THIS PLACE?

I THINK IT'S HELL.

I DON'T THINK IT IS. I'M NOT IN PAIN. ARE YOU IN PAIN?

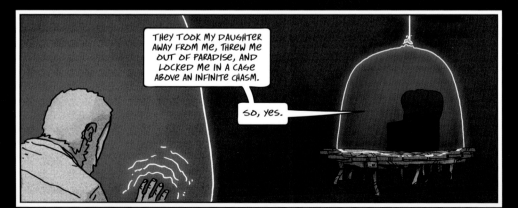

THEY TOOK MY DAUGHTER AWAY FROM ME, THREW ME OUT OF PARADISE, AND LOCKED ME IN A CAGE ABOVE AN INFINITE CHASM.

SO, YES.

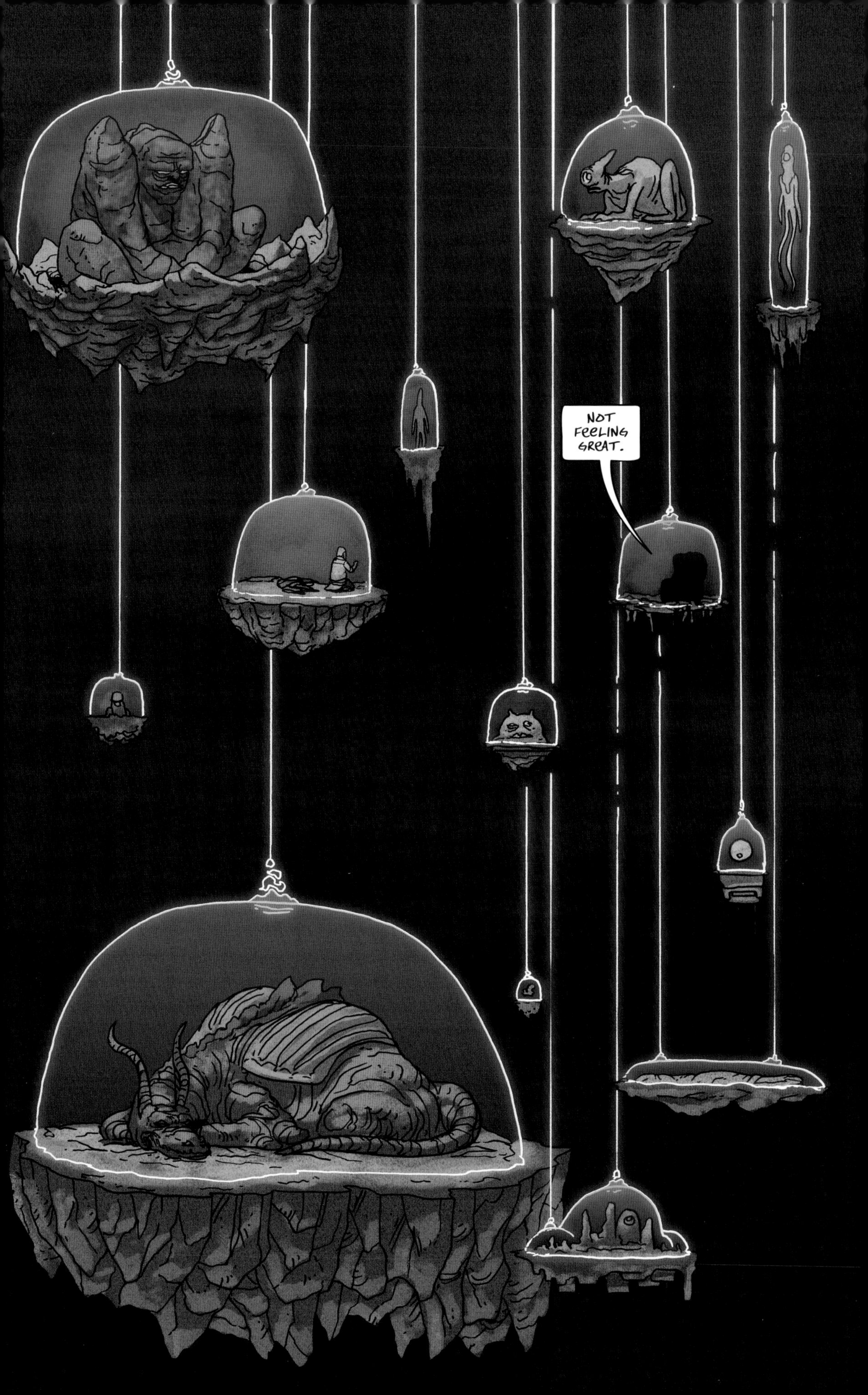
NOT FEELING GREAT.

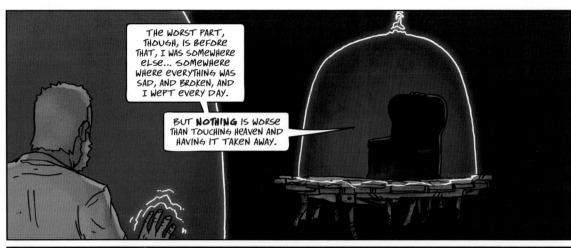

THE WORST PART, THOUGH, IS BEFORE THAT, I WAS SOMEWHERE ELSE... SOMEWHERE WHERE EVERYTHING WAS SAD, AND BROKEN, AND I WEPT EVERY DAY.

BUT **NOTHING** IS WORSE THAN TOUCHING HEAVEN AND HAVING IT TAKEN AWAY.

MY DAUGHTER WAS STILL BORN, EVERY DAY, FOR AN ETERNITY.

AND THEN SOME **MONSTER** SENT ME TO PARADISE.

JUST TO TORTURE ME. TO PUNISH ME FOR MY SINS.

WHEN HE TOUCHED ME, HE SHOWED ME HOPE.

A SPARK OF ELECTRICITY, AND THEN, A WHITE LIGHT, AND THEN, HAPPINESS.

WHICH WAS **STOLEN** FROM ME.

AND IF I EVER FIND THAT MAN, I'M GOING TO MURDER HIM FOR WHAT HE'S DONE.

AND HE SAID ALL HE WANTED TO DO WAS GIVE ME BACK MY HANDKERCHIEF.

ALL I REMEMBER IS A NAME...

JUDE.

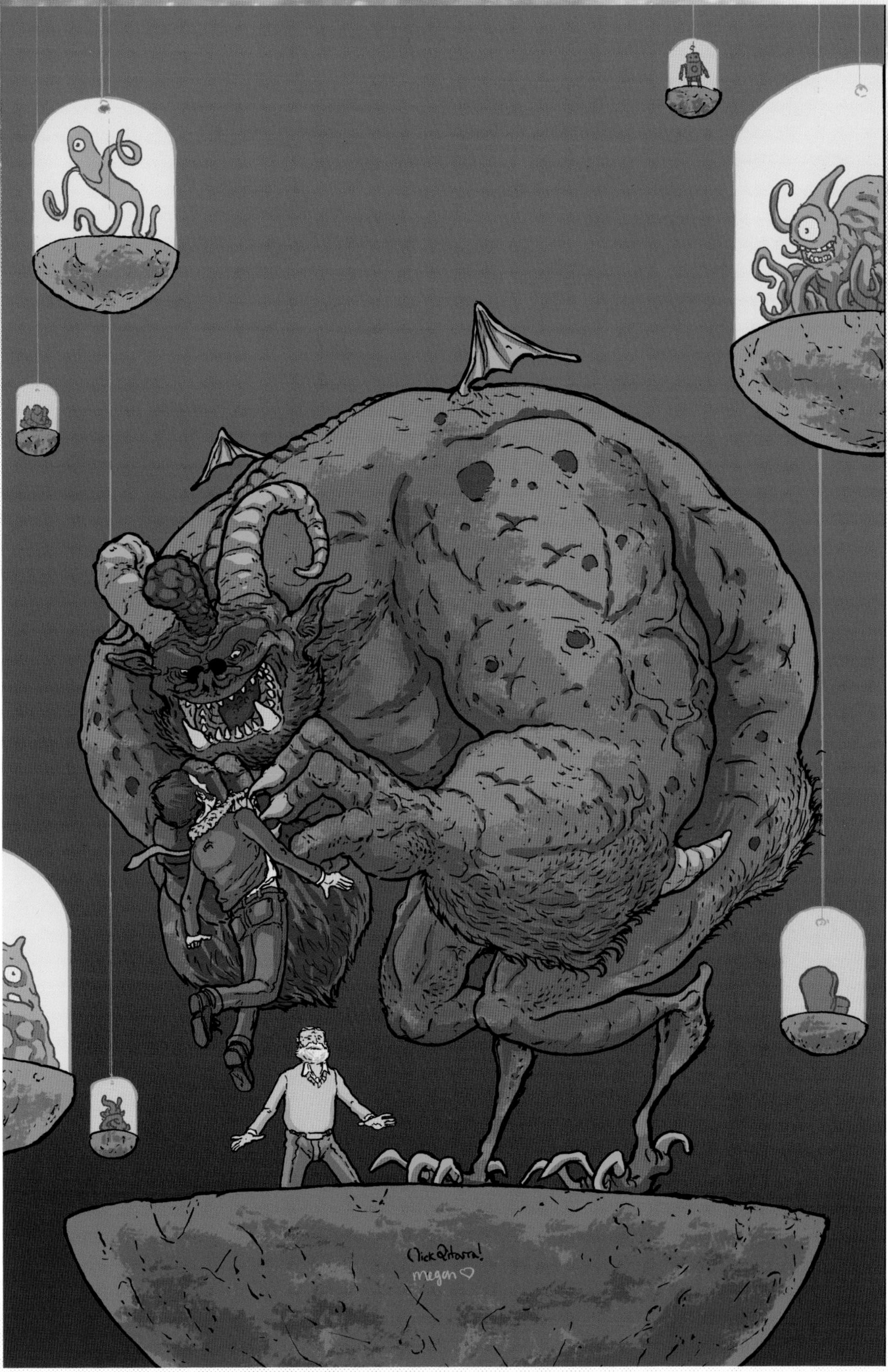
megan

Chapter Five

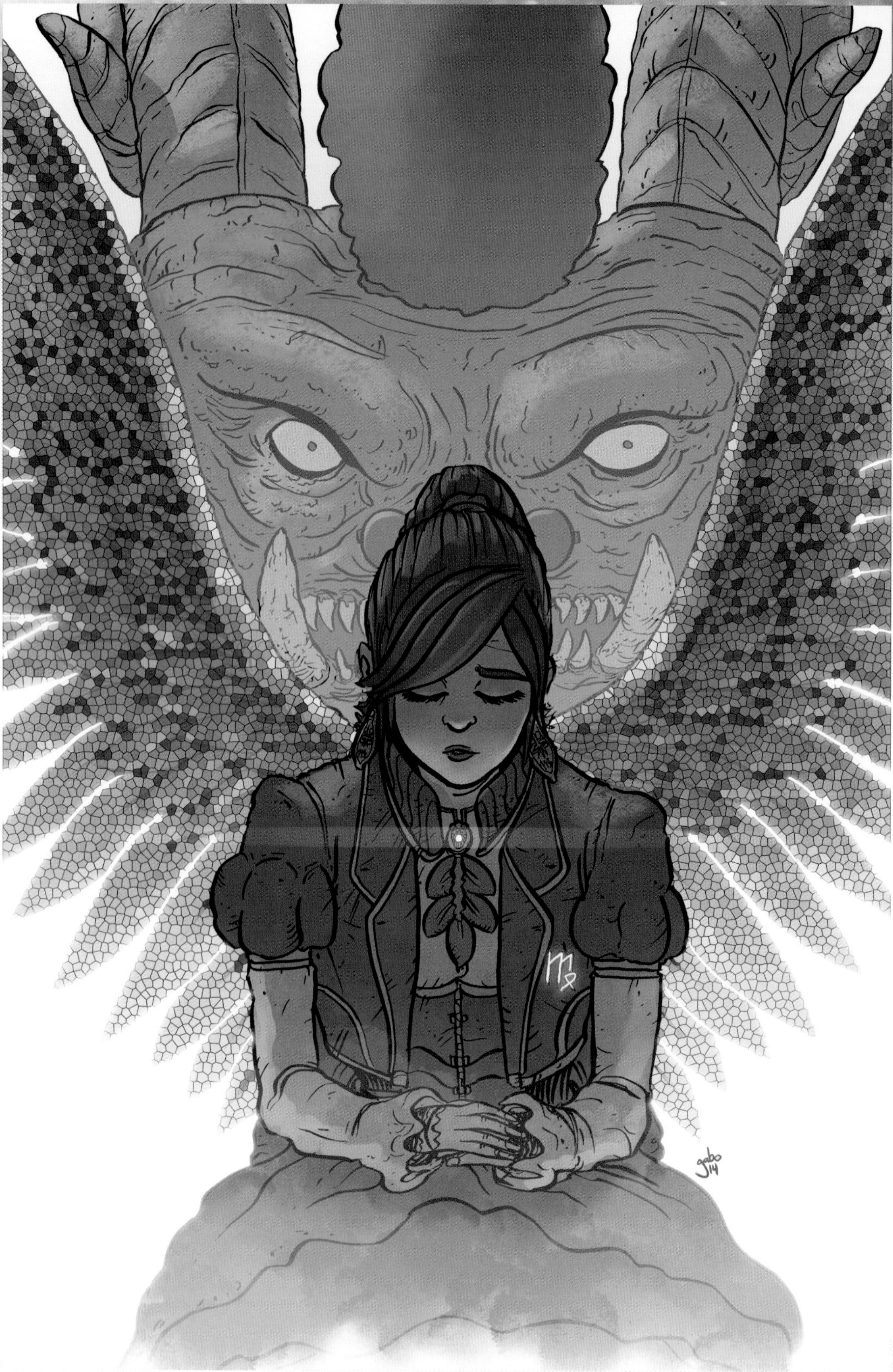
gabo
14

THE LIFE
AFTER

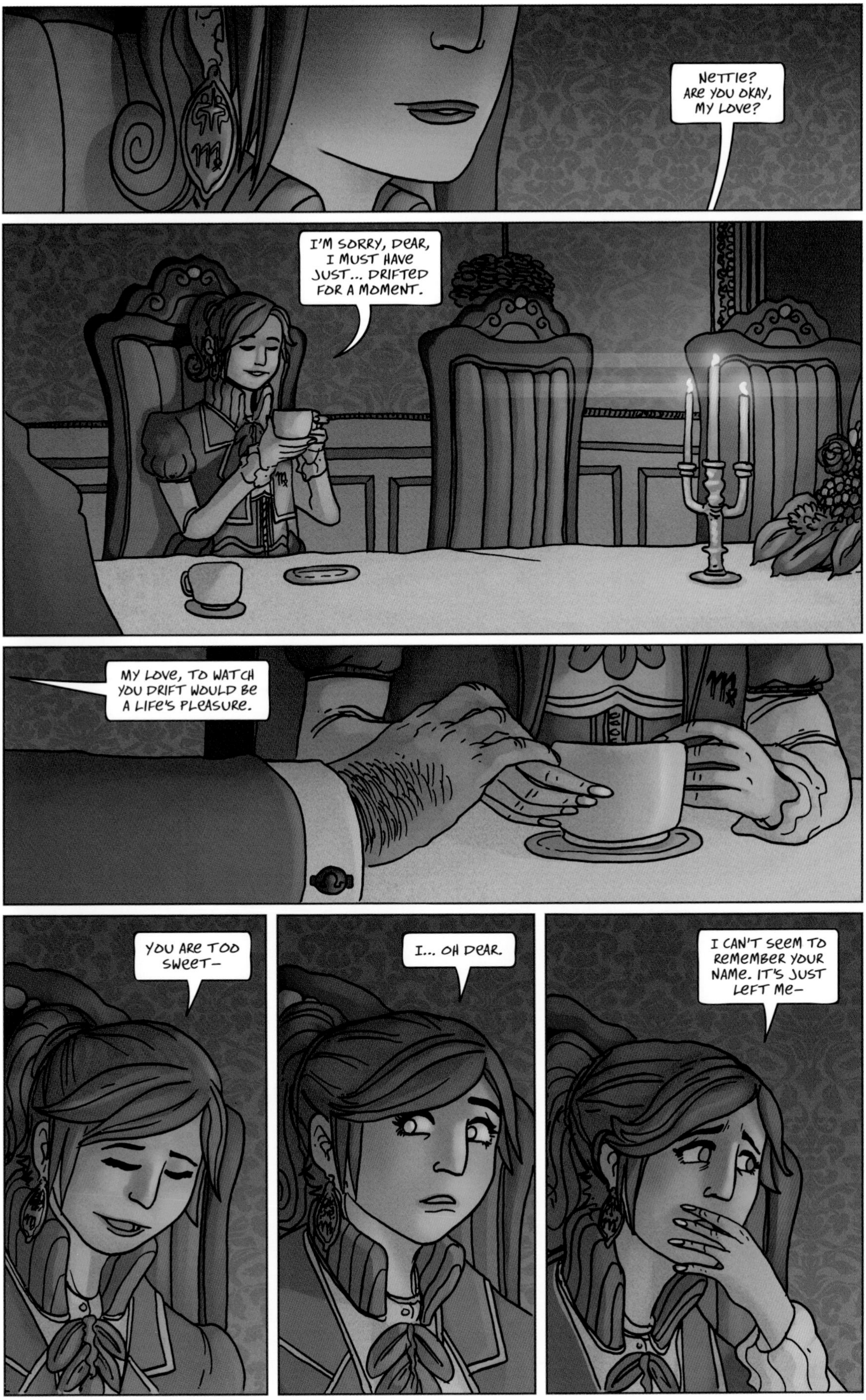
NETTIE? ARE YOU OKAY, MY LOVE?
I'M SORRY, DEAR, I MUST HAVE JUST... DRIFTED FOR A MOMENT.
MY LOVE, TO WATCH YOU DRIFT WOULD BE A LIFE'S PLEASURE.
YOU ARE TOO SWEET—
I... OH DEAR.
I CAN'T SEEM TO REMEMBER YOUR NAME. IT'S JUST LEFT ME—

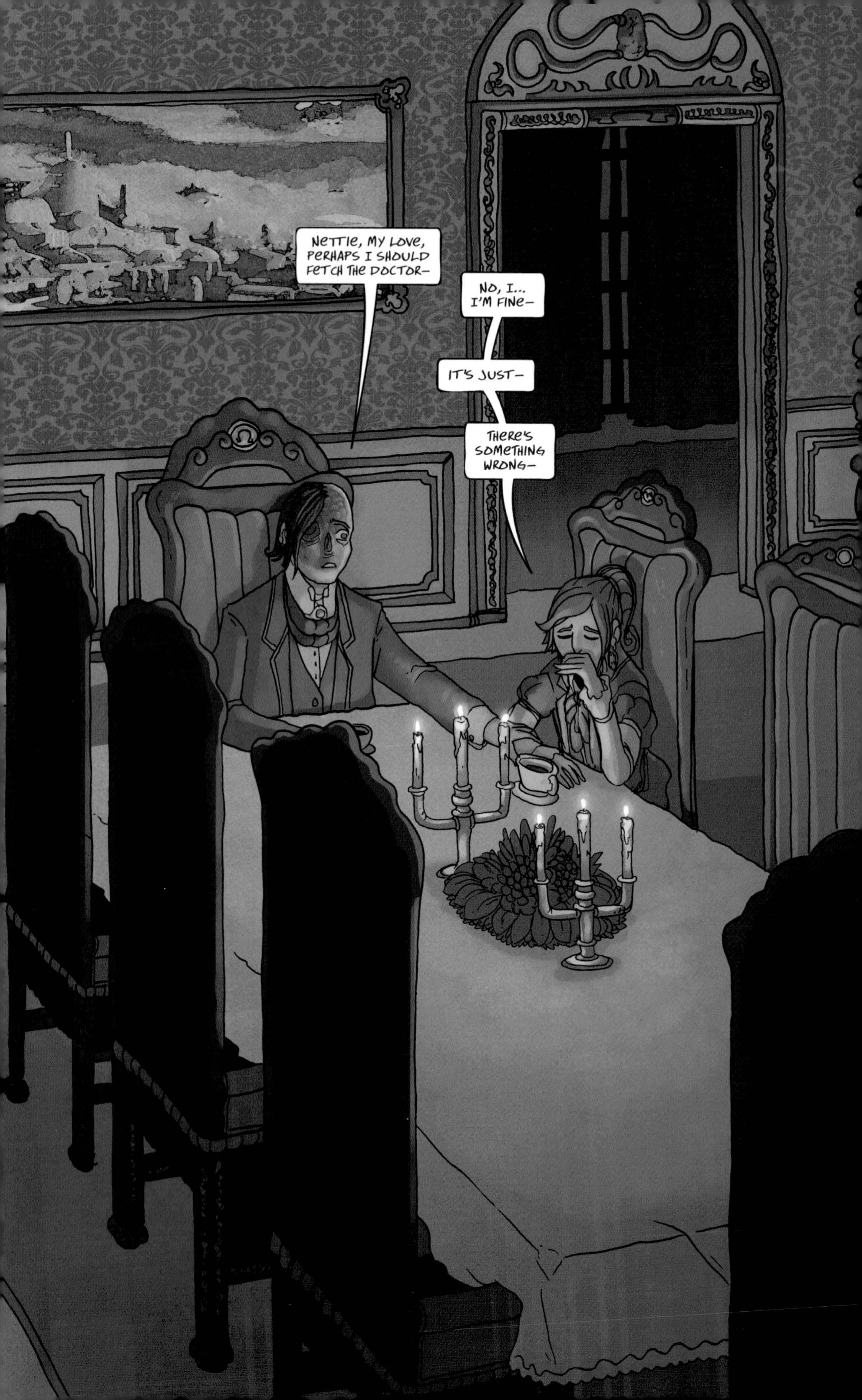

NETTIE, MY LOVE, PERHAPS I SHOULD FETCH THE DOCTOR–
NO, I... I'M FINE–
IT'S JUST–
THERE'S SOMETHING WRONG–

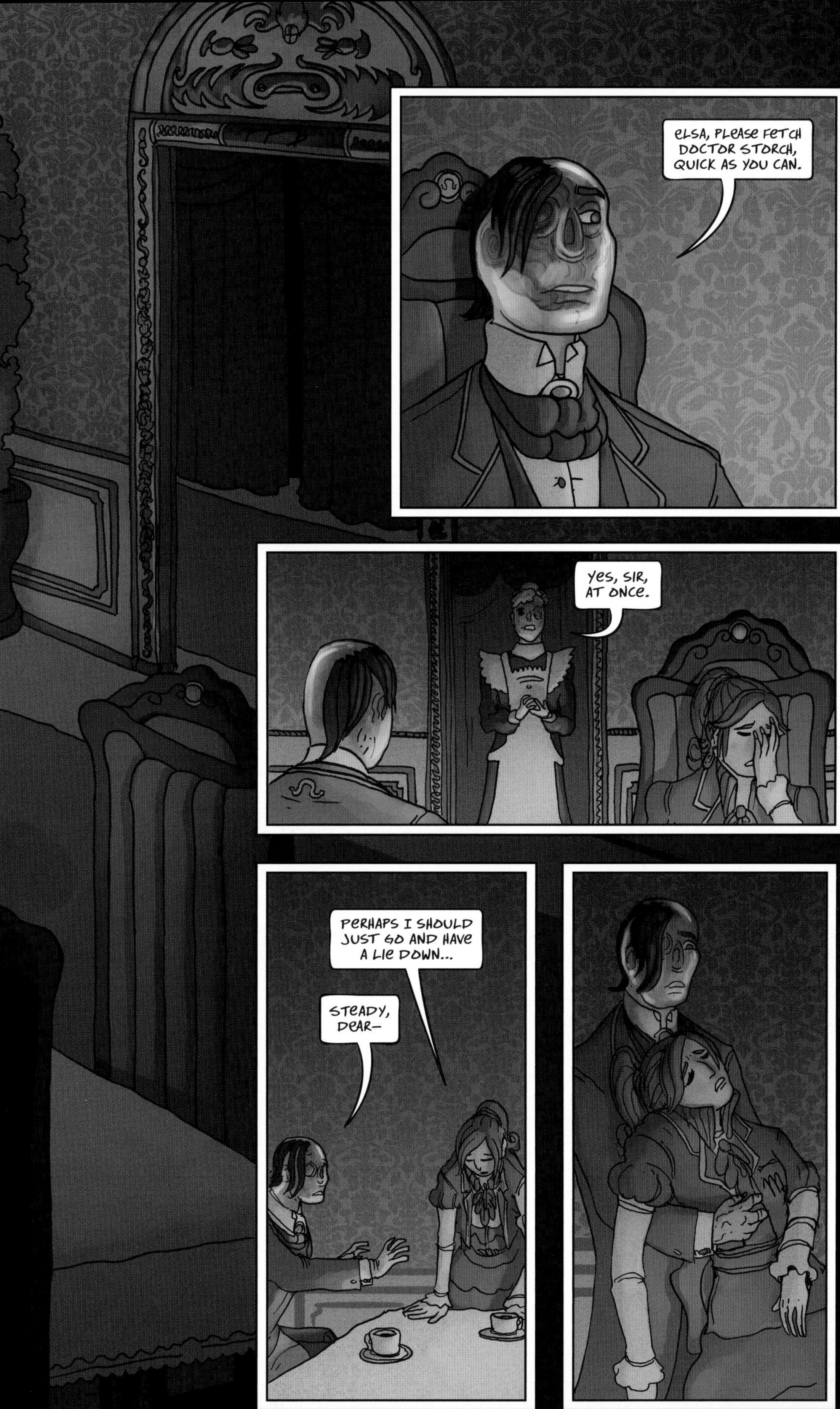
ELSA, PLEASE FETCH DOCTOR STORCH, QUICK AS YOU CAN.
YES, SIR, AT ONCE.
PERHAPS I SHOULD JUST GO AND HAVE A LIE DOWN...
STEADY, DEAR–

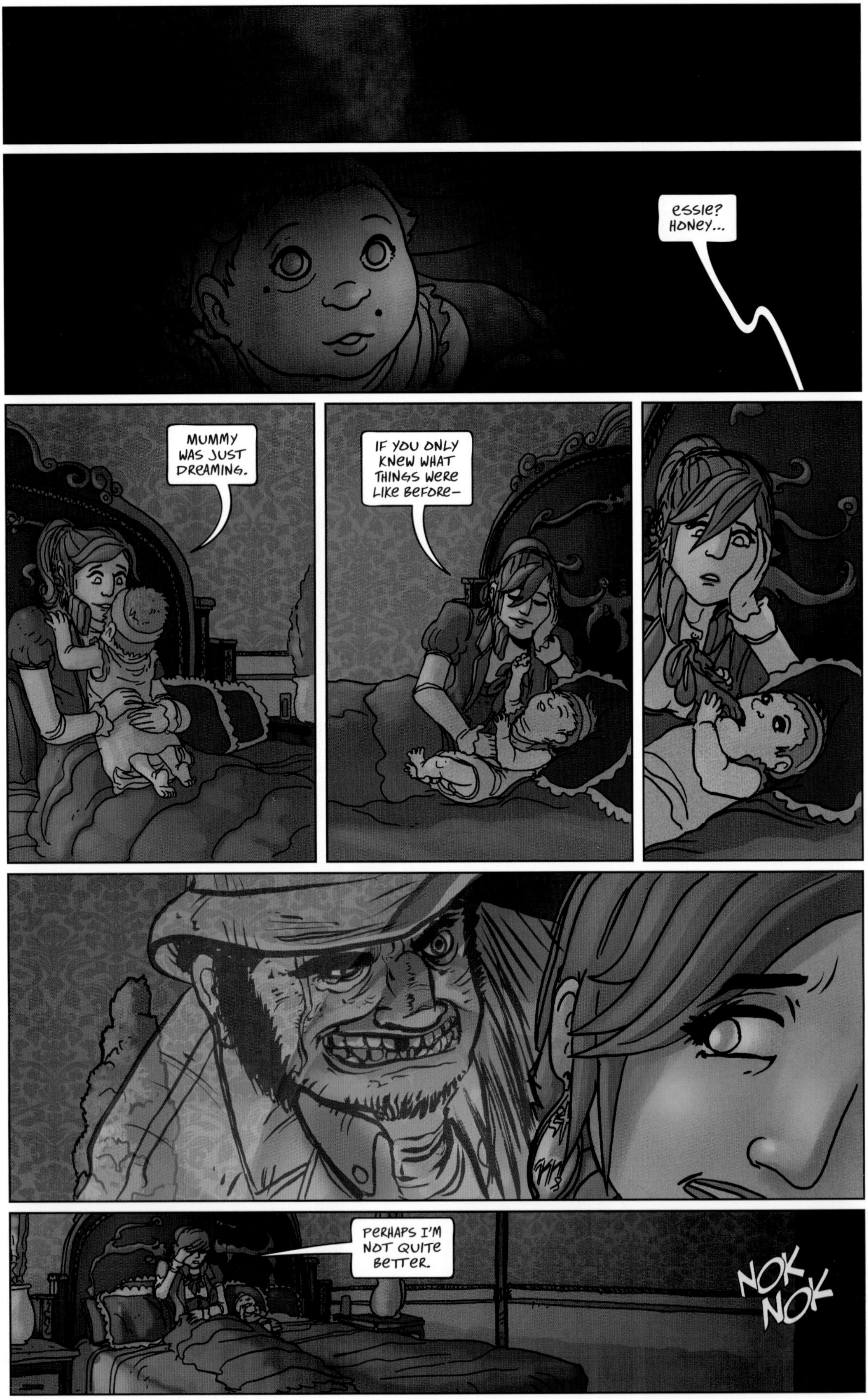
essie? HONEY...
MUMMY WAS JUST DREAMING.
IF YOU ONLY KNEW WHAT THINGS WERE LIKE BEFORE–
PERHAPS I'M NOT QUITE BETTER.
NOK NOK

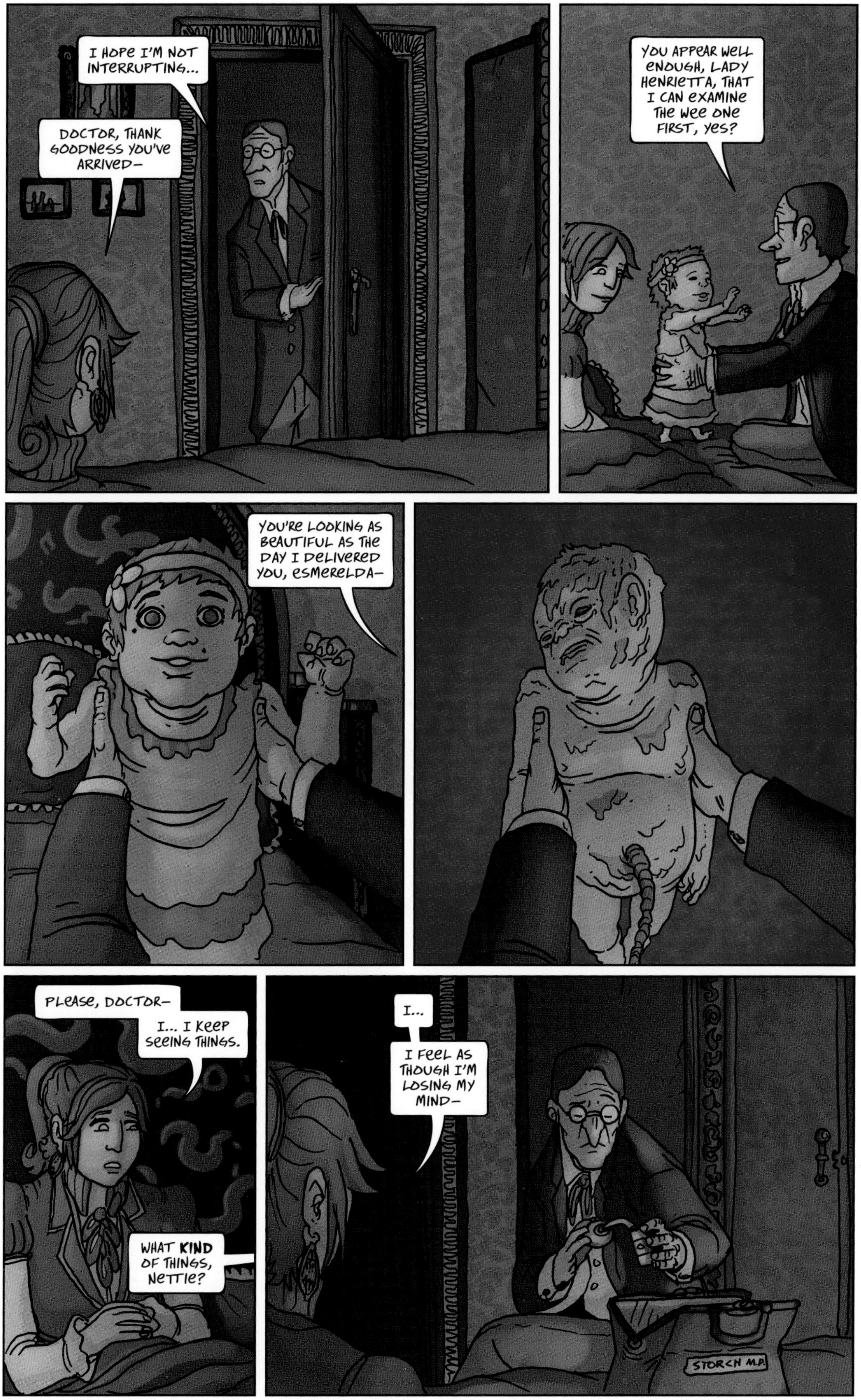
I HOPE I'M NOT INTERRUPTING...
DOCTOR, THANK GOODNESS YOU'VE ARRIVED—
YOU APPEAR WELL ENOUGH, LADY HENRIETTA, THAT I CAN EXAMINE THE WEE ONE FIRST, YES?
YOU'RE LOOKING AS BEAUTIFUL AS THE DAY I DELIVERED YOU, ESMERELDA—
PLEASE, DOCTOR—
I... I KEEP SEEING THINGS.
WHAT **KIND** OF THINGS, NETTIE?
I...
I FEEL AS THOUGH I'M LOSING MY MIND—
STORCH M.P.

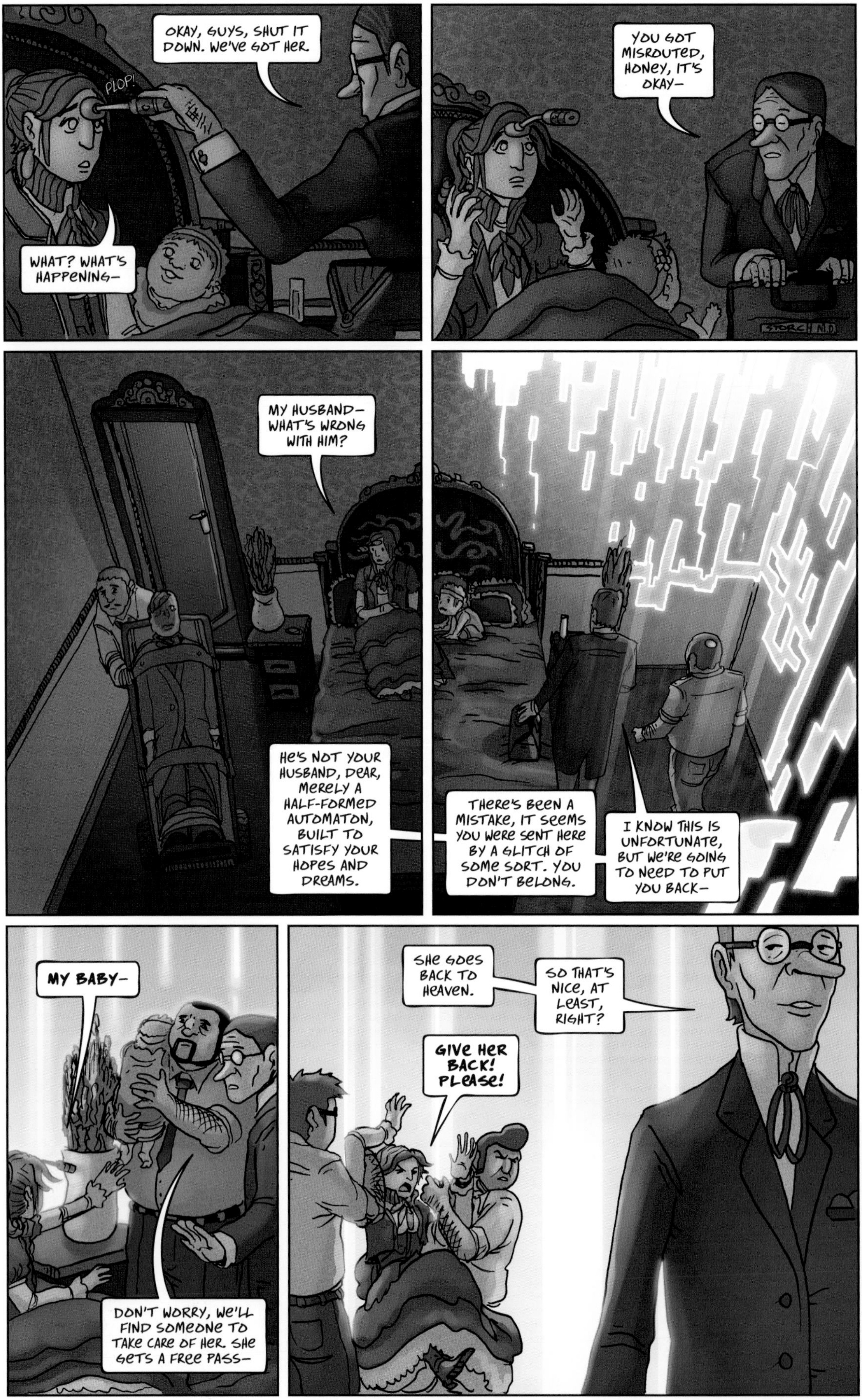
OKAY, GUYS, SHUT IT DOWN. WE'VE GOT HER.
PLOP!
WHAT? WHAT'S HAPPENING—
YOU GOT MISROUTED, HONEY, IT'S OKAY—
STORCH M.D.
MY HUSBAND— WHAT'S WRONG WITH HIM?
HE'S NOT YOUR HUSBAND, DEAR, MERELY A HALF-FORMED AUTOMATON, BUILT TO SATISFY YOUR HOPES AND DREAMS.
THERE'S BEEN A MISTAKE, IT SEEMS YOU WERE SENT HERE BY A GLITCH OF SOME SORT. YOU DON'T BELONG.
I KNOW THIS IS UNFORTUNATE, BUT WE'RE GOING TO NEED TO PUT YOU BACK—
MY BABY—
DON'T WORRY, WE'LL FIND SOMEONE TO TAKE CARE OF HER. SHE GETS A FREE PASS—
SHE GOES BACK TO HEAVEN.
SO THAT'S NICE, AT LEAST, RIGHT?
GIVE HER BACK! PLEASE!

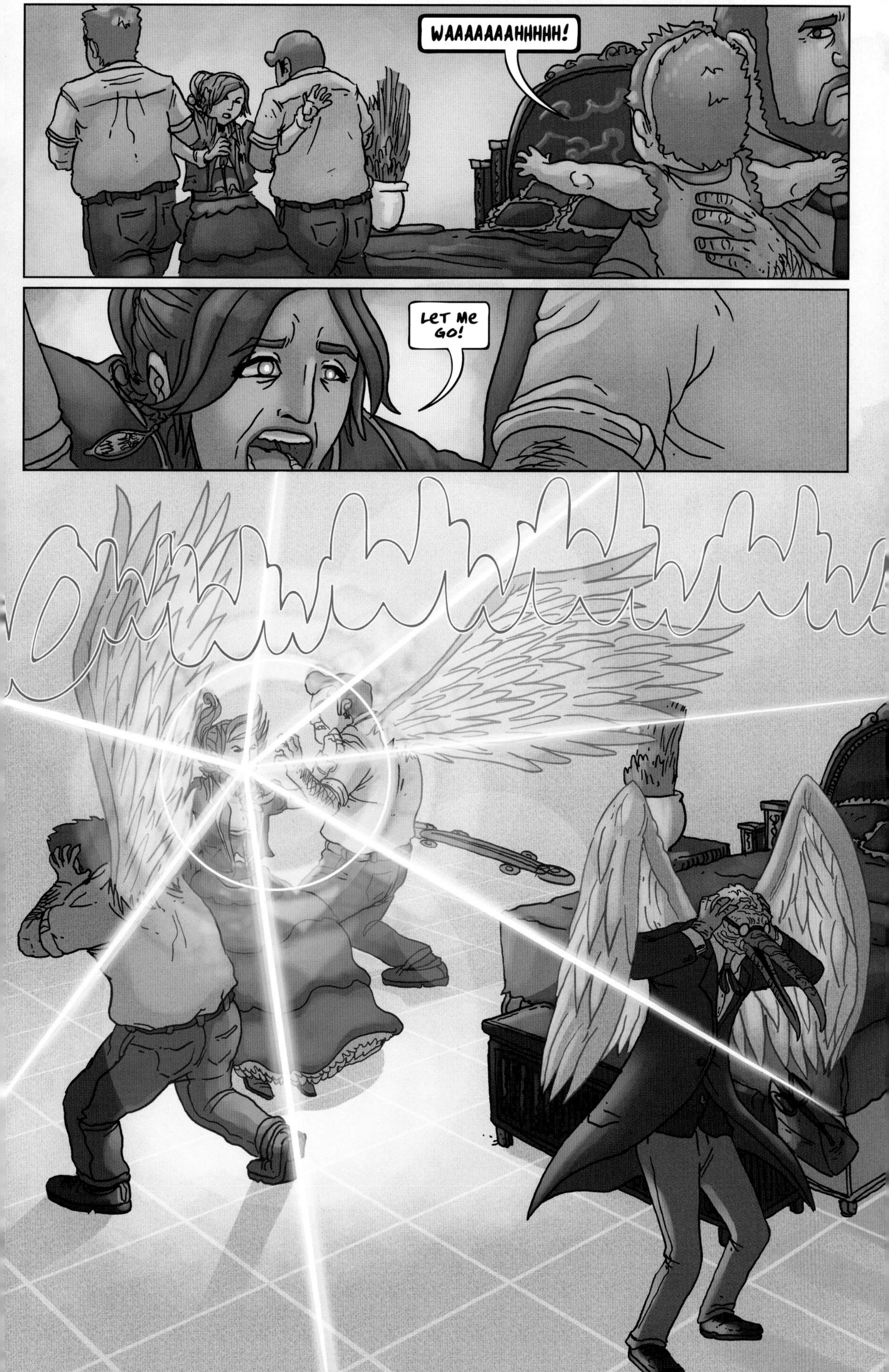
WAAAAAAAAHHHHH!
LET ME GO!

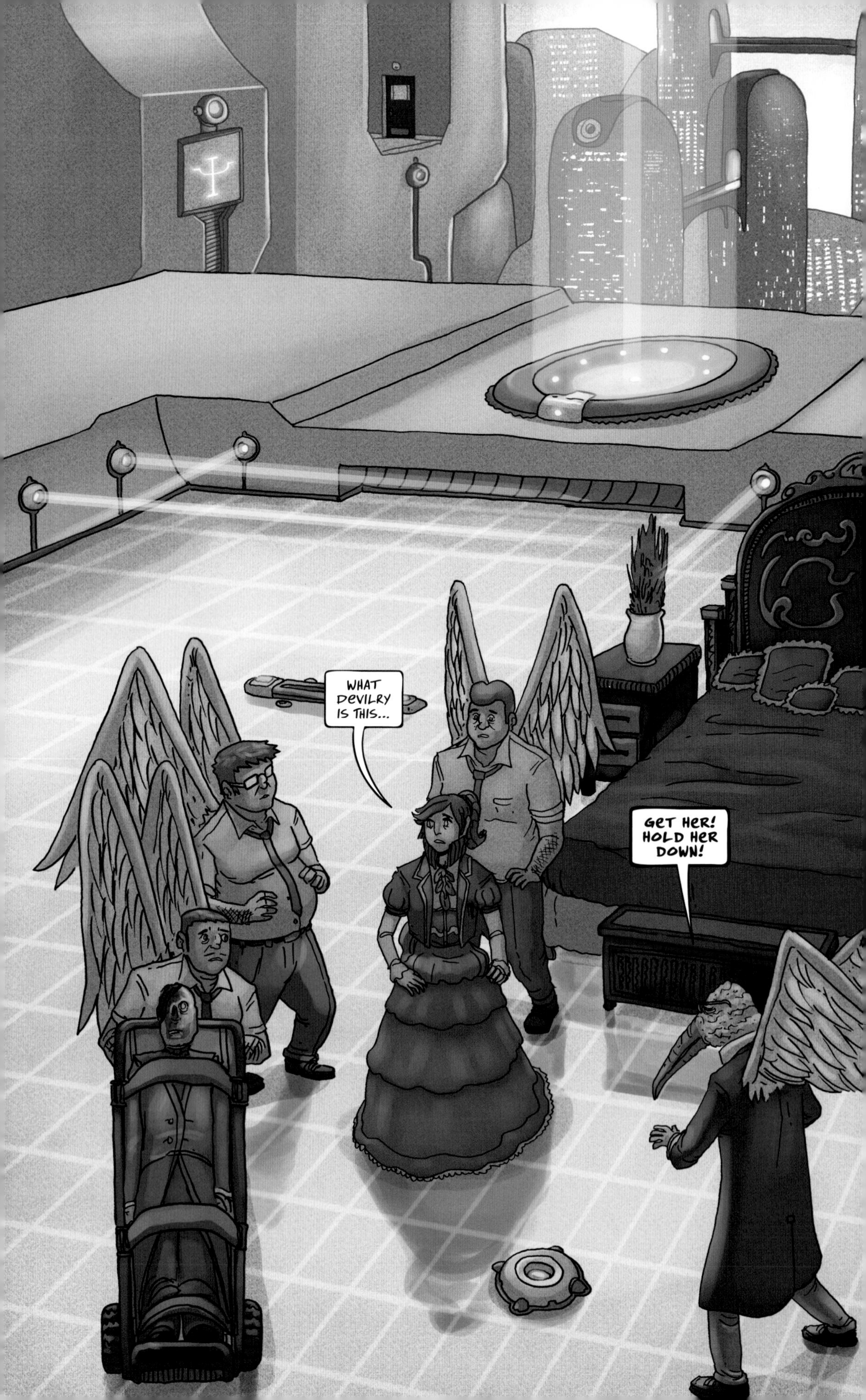
WHAT DEVILRY IS THIS...
GET HER! HOLD HER DOWN!

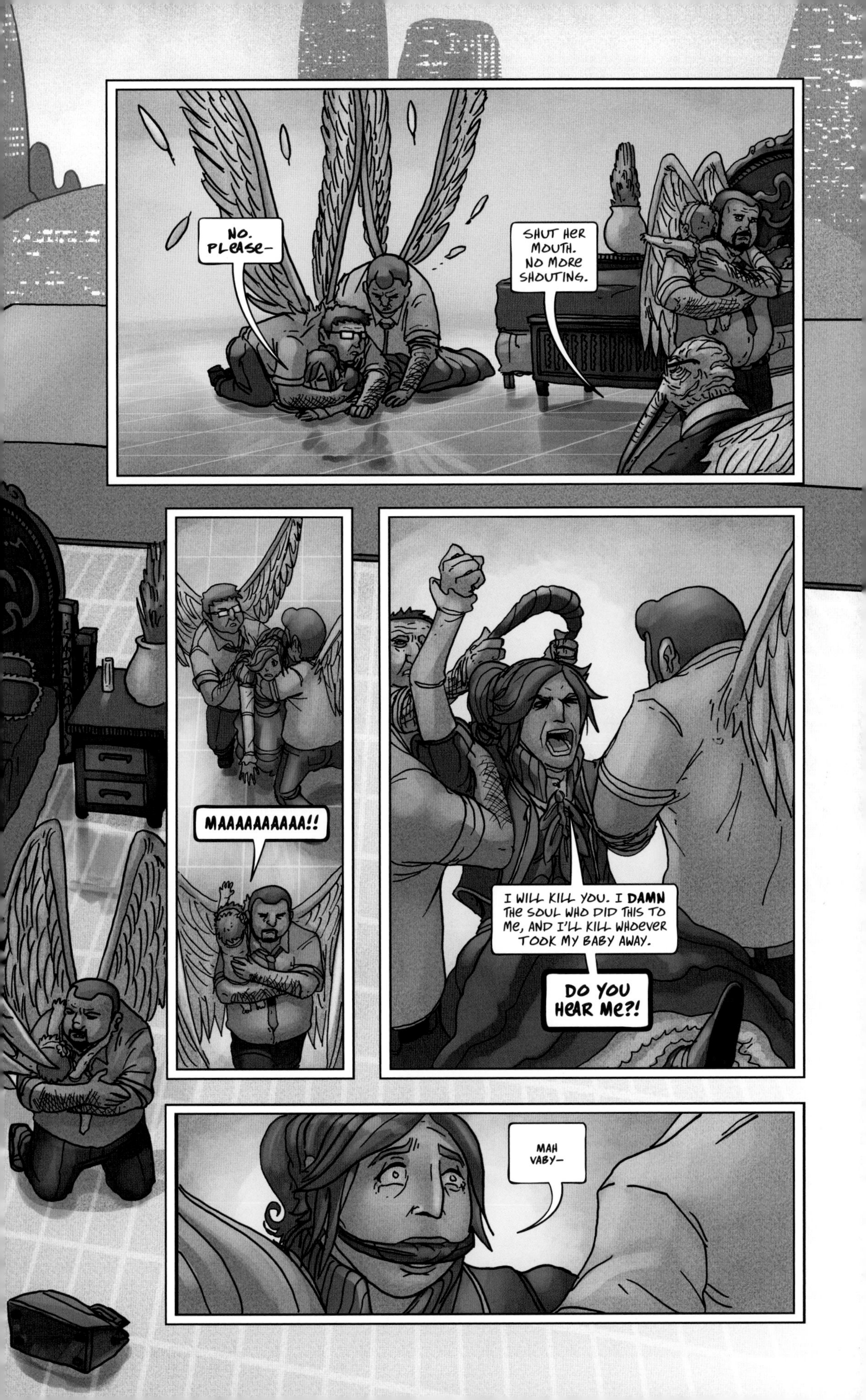
NO. PLEASE-
SHUT HER MOUTH. NO MORE SHOUTING.
MAAAAAAAAAA!!
I WILL KILL YOU. I DAMN THE SOUL WHO DID THIS TO ME, AND I'LL KILL WHOEVER TOOK MY BABY AWAY.
DO YOU HEAR ME?!
MAH VABY—

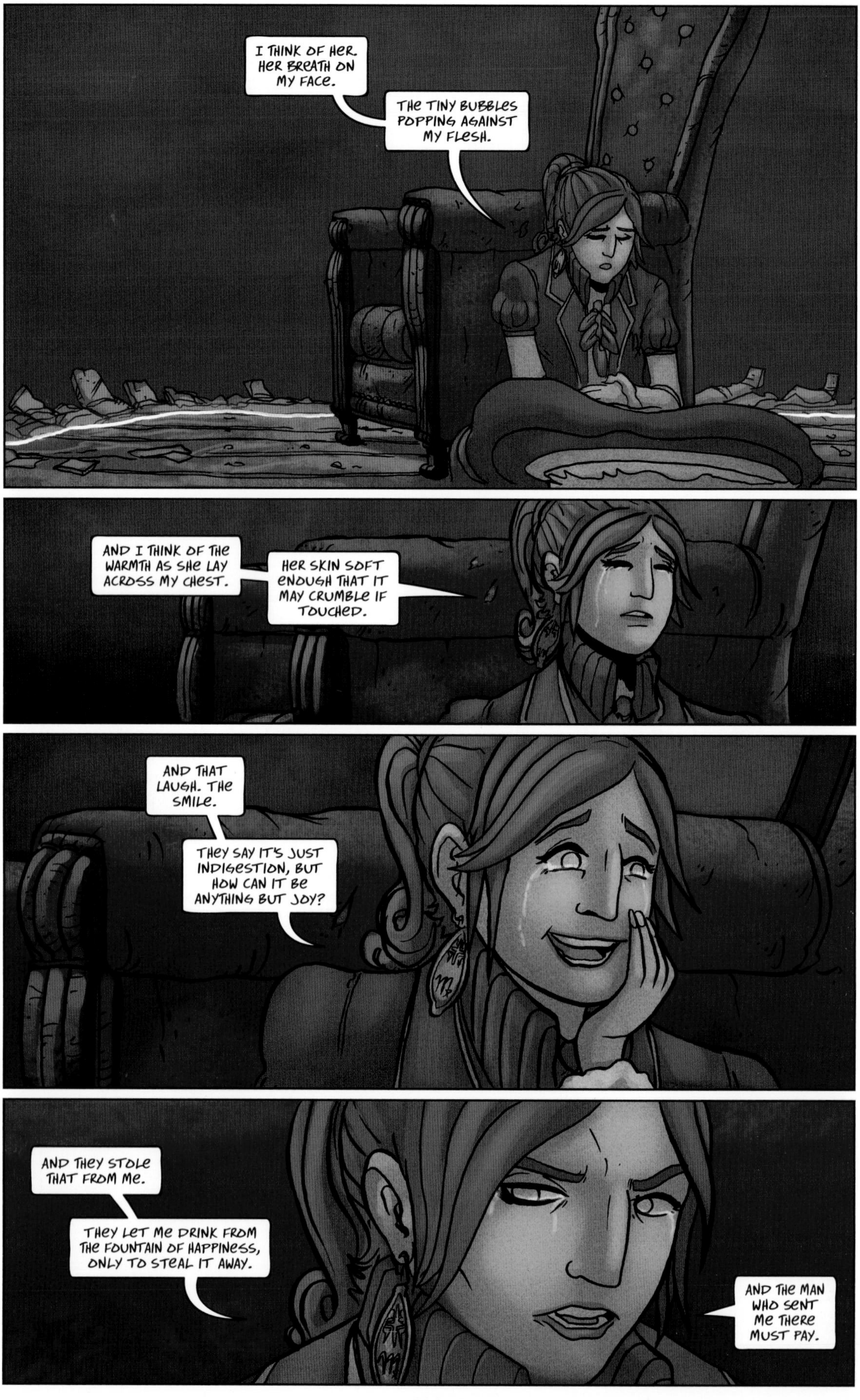
I THINK OF HER. HER BREATH ON MY FACE.
THE TINY BUBBLES POPPING AGAINST MY FLESH.
AND I THINK OF THE WARMTH AS SHE LAY ACROSS MY CHEST.
HER SKIN SOFT ENOUGH THAT IT MAY CRUMBLE IF TOUCHED.
AND THAT LAUGH. THE SMILE.
THEY SAY IT'S JUST INDIGESTION, BUT HOW CAN IT BE ANYTHING BUT JOY?
AND THEY STOLE THAT FROM ME.
THEY LET ME DRINK FROM THE FOUNTAIN OF HAPPINESS, ONLY TO STEAL IT AWAY.
AND THE MAN WHO SENT ME THERE MUST PAY.

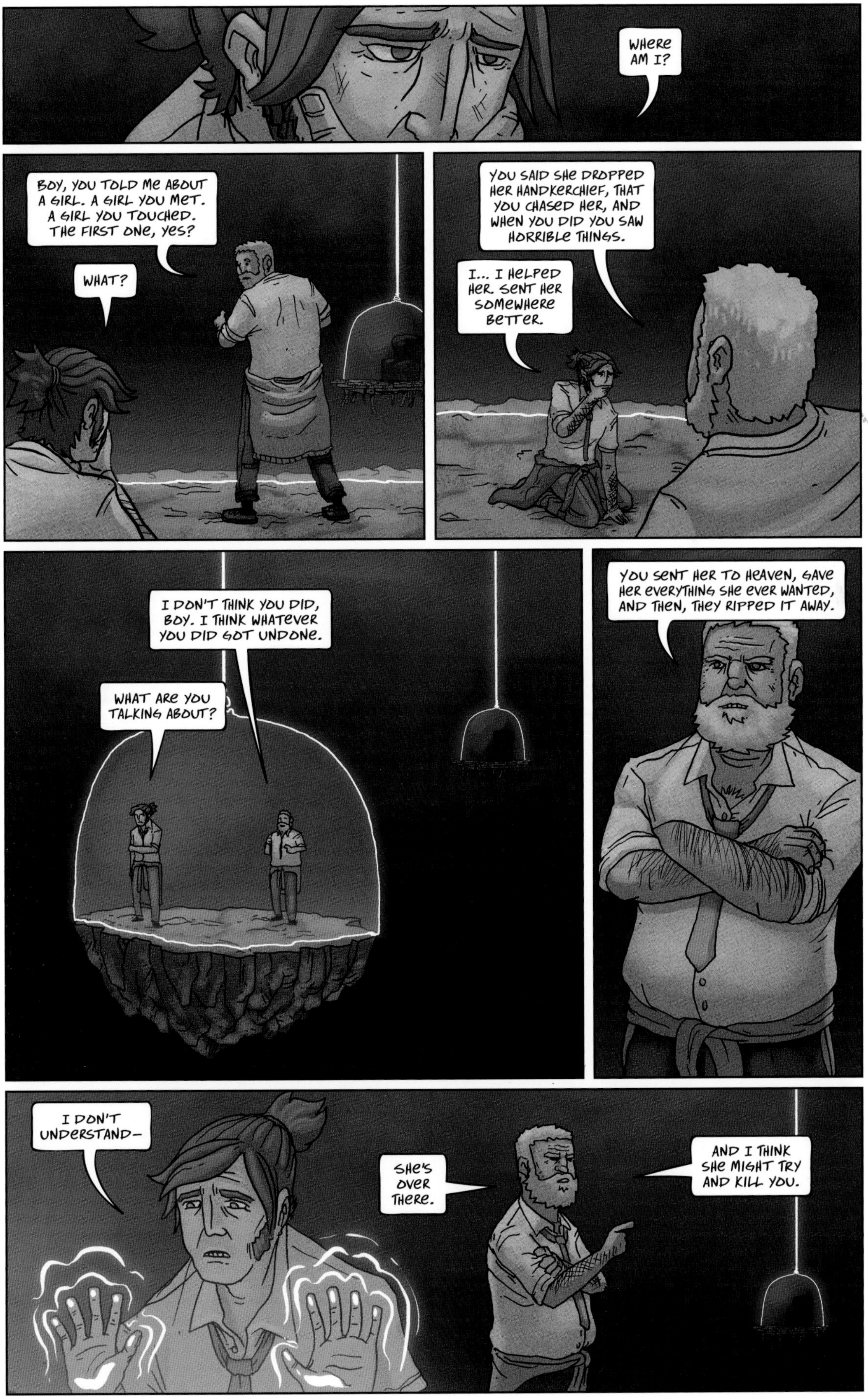
WHERE AM I?
BOY, YOU TOLD ME ABOUT A GIRL. A GIRL YOU MET. A GIRL YOU TOUCHED. THE FIRST ONE, YES?
WHAT?
YOU SAID SHE DROPPED HER HANDKERCHIEF, THAT YOU CHASED HER, AND WHEN YOU DID YOU SAW HORRIBLE THINGS.
I... I HELPED HER. SENT HER SOMEWHERE BETTER.
I DON'T THINK YOU DID, BOY. I THINK WHATEVER YOU DID GOT UNDONE.
WHAT ARE YOU TALKING ABOUT?
YOU SENT HER TO HEAVEN, GAVE HER EVERYTHING SHE EVER WANTED, AND THEN, THEY RIPPED IT AWAY.
I DON'T UNDERSTAND—
SHE'S OVER THERE.
AND I THINK SHE MIGHT TRY AND KILL YOU.

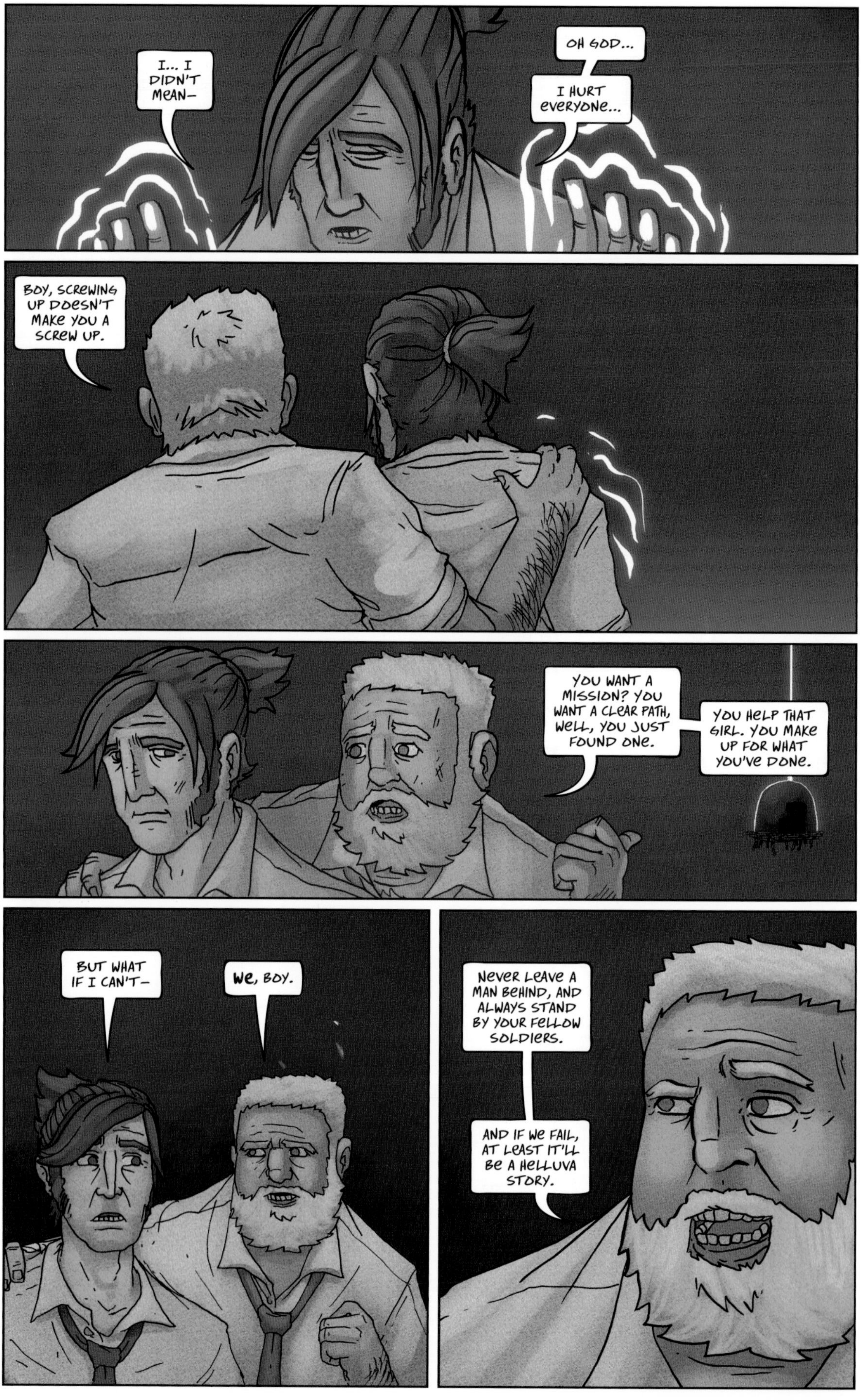
I... I DIDN'T MEAN—
OH GOD...
I HURT EVERYONE...
BOY, SCREWING UP DOESN'T MAKE YOU A SCREW UP.
YOU WANT A MISSION? YOU WANT A CLEAR PATH, WELL, YOU JUST FOUND ONE.
YOU HELP THAT GIRL. YOU MAKE UP FOR WHAT YOU'VE DONE.
BUT WHAT IF I CAN'T—
WE, BOY.
NEVER LEAVE A MAN BEHIND, AND ALWAYS STAND BY YOUR FELLOW SOLDIERS.
AND IF WE FAIL, AT LEAST IT'LL BE A HELLUVA STORY.

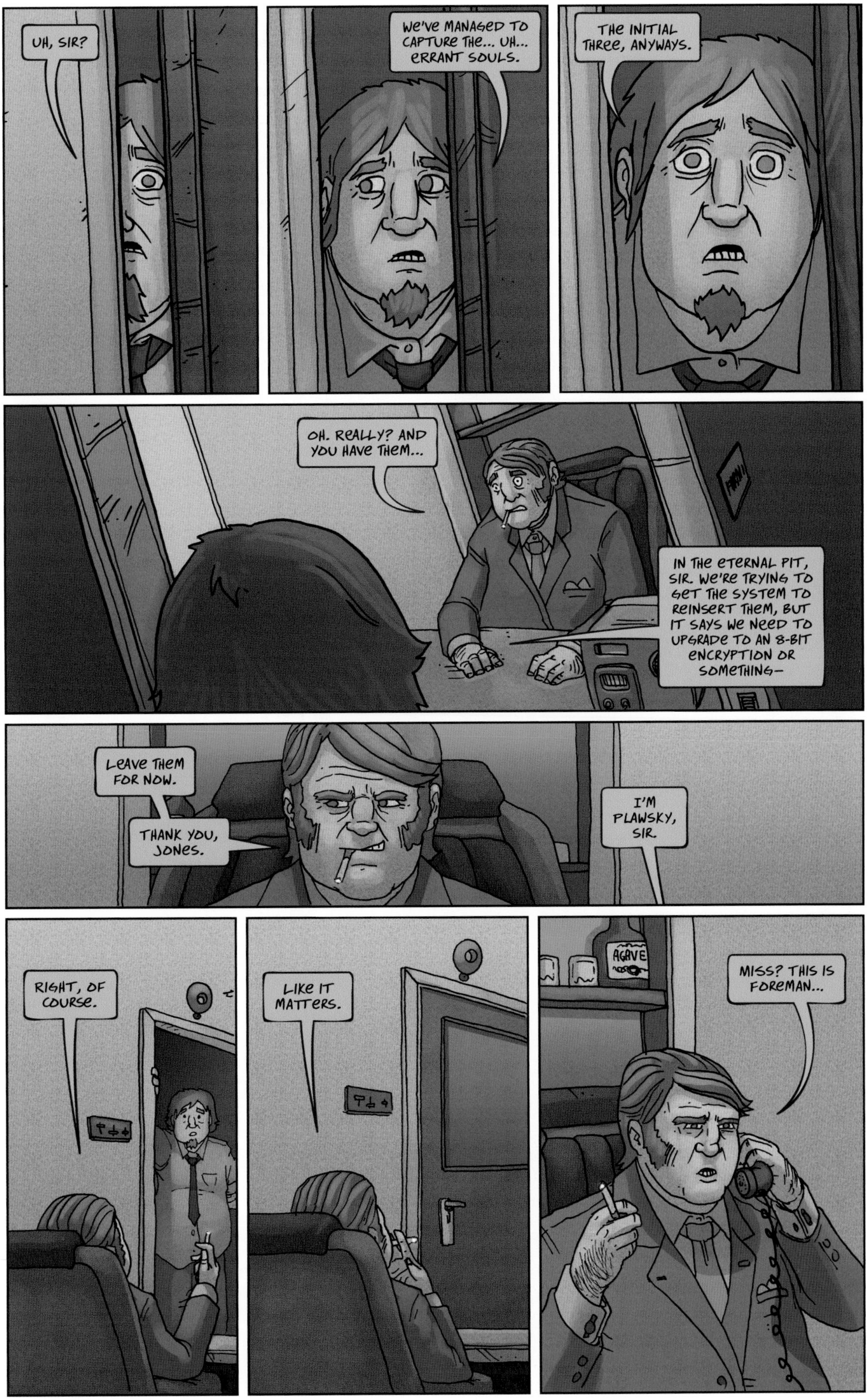
UH, SIR?
WE'VE MANAGED TO CAPTURE THE... UH... ERRANT SOULS.
THE INITIAL THREE, ANYWAYS.
OH. REALLY? AND YOU HAVE THEM...
IN THE ETERNAL PIT, SIR. WE'RE TRYING TO GET THE SYSTEM TO REINSERT THEM, BUT IT SAYS WE NEED TO UPGRADE TO AN 8-BIT ENCRYPTION OR SOMETHING—
LEAVE THEM FOR NOW.
THANK YOU, JONES.
I'M PLAWSKY, SIR.
RIGHT, OF COURSE.
LIKE IT MATTERS.
AGAVE
MISS? THIS IS FOREMAN...

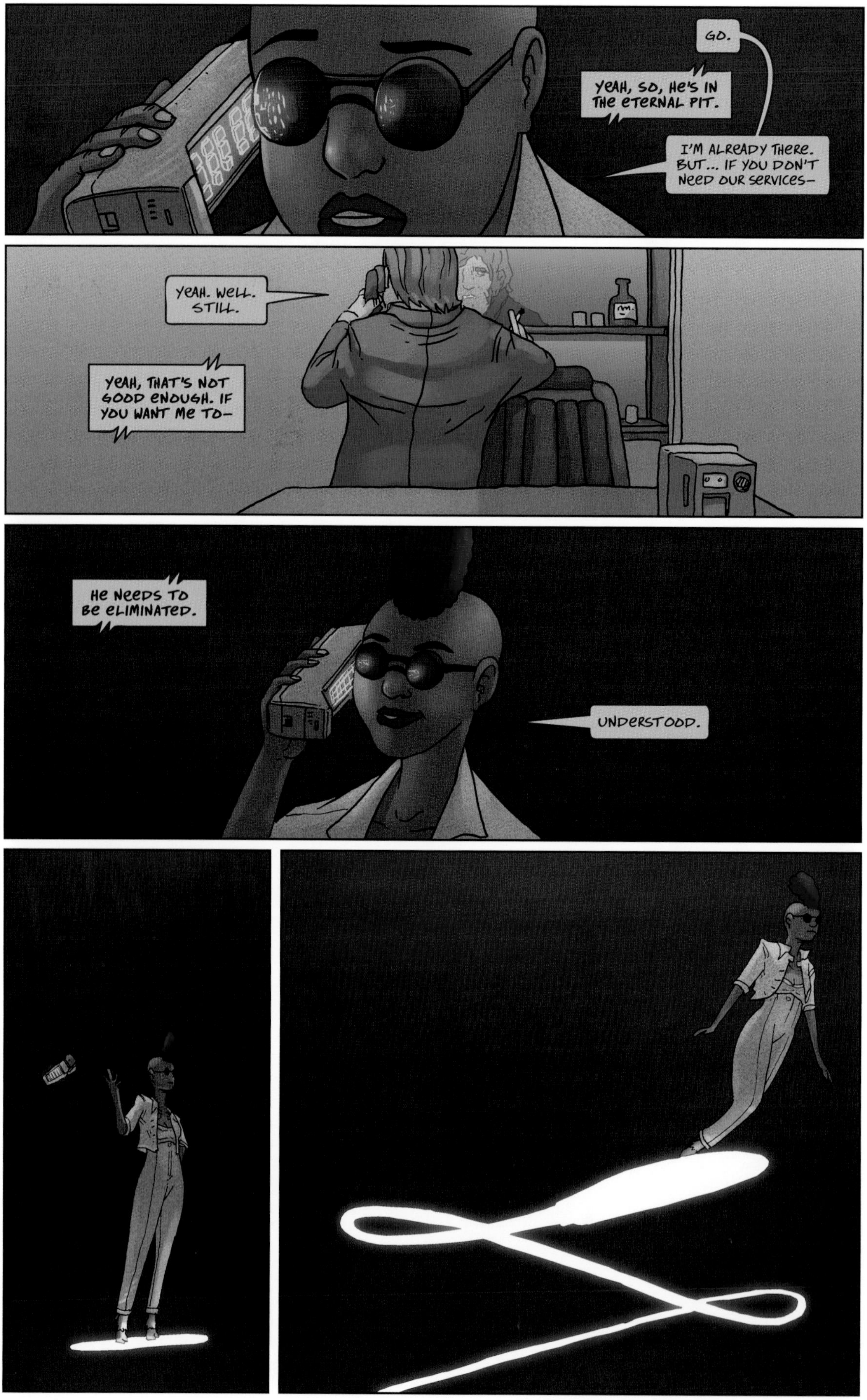
GO.
YEAH, SO, HE'S IN THE ETERNAL PIT.
I'M ALREADY THERE. BUT... IF YOU DON'T NEED OUR SERVICES—
YEAH. WELL. STILL.
YEAH, THAT'S NOT GOOD ENOUGH. IF YOU WANT ME TO—
HE NEEDS TO BE ELIMINATED.
UNDERSTOOD.

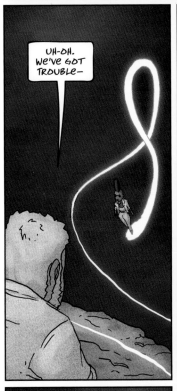

UH-OH. WE'VE GOT TROUBLE—

YOU'RE HIM, HUH?

THAT'S RIGHT. ERNEST HEMING—

NOT YOU, BEARD-O.

HIM.

I DON'T KNOW **WHO** EXACTLY YOU ARE, MISTER, BUT I'VE NEVER SEEN BOTH SIDES SO KEEN TO KILL A SOUL BEFORE.

SO WHAT DO YOU SAY YOU JUST COME WITH ME, AND I'LL EAT YOU UP REAL QUICK.

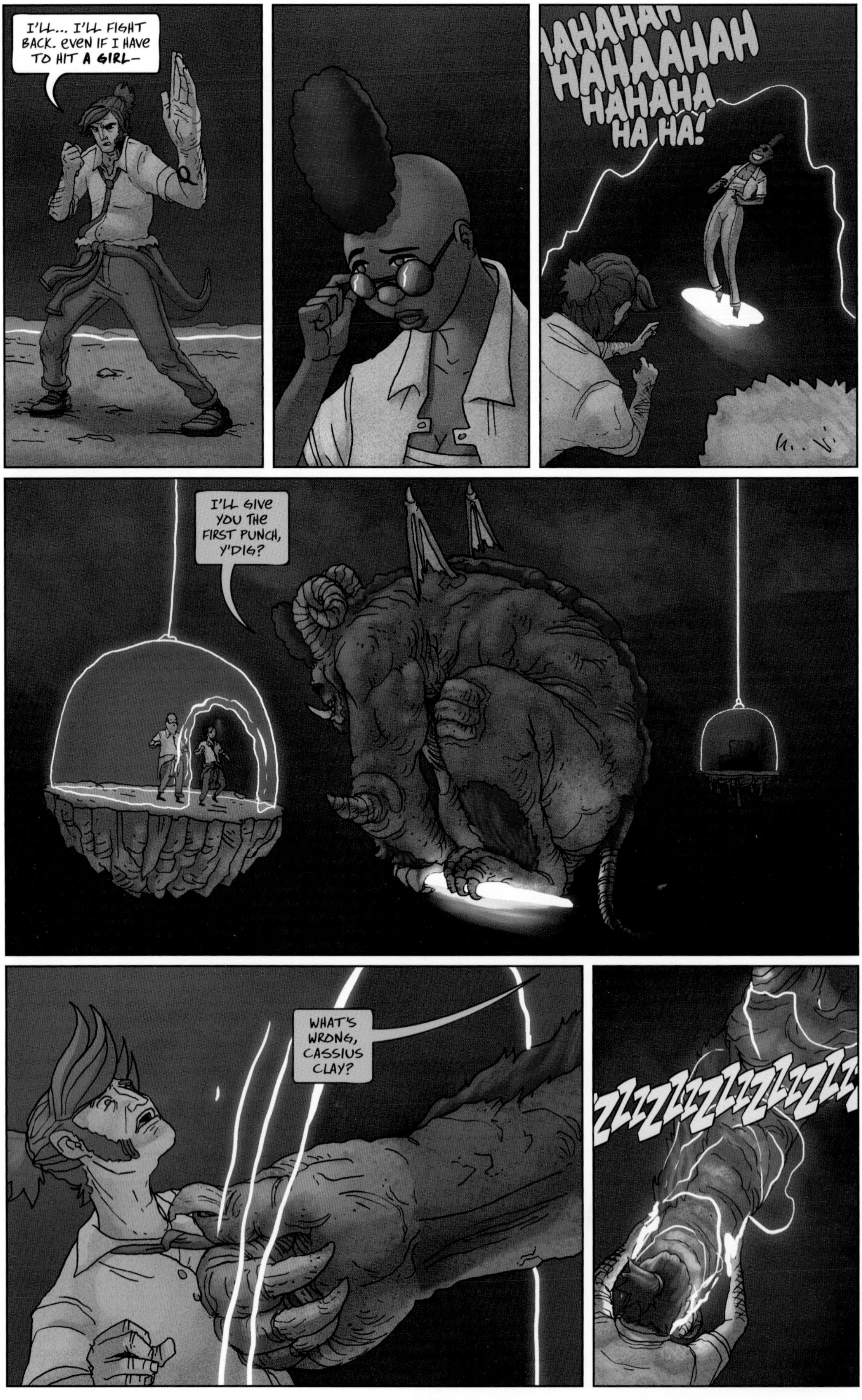
I'LL... I'LL FIGHT BACK. EVEN IF I HAVE TO HIT A GIRL—
HAHAHAH HAHAAAHAH HAHAHA HA HA!
I'LL GIVE YOU THE FIRST PUNCH, Y'DIG?
WHAT'S WRONG, CASSIUS CLAY?
ZZZZZZZZZZZZZZZZ

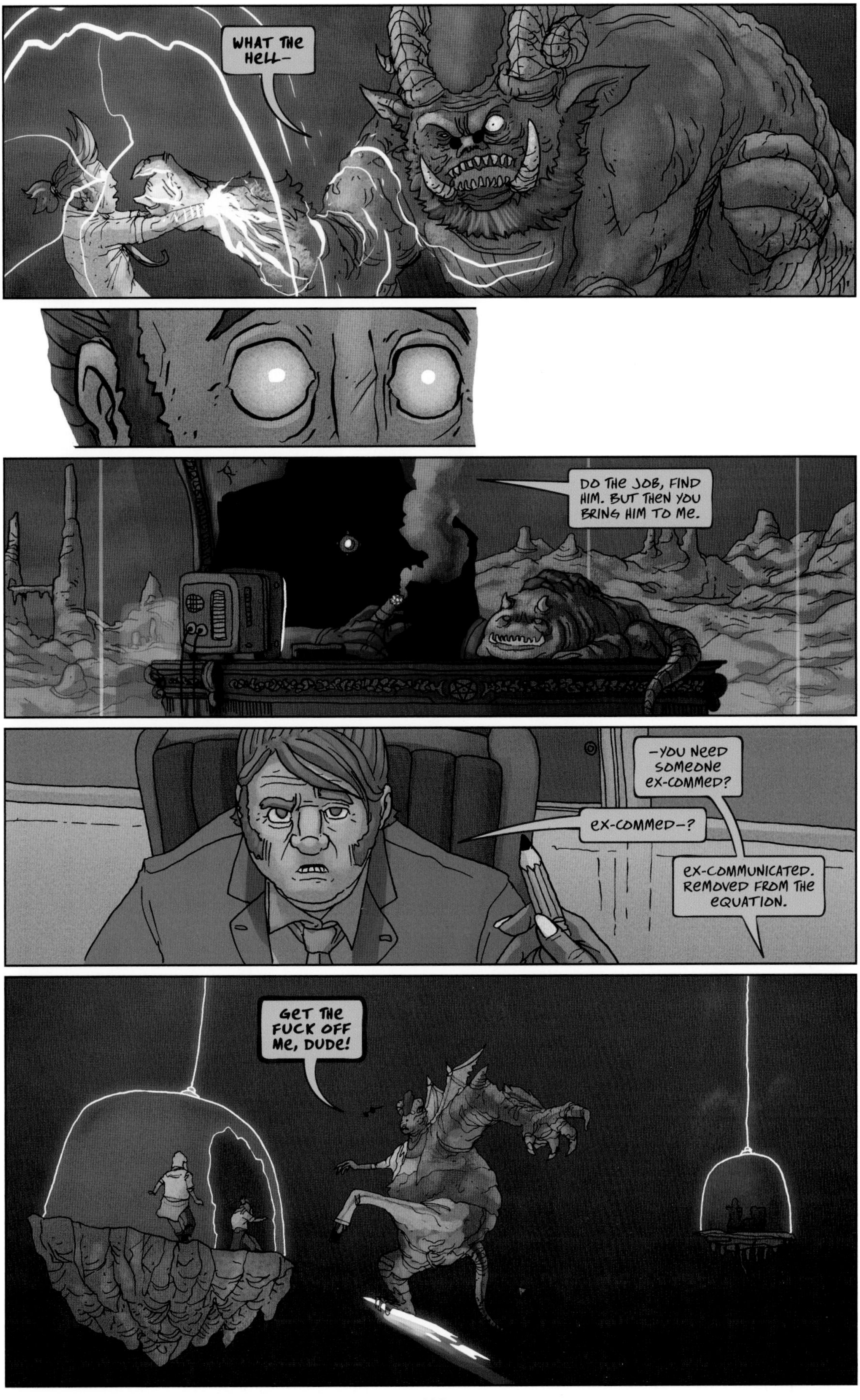
WHAT THE HELL-
DO THE JOB, FIND HIM. BUT THEN YOU BRING HIM TO ME.
-YOU NEED SOMEONE EX-COMMED?
EX-COMMED-?
EX-COMMUNICATED. REMOVED FROM THE EQUATION.
GET THE FUCK OFF ME, DUDE!

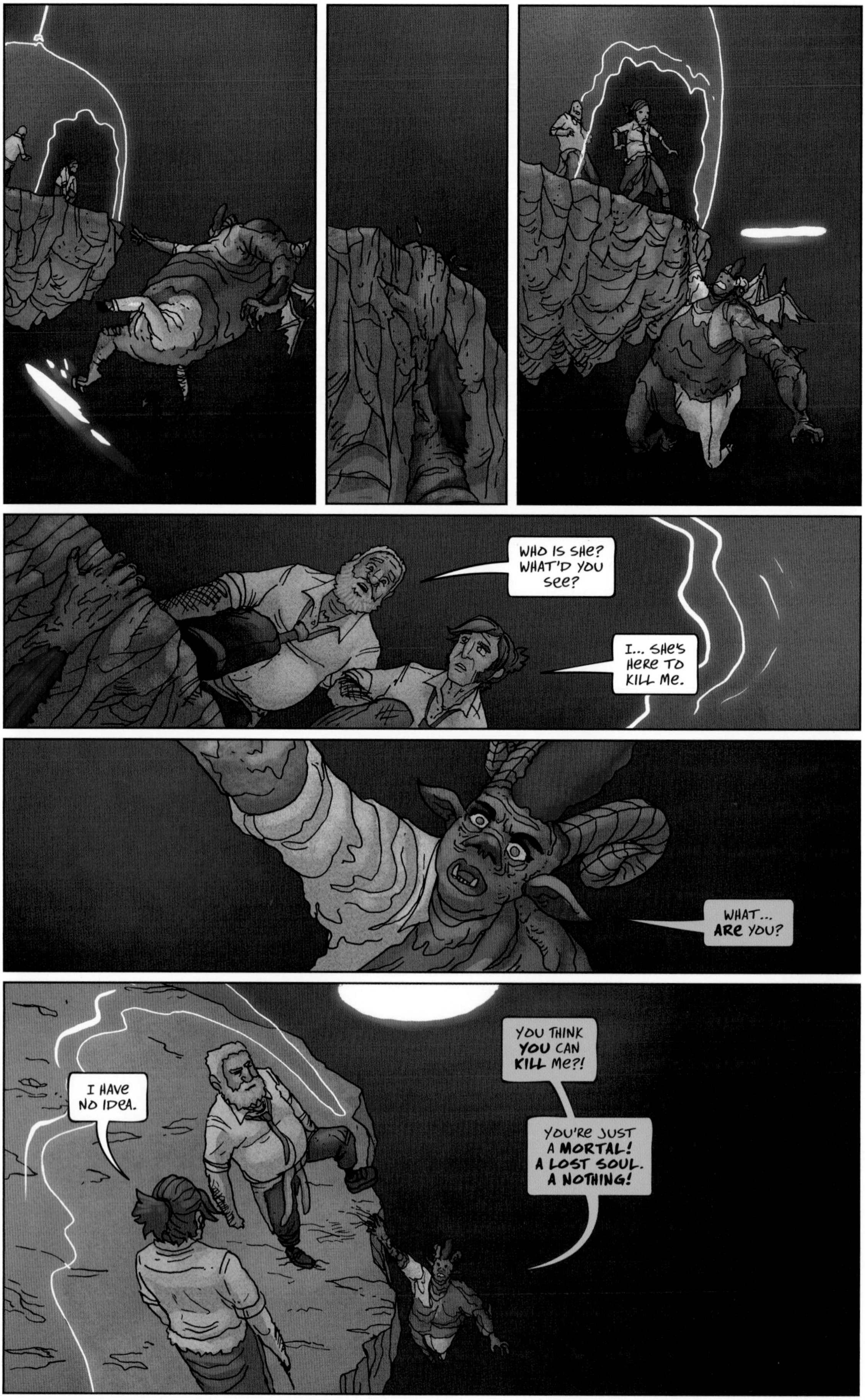
WHO IS SHE? WHAT'D YOU SEE?
I... SHE'S HERE TO KILL ME.
WHAT... ARE YOU?
I HAVE NO IDEA.
YOU THINK YOU CAN KILL ME?!
YOU'RE JUST A MORTAL! A LOST SOUL. A NOTHING!

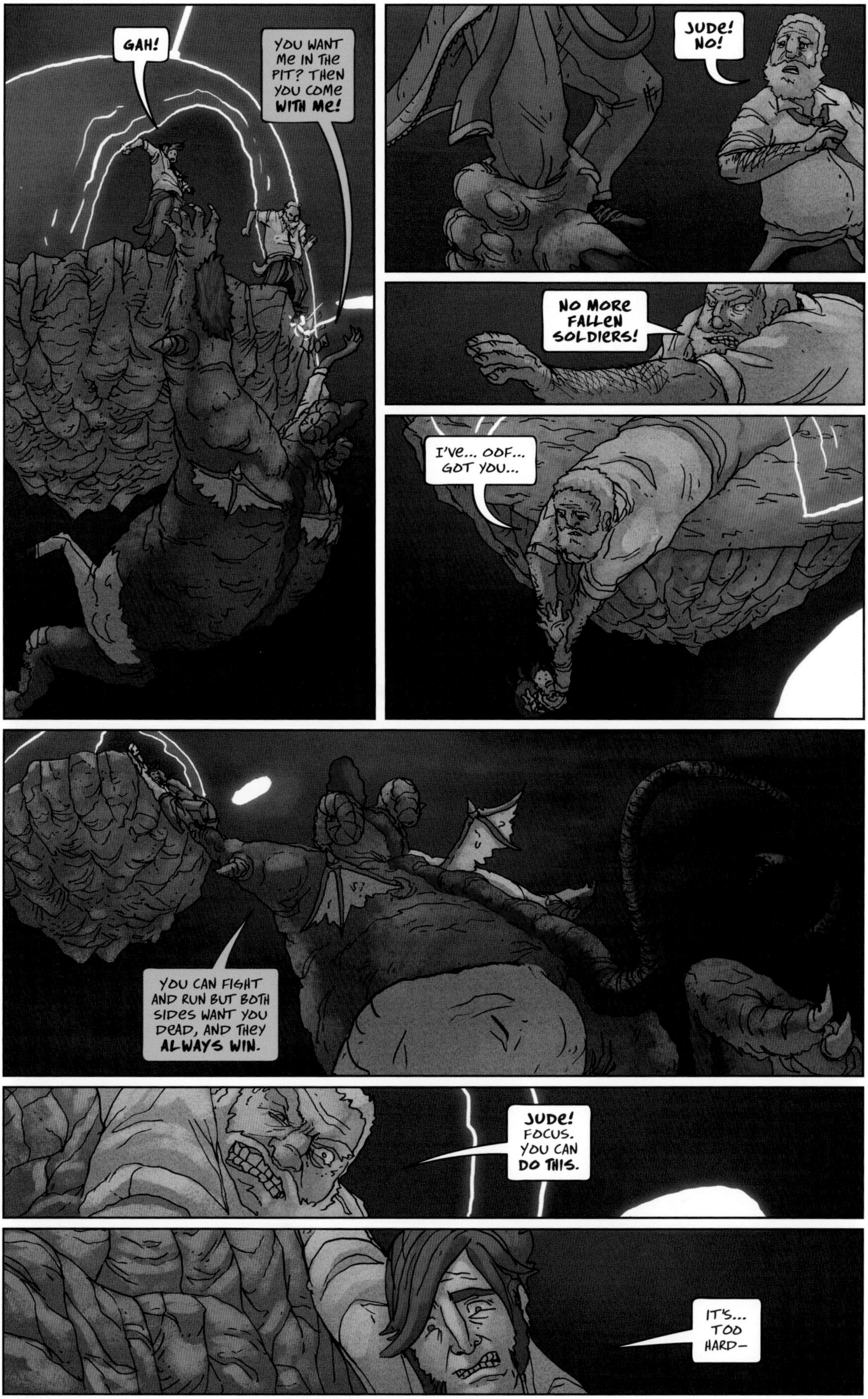
GAH!
YOU WANT ME IN THE PIT? THEN YOU COME WITH ME!
JUDE! NO!
NO MORE FALLEN SOLDIERS!
I'VE... OOF... GOT YOU...
YOU CAN FIGHT AND RUN BUT BOTH SIDES WANT YOU DEAD, AND THEY ALWAYS WIN.
JUDE! FOCUS. YOU CAN DO THIS.
IT'S... TOO HARD–

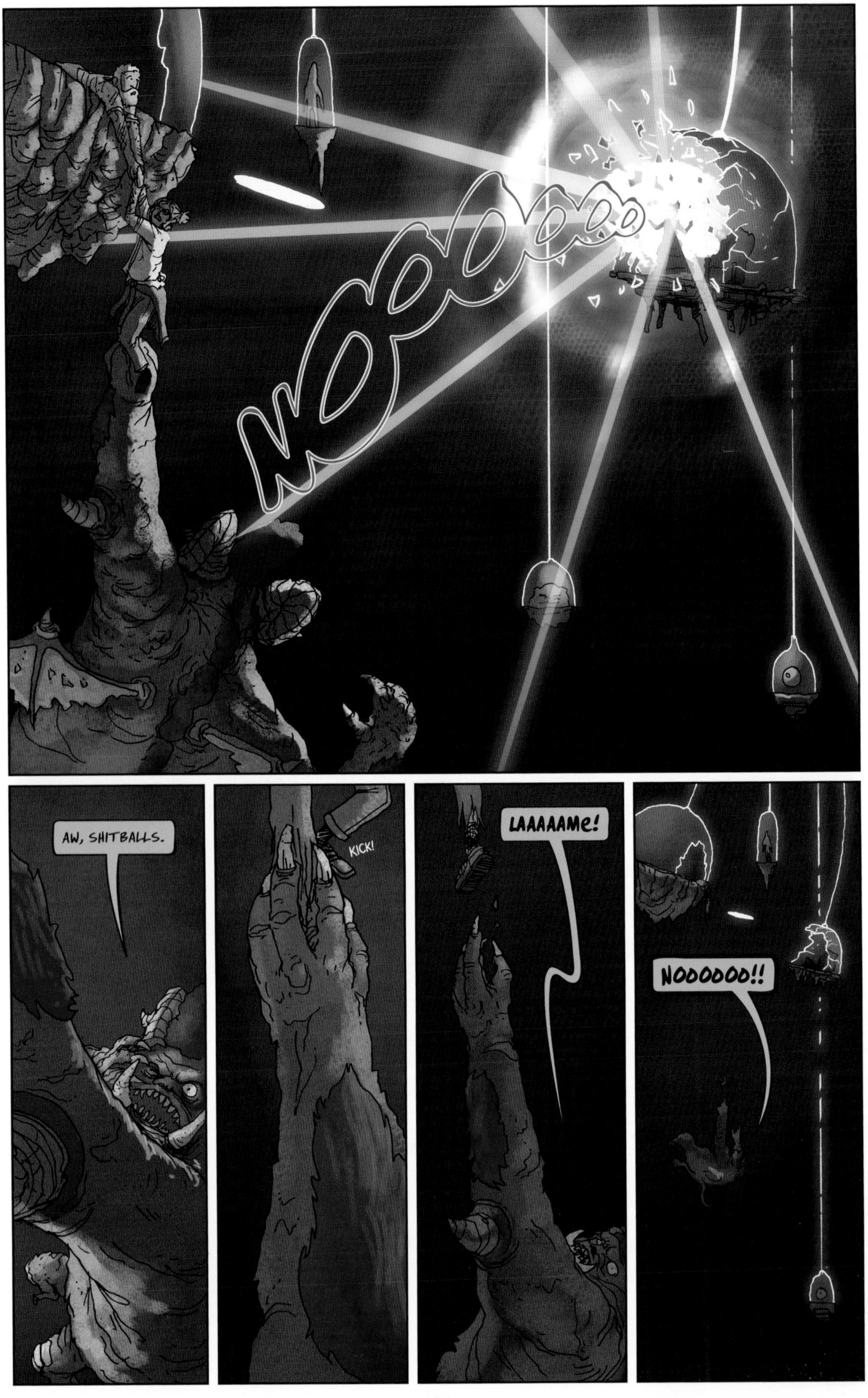
NOOOOOOO
AW, SHITBALLS.
KICK!
LAAAAAME!
NOOOOOO!!

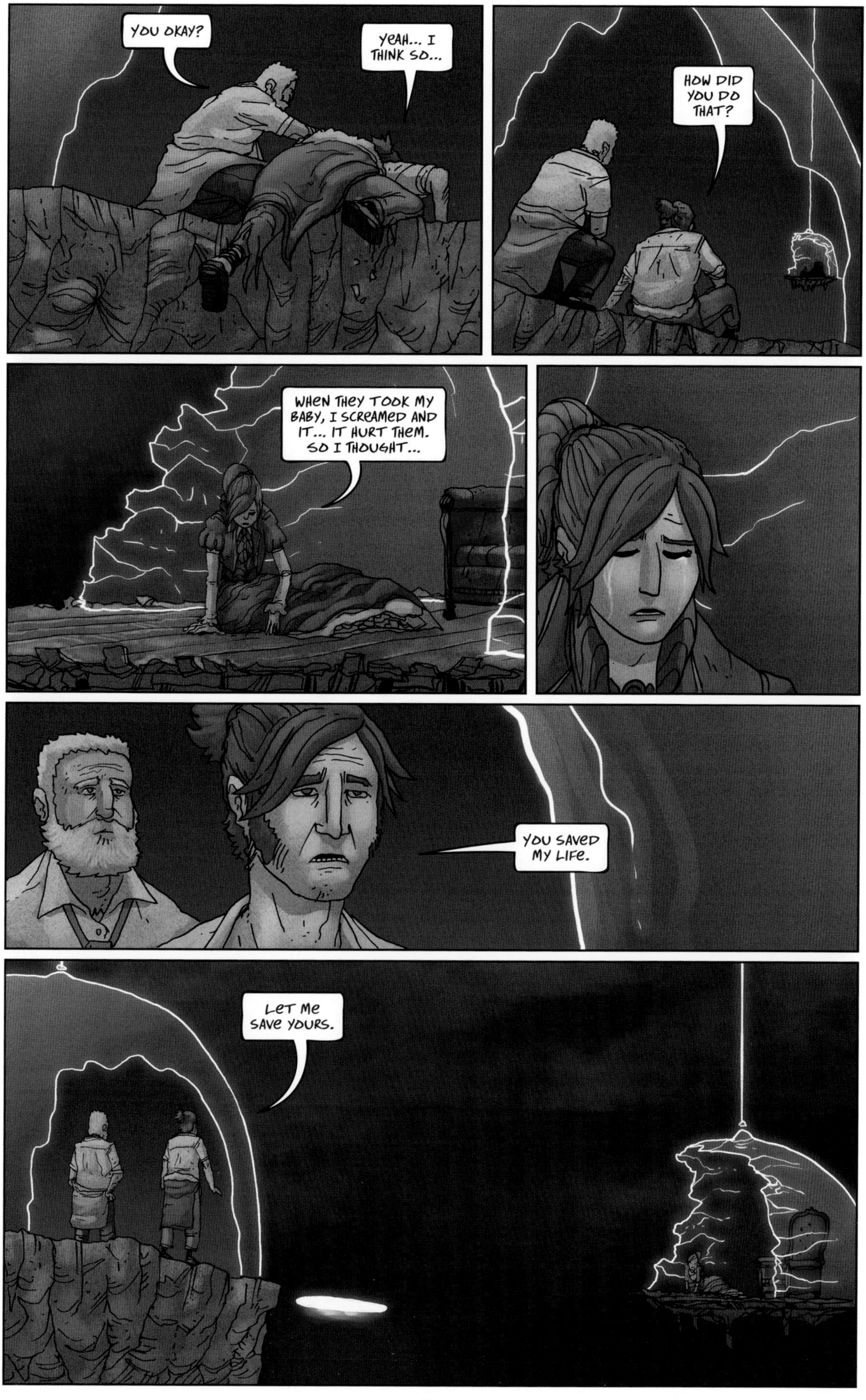
YOU OKAY?
YEAH... I THINK SO...
HOW DID YOU DO THAT?
WHEN THEY TOOK MY BABY, I SCREAMED AND IT... IT HURT THEM. SO I THOUGHT...
YOU SAVED MY LIFE.
LET ME SAVE YOURS.

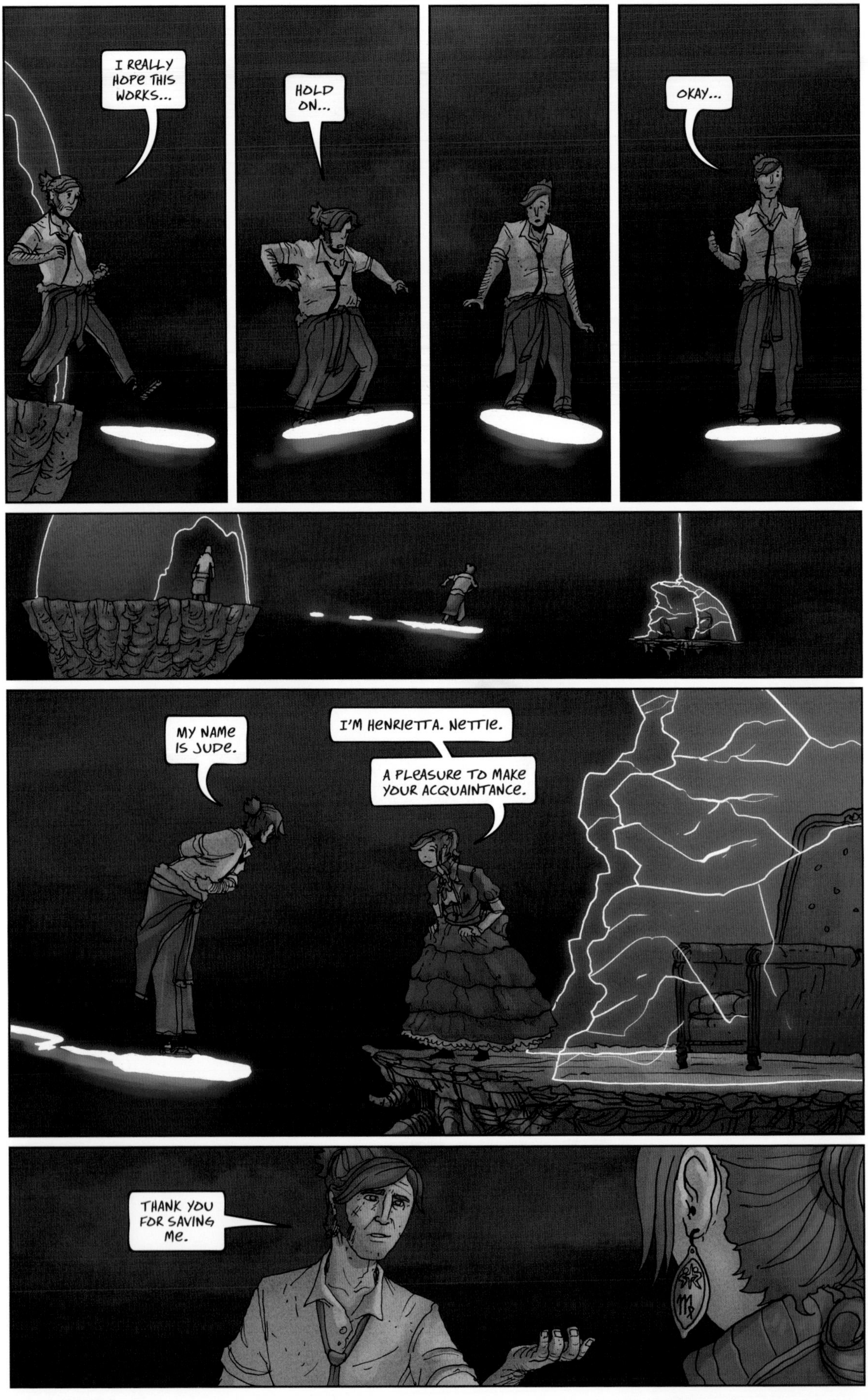
I REALLY HOPE THIS WORKS...
HOLD ON...
OKAY...
MY NAME IS JUDE.
I'M HENRIETTA. NETTIE.
A PLEASURE TO MAKE YOUR ACQUAINTANCE.
THANK YOU FOR SAVING ME.

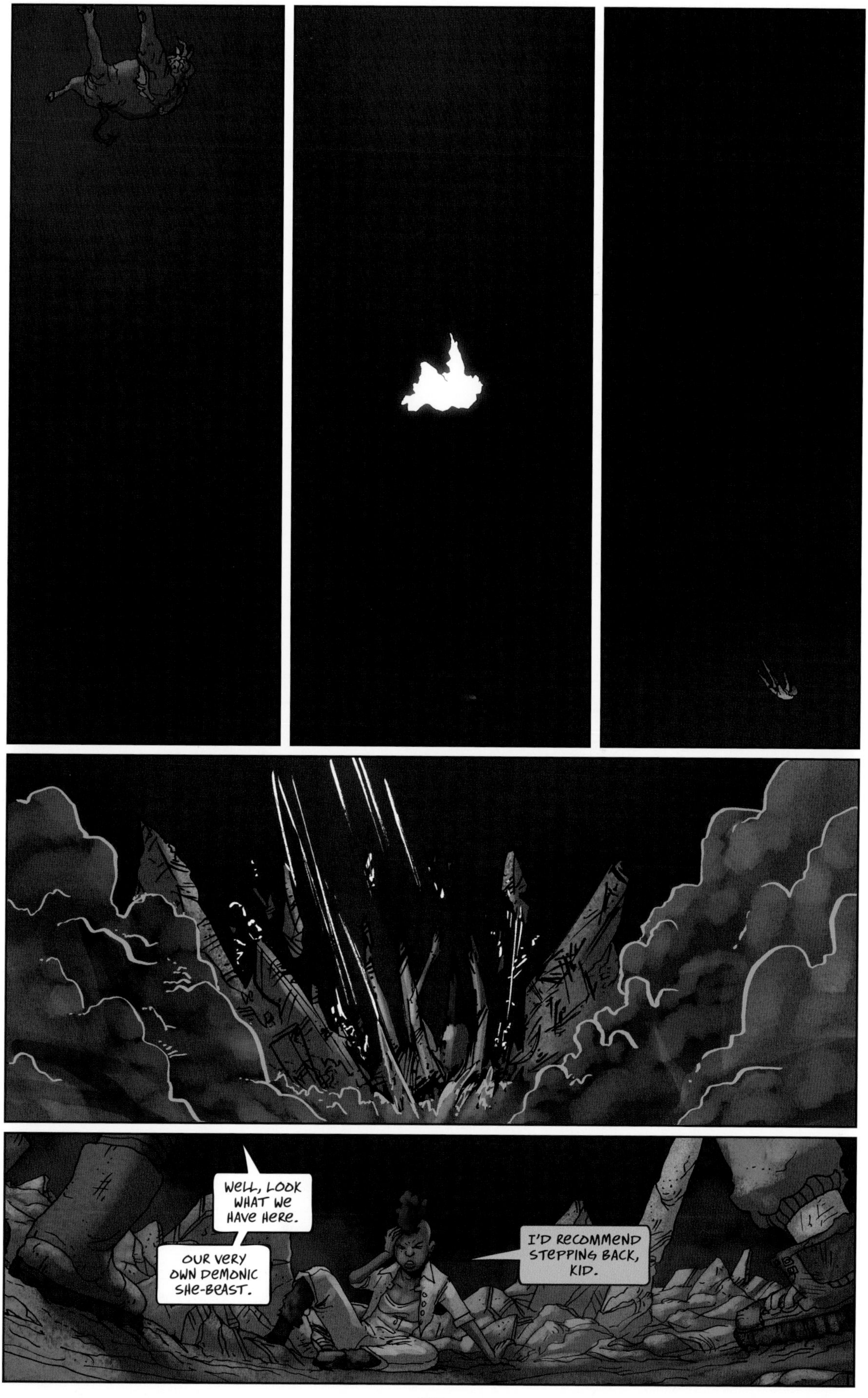
WELL, LOOK WHAT WE HAVE HERE.
OUR VERY OWN DEMONIC SHE-BEAST.
I'D RECOMMEND STEPPING BACK, KID.

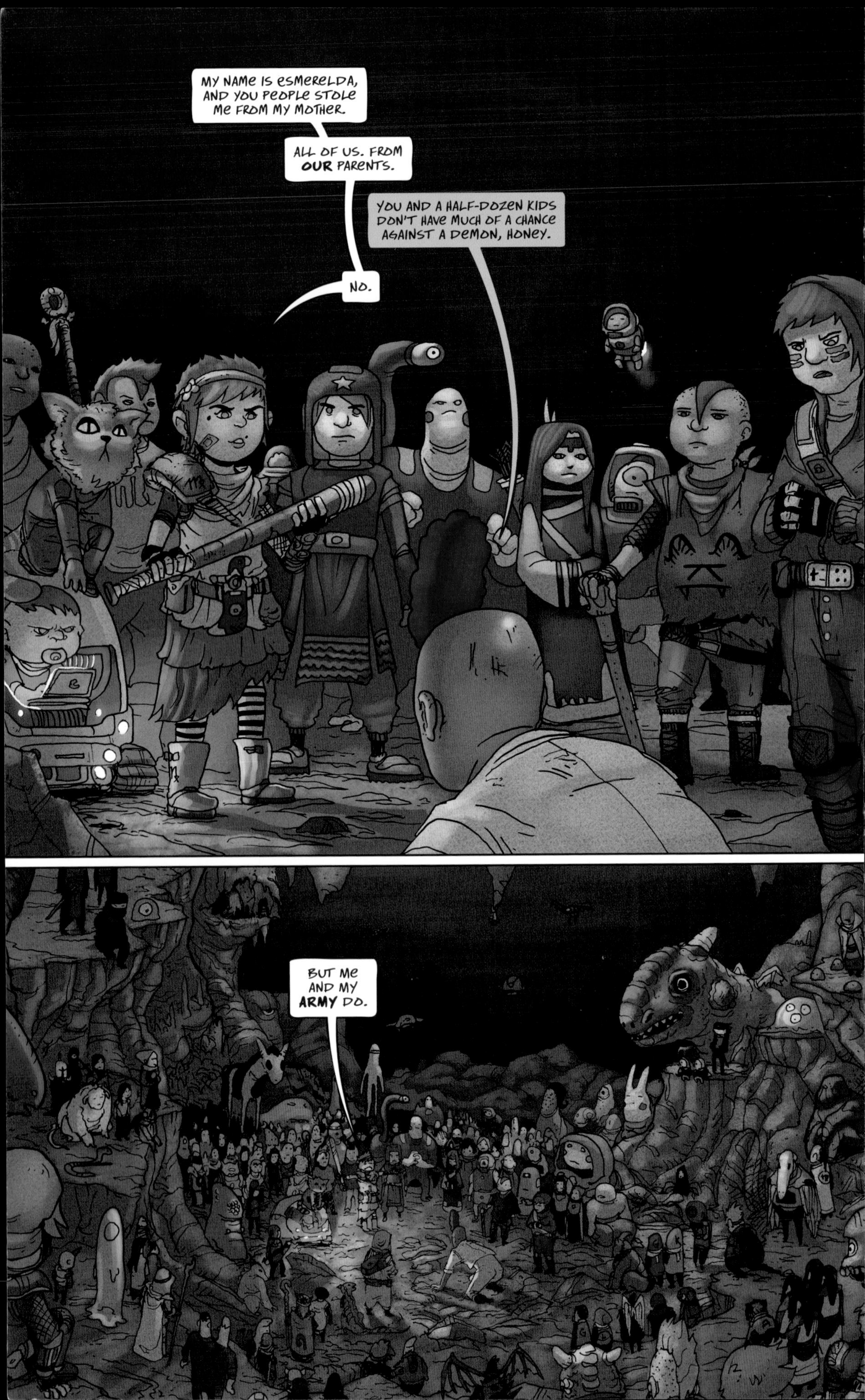
MY NAME IS ESMERELDA, AND YOU PEOPLE STOLE ME FROM MY MOTHER.
ALL OF US. FROM **OUR** PARENTS.
YOU AND A HALF-DOZEN KIDS DON'T HAVE MUCH OF A CHANCE AGAINST A DEMON, HONEY.
NO.
BUT ME AND MY **ARMY** DO.

THE LIFE
AFTER

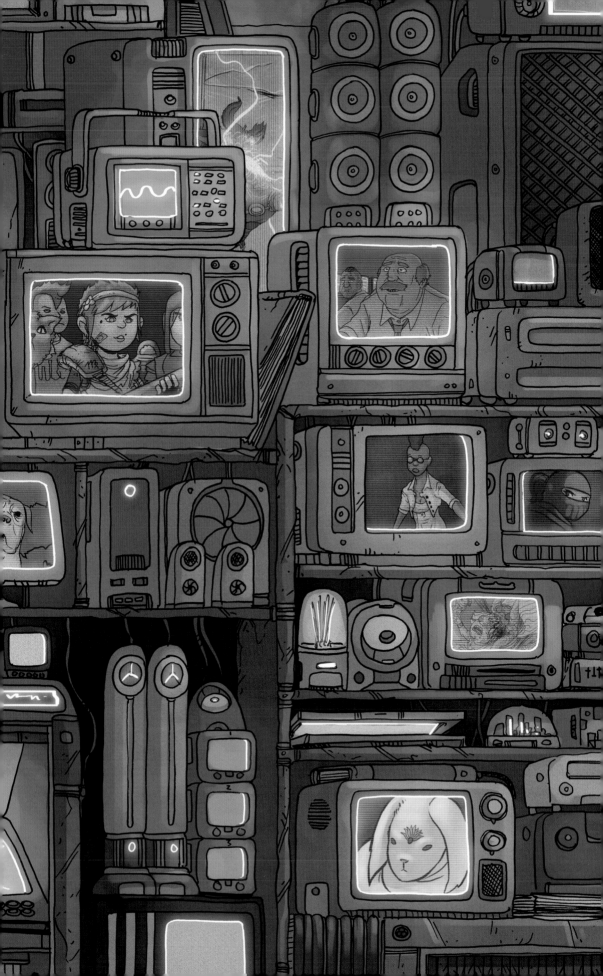

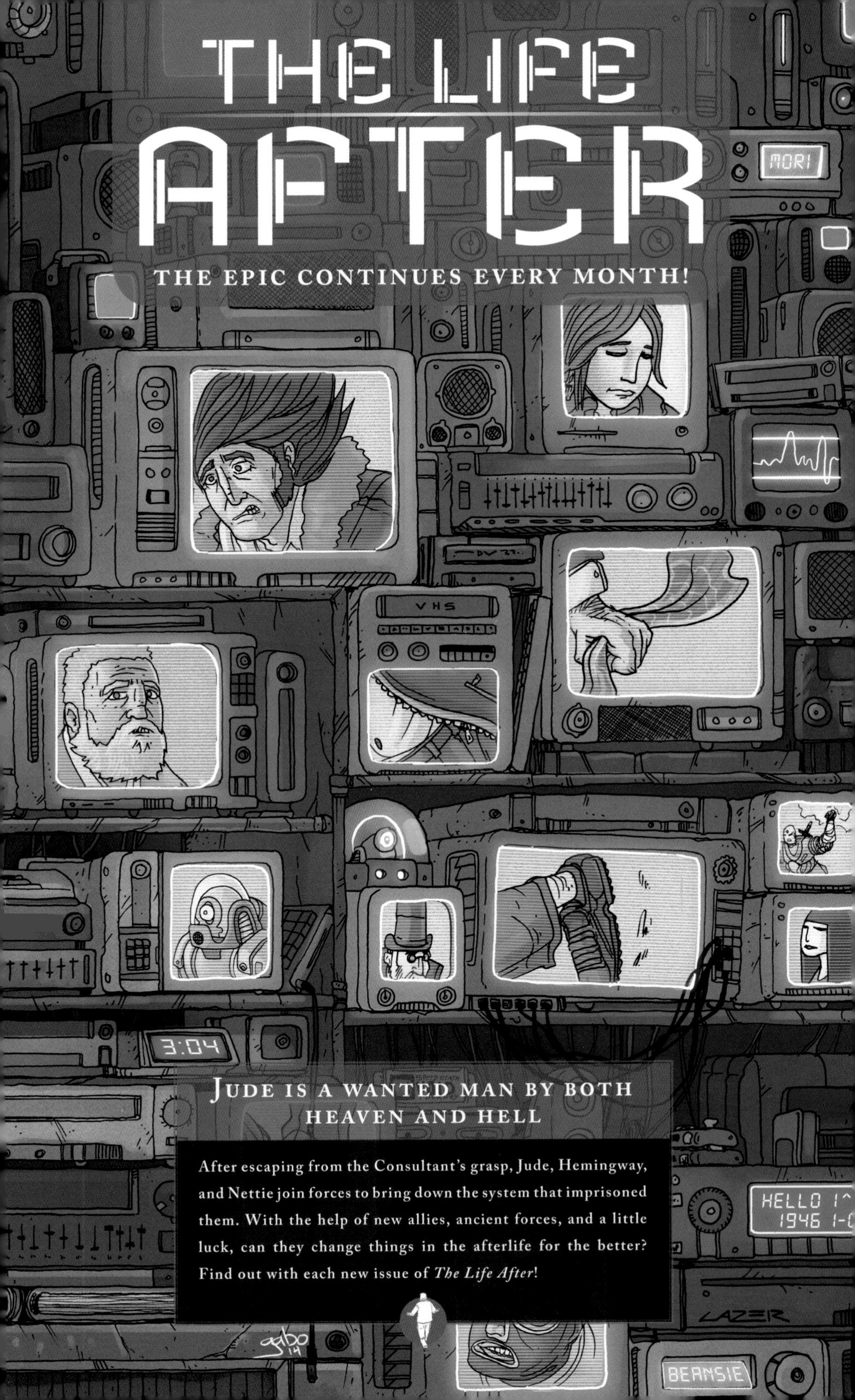
THE LIFE AFTER
THE EPIC CONTINUES EVERY MONTH!
MORI
VHS
3:04
JUDE IS A WANTED MAN BY BOTH HEAVEN AND HELL
After escaping from the Consultant's grasp, Jude, Hemingway, and Nettie join forces to bring down the system that imprisoned them. With the help of new allies, ancient forces, and a little luck, can they change things in the afterlife for the better? Find out with each new issue of *The Life After*!
LAZER
BEARNSIE

Joshua Hale Fialkov

Joshua Hale Fialkov is the Harvey-, Eisner-, and Emmy-nominated creator of graphic novels, including *The Bunker*, *Punks*, *Tumor*, *Echoes*, and *Elk's Run*. He's worked for Marvel, DC, Dark Horse, Top Cow, Dynamite, and pretty much anybody else foolish enough to pay him money. He lives in Los Angeles with his wife, author Christina Rice, their daughter (who shall not be named), their dogs, Cole and Olaf, and their cat, Smokey. The cat is quite unhappy with this arrangement.

GABO

Gabo, also known as Gabriel Bautista, is a Chicago-based illustrator. He is a recurring artist on *Elephantmen* (Image Comics), and series artist on *Albert The Alien* (Thrillbent). He is also an Eisner and Harvey award-winning colorist for his work in *Comic Book Tattoo* (Image Comics). He is also the creator of the world's best comic book battle website, EnterVoid.com. He lives in a large house full of cereal and almond milk and is assisted by his pug assistant Loux Loux "Shark Week" LaRoux in all matters regarding comics and tasty snacks.

MORE BOOKS FROM ONI PRESS...

THE BUNKER
JOSHUA HALE FIALKOV | JOE INFURNARI

the Auteur

LETTER 44

SCOTT PILGRIM
SCOTT PILGRIM'S PRECIOUS LITTLE LIFE
1
BY BRYAN LEE O'MALLEY
COLOR EDITION

THE SIXTH GUN
CULLEN BUNN
BRIAN HURTT

HELHEIM

WASTELAND
ANTONY JOHNSTON
CHRISTOPHER MITTEN
BOOK 01
CITIES IN DUST

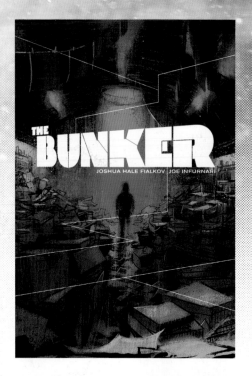

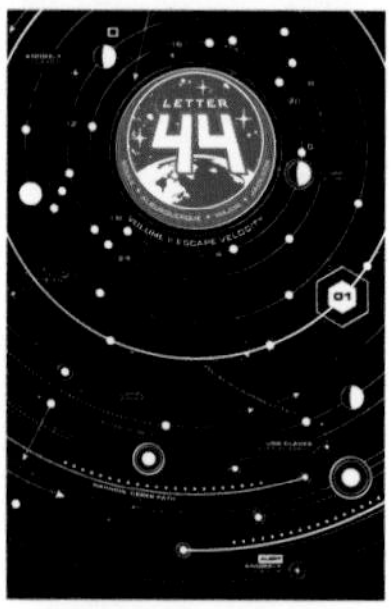

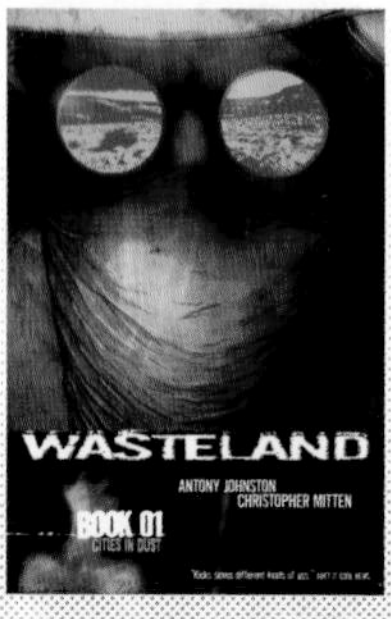

THE BUNKER, VOLUME ONE
By Joshua Hale Fialkov and Joe Infurnari
136 pages, softcover, color
ISBN 978-1-62010-164-3

THE AUTEUR, BOOK ONE:
PRESIDENTS DAY
By Rick Spears and James Callahan
144 pages, softcover, color
ISBN 978-1-62010-135-3

LETTER 44, VOLUME ONE:
ESCAPE VELOCITY
By Charles Soule and Alberto Jiménez Alburquerque
160 pages, softcover, color
ISBN 978-1-62010-133-9

SCOTT PILGRIM, VOLUME ONE:
PRECIOUS LITTLE LIFE
By Bryan Lee O'Malley
192 pages, hardcover, color
ISBN 978-1-62010-000-4

THE SIXTH GUN, BOOK ONE:
COLD DEAD FINGERS
By Cullen Bunn and Brian Hurtt
176 pages, softcover, color
ISBN 978-1-934964-60-6

HELHEIM, VOLUME ONE:
THE WITCH WAR
By Cullen Bunn, Joëlle Jones and Nick Filardi
160 pages, softcover, color
ISBN 978-1-62010-014-1

WASTELAND, BOOK ONE:
CITIES IN DUST
By Antony Johnston and Christopher Mitten
160 pages, softcover, black and white
ISBN 978-1-932664-59-1

ONI PRESS
REVOLUTIONIZE COMICS
www.onipress.com

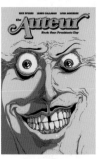

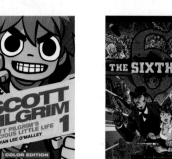

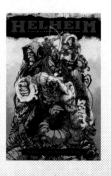

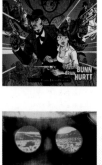

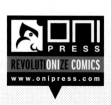

For more information on these and other fine Oni Press comic books and graphic novels visit www.onipress.com. To find a comic specialty store in your area visit www.comicshops.us.